The Press and Society

Themes in British Social History

edited by Dr J. Stevenson

*already published

The Press and Society
From Caxton to Northcliffe

G. A. Cranfield

Longman
London and New York

To my wife

Longman Group Limited London

Associated companies, branches and representatives
throughout the world

Published in the United States of America
by Longman Inc., New York

© Longman Group Limited 1978

All rights reserved. No part of this publication may be
reproduced, stored in a retrieval system, or transmitted
in any form or by any means, electronic, mechanical,
photocopying, recording, or otherwise, without the
prior permission of the copyright owner.

First published 1978

ISBN 0 582 48983 0 cased
ISBN 0 582 48984 9 paper

Library of Congress Cataloging in Publication Data

Cranfield, Geoffrey Alan.
    The press and society.

    (Themes in British social history)
    Bibliography: p. 232
    1. Press—Great Britain—History. 2. Journalism—
Social aspects—Great Britain. 3. Great Britain—Social
conditions. I. Title.
PN5124. S6C7   079'.41   77-21904
ISBN 0-582-48983-0
ISBN 0-582-48984-9 pbk.

Printed in Great Britain by
Richard Clay (The Chaucer Press) Ltd, Bungay, Suffolk

Contents

Preface

This book attempts to survey the history of the Press as a whole in relation to the development of society – beginning with the introduction of the art of printing into England in 1476. Sheer pressure has meant that the survey ends with the arrival on the scene of Alfred Harmsworth, later Lord Northcliffe – and the so-called 'Northcliffe Revolution' is touched on only very briefly. To the author's mind, the history of the Press after this is a subject in its own right. Even so, the author has had to rely heavily upon secondary sources. The problem is particularly acute in the nineteenth century, when to read every issue of *The Times* would be a Herculean task in itself. When one considers that there were many other newspapers in existence, together with a vast mass of periodicals and magazines, the task becomes impossible. But the problem is by no means confined to the nineteenth century. The author has read as many of the newspapers and periodicals as possible. Of necessity, he has been forced to draw heavily on those writers who have had the great advantage of being able to concentrate on particular newspapers, particular fields, and particular periods. The references (positioned at the end of the text) indicate this heavy dependence. But he has tried to avoid excessive referencing, and apologises in advance to any writer whose work he has pirated without due acknowledgement.

Finally, he would like to express his sincere thanks to Dr Stevenson, the general editor of the series, for his unfailing encouragement and constructive criticism, and to the staff of Longman for their efficiency, helpful comments and patience in dealing with what must have been a 'dirty script'. Their task was not made easier by the fact that the author was 12,000 miles away.

G. A. Cranfield
The University of Newcastle,
New South Wales,
Australia

1   From the beginnings to 1695

The introduction of the art of printing did not effect a social or political revolution overnight: few people could read, and the printing press was regarded as a harmless novelty. But as the trade in printed books increased, printers began to show a distinct tendency to stray from the innocuous field of letters into the more exciting fields of religious and political controversy. Such a tendency no authoritarian government could permit – particularly one which, like Henry VIII's, was already grappling with problems of unprecedented size and complexity. In religion, changes were in the air which were eventually to bring about a revolution rather than a mere reformation; in politics, what has, perhaps extravagantly, been called 'the Tudor revolution in government' was under way; and, in the background, there was the slow but sometimes painful adaptation to new social and economic conditions as the feudally organised society disintegrated, to be replaced by a society in which capitalism was to be the increasingly dominant force. The period was, in fact, one of unusual strain and tension, in which the development of the printing press as a critical and possibly subversive force could not be tolerated: and from the time of Henry VIII onwards, Authority sought to control this new threat.

The process was a lengthy one. The problem, like so many of those facing the Tudor monarchy, was entirely new. The first list of prohibited books appeared in 1529, and the following year saw the establishment of the first licensing system. This system was to be operated by ecclesiastics and applied only to books 'concernynge holy scripture', but it was extended by royal proclamation in 1538 to cover all types of printing, and the clerics were made responsible not only for suppressing theological errors but also for 'expellinge and avoydinge the occasion of erroneous and seditious opinions'. In that age, in fact, religion was politics and politics religion. Gradually the system of control was improved. Mary Tudor brought the Stationers' Company into it in 1557, when she granted the Company its charter and gave it wide powers over the craft, and it was completed by Elizabeth's great Star Chamber decree of 1586 which set the pattern of regulation for the next hundred years. *All* books were to be licensed, the Company's powers of search and seizure were confirmed, and the number of master printers, apprentices and printing presses severely limited.

Such was the Tudor system of control. But perhaps too much attention has been paid in the past to its purely negative aspects by historians whose judgement has been clouded by the modern doctrine of the freedom of the Press. Certainly, the Tudors worked on the principle that the peace of the realm demanded the suppression of all dissenting opinion: and in their efforts to stamp out what were called 'lewd and naughty matters' they were remarkably successful. But it has to be remembered that this was a period of uncertainty and insecurity – of religious upheavals, economic crises, dynastic doubts, plots and rebellions, of constant fears of foreign invasion. Under such conditions, the government naturally did its utmost to suppress criticism. However, the system was by no means as severe as it may seem on paper and permitted the publication of a surprisingly extensive and varied amount of printed matter, including news.

Long before the evolution of the newspaper proper, reports of news were being printed and sold, becoming quite common by the middle of the sixteenth century. The main agent in this development was, curiously enough, the government. Riots, rebellions and public executions could not be covered up, and often the government's case had to be stated – and publicised – to instruct the nation in its duty and to scotch wild rumours. However much they might reject any notion of appealing to the vulgar, the fact remained that the Tudors were forced in their own interests to make frequent use of the printing press: in the last resort, they depended on popular support, or at least the good will of the governed. The first Tudor monarch to make extensive use of the printing press was Henry VIII; but as early as 1486 Henry VII had published the Bull of Pope Innocent VIII confirming his title to the throne and his marriage to Elizabeth of York, republishing it in 1494, a year of rebellion, to remind his subjects where their loyalty lay. Henry VIII found the press useful in his dispute with Rome, and in 1531 published *The determination of the universities of Italy and Fraunce, that it is so unlafull for a man to marie his brothers wyfe, that the pope hath no power to dispence therewith.* In 1536, another year of rebellion, he issued the *Answere made by the Kynges hyghnes to the Petition of the rebelles in Yorkeshire.* And, of course, proclamations were regularly printed. But not all the material published to inform public opinion, or lead it, was of so official and heavy a character, and the government also permitted the printing of publications aimed at a somewhat different level of the population. In particular, the ballad took on a new lease of life with the introduction of printing, and was to remain for many years to come the characteristic form of popular English art. Every plot, every rebellion, every public execution produced its ballads, aimed at the least critical class of reader and listener. Many of them were to all intents and purposes news-sheets. But from the point of view of Authority most were harmless enough: no printer was prepared to risk his neck over such trifles. Thus the Northern Rebellion of 1569–70 produced a flood of ballads: they contained some news, but more patriotism, with eulogies of the Queen which must have made even Elizabeth blush, denunciations of the rebels, and gloating forecasts of the painful end in store for those rebels.

At the same time the government also permitted the publishing of pamphlets and broadsheets dealing with news of a more general kind. Then, as now, war was the great attraction, and one of the earliest known news pamphlets concerned the Battle of Flodden in 1513: *Hereafter ensue the trewe encountre or Batayle lately don betwene Englande and Scotlande*. Printers and public, not to mention Authority, would undoubtedly have liked to read of the heroic exploits and triumphs of Englishmen against the foreign devil. Unfortunately, the achievements of English armies throughout most of the sixteenth century were, to say the least, disappointing, and the printers very wisely tended to ignore the various fiascos. Not until the 1580s, with the advent of the sea-dogs, could they give full vent to their patriotic ardour, with the sea-dogs invariably fighting against overwhelming odds, and equally invariably emerging victorious. Readers eagerly devoured accounts of a battle between 'A Ship of 200 Tun having in her but 36. men and 2. Boyes who were ... set upon by 6 Men of Warre of the Turkes, having at least 1500. men in them', or of the encounter between 'fyve shippes of London against xj. galleis and ij. fragates the strongest in christendom'. And the propaganda element was well to the fore during the excitement of the Armada, with such publications as the *New Ballet of the straunge and most cruel Whippes which the Spanyards had prepared to whippe and torment English men and women*, or the detailed account of massacre and rape, village by village, perpetrated by Spanish troops in the Netherlands:

> James Messier being stricken over his belly, so that his intrailes did issue forth, dyed a few dayes after. The wife of the said Messier was so sore beaten, that she can never be her owne woman again. Peter Riondet, killed as he came out of his bed, although he was seventie yeares olde, his wife is sore hurt, and is like hardly to recover it. Both her daughters defloured, and the one so hurt that the intrals came forth of her body, fifteene and eighteen years of age.

Already the atrocity story had taken the lead. But the tastes of the general public have changed little since the sixteenth century. Then, as now, blood and sex reigned supreme. This emphasis was obvious in reports of crime: unusually ghastly crimes were assured of a splendid coverage, with vivid descriptions of the crime itself and (often even more harrowing) of the punishment inflicted. In 1601 appeared a detailed account of the execution of six witches in Germany:

> First they were all six brought before the towne house of Manchen where the woman (being plaest betwixt her two Sonnes) had both her Brestes cut off: and with the which Brestes the Executioner stroke her three times about the face;

and in like manner her two Sonnes, who satt on each side of her were likewise beaten about the face with their Mothers Brests three times apiece. This beeing done in the presence of many people, the woman had sixe stripes given her with a Whip of twisted Wier: and after, had both her armes broken with a Wheel, and then set in a settle made of purpose: her body was immediately burnt. After this the other five witches had also six stripes apiece, and both their armes likewise broken with a Wheele, and foure of them tyde unto a stake in the same place, and burnt: But *Paule Gamherle*, the father and maister Witch of them all, was spitted alive, and so roasted to death.

Another type of news of which the sixteenth-century reader never seems to have wearied was that concerning miracles, prodigies and wonders. Such items were to remain standard fare for many years to come – and are not unknown today. A particularly outstanding collection was published in 1594 under the title *Strange Signes seene in the Aire, strange Monsters behelde on the Lande, and wonderfull Prodigies both by Land and Sea, over, in and about the Citie of Rosenberge in high Germany . . . Truely translated out of the high Dutch Copie.* In the air there had appeared a double rainbow full of 'furious countenances', three suns all shining at once, 'through each was thrust a bloody sword from which many drops of blood fell on the earth', and a huge cross covered with fresh blood. But this was not all:

> At the same time as these portents in the air, a strange woman was delivered in the town of four monstrous children. The first without a head with eyes in his breast. The second with a roll of flesh growing on his head like a Turk's Turban. The third with long upright hair long teeth and a nose like an Eagle's beak, and on his fingers and toes long and sharp claws. The fourth was not deformed but wept tears of blood till he died.'

The woman and her unusual progeny all died and were placed in a coffin. But eight men had been unable to lift the coffin off the ground, although when it was opened there was nothing inside but three drops of blood.

Perhaps fortunately not all the news was of this nature. Then, as now, news of the Court and of royal pageantry was always popular, and the news-writers could regale their readers with descriptions *Of the Tryumphe and the uses that Charles themperour & the Kyng of England were saluted with passyng through London* (1522), or *The Passage of most dred Soveraigne Lady Quene Elyzabeth to Westminster the daye before her Coronacion* (1558).

In these various ways a surprising amount of printed news was available to the sixteenth century. It was news with limitations. By and large, printers confined themselves to foreign affairs, and steered well clear of such controversial subjects as religion and politics. In fact, the Tudors were remarkably successful in their efforts to control the press.

The reasons are not difficult to find. The dominant classes – the merchants and the landowners – wanted above all else peace and prosperity, and they realised that a strong government was the best assurance against a return to the anarchy of the recent past. There was the emergent feeling of nationalism, and both Henry VIII and Elizabeth succeeded in identifying themselves with the outlook and ambitions of the nation. Even the seriousness of the religious problem can easily be exaggerated, for Catholicism and Protestantism did not really harden and crystallise until Elizabeth's reign at the earliest. Finally, there was the fact that, pronounced as the spread of literacy may have been among the middle classes, the vast mass of the population was illiterate. And not only was it illiterate, but it was not politically conscious, save when its pockets were concerned or when events of quite exceptional interest occurred. Nevertheless, a great deal had been achieved. Printers had appeared who were prepared to publish news. They accustomed people to the idea of printed news, and assisted in the growth of an appetite for it. At the same time, conditions were changing as the century progressed. The 'growth of capitalism' was producing a strong and increasingly confident middle class, impatient of restraints of any kind: this class was the one most influenced by militant Puritanism. A new spirit was abroad and Elizabeth, despite the awe in which she was held, had to face evergrowing criticism from her parliaments. This new spirit manifested itself in the Press, and the later years of the century were marked by increasing violations of the press regulations. First, Elizabeth had trouble with the Catholics. More serious was the clash with the Puritans, who made the first effective challenge to the Tudor system, demonstrating for the first time the power of the Press. Despite all official efforts, the *Martin Marprelate* tracts of 1588 and 1589 achieved a wide circulation, and although the government eventually succeeded in suppressing them, it was not before they had made a deep impression on the literate public. And James I immediately found himself the centre of a widespread and articulate religious and political controversy. He naturally, and with some success, continued the Tudor system. But England was now lagging behind the continent in the publishing of news. By 1620 weekly periodicals or 'corantos' had evolved in Germany and the Netherlands. The idea was bound to be communicated to England, especially as so many corantos were published in translation there. Some stimulus was needed.

By the early seventeenth century interest in public affairs, both foreign and domestic, was growing steadily in England. The rise of England as a naval and maritime power had enlarged her horizons, and a wealthy and ambitious commercial class had developed. There were the economic and political problems caused mainly by the financial difficulties of James. But the dominant force of the age was religion, and it was the Thirty Years War which provided the required stimulus. That war seemed to be a war to the death between Protestantism and Catholicism, and one which the Protestant cause was losing. At the same time there was growing concern in England over a foreign policy which appeared to be lukewarm in its support of Protestantism. News was at a premium, and the traditional sources of news were no longer adequate.

The first printers to attempt to satisfy this demand for up-to-date news in England seem to have been a Dutch combination. The earliest known issue of their publication is dated 2 December 1620, and consists of a single sheet of small folio, printed in two columns, and bearing no title. It was 'Imprinted at Amsterdam by George Veseler, Ao. 1620... And are to be soulde by Petrus Keerius, dwelling in the Calverstreete, in the uncertaine time'. At least fifteen more numbers appeared between this and 18 September 1621. But although this is usually regarded as the first English news-sheet, it was English only in language, and when the Dutch coranto from which it was translated contained actual English news, that section was carefully omitted. Even its presentation of foreign news was hardly exciting. At times a Protestant bias was apparent, but by and large the printer did everything to maintain a strictly neutral approach, even to the war – *the* great issue of the period. Nevertheless, it did contain reasonably up-to-date news, and seems to have been imitated by other Amsterdam printers, although actual evidence is lacking. Indeed, according to Dahl, only 0.13 per cent of the copies of the early corantos (and, in fact, of the later newsbooks) have survived. As Frank puts it, 'three centuries ago, as now, old newspapers had little individual value, and from the beginning they served to line pots or to wrap fish'. It was clearly only a matter of time before an English printer entered the market. Of course, there was a risk involved: no printer would dare to include, much less comment on, domestic news. Unfortunately, at this particular stage the government was growing steadily more sensitive on the subject of foreign affairs, and when some time before August 1621 a London bookseller, Thomas Archer, began to issue a coranto, he was promptly charged with publishing a news-sheet on the war in the Palatinate without licence and imprisoned. His offence seems to have been 'making, or adding to, his corrantos'; but accurate translations from the Dutch were apparently acceptable, for, according to a letter of the period, 'now there is another that hath got license to print them and sell them, honestly translated out of the Dutch'.

This new printer 'N.B.' – presumably Nathaniel Butter, although Nicholas Bourne is a possible candidate – immediately began to publish a *Corante, or newes from Italy, Germany, Hungarie, Spaine, and France... out of the Hie Dutch Coppy printed at Franckford.* Butter and Bourne were virtually to monopolise the scene until the 1640s. They took the first step away from their Dutch model by issuing a quarto pamphlet of anything from eight to twenty-four pages, thus introducing the 'book' of news, a format which remained standard until 1655. Also, whereas the earlier corantos had not been numbered and bore varying titles, they now, from 1622, began to be numbered consecutively, and by 1624 had acquired a more or less permanent title, *Mercurius Britannicus.* They also began to appear at approximately weekly intervals, although this last step was not achieved easily, and the printers were still inclined to vary the frequency of publication according to the supply of news available. A glut of news could produce two newsbooks on the same day, but there could also be an interval of seventeen days between issues in a period of 'slow' news. As to content, no such advances were made. The supreme note remained one of caution. English news was virtually excluded, but even foreign news could easily lead to trouble. On 9 September 1622 the newsbook contained a somewhat rash report of the activities of Count Mansfield, the leading general on the Protestant side: 'He hath burned and spoyled in *Loraine*, and upon the borders of *France*, sixtie Villages and Castles, and he is very rich in robbing the Churches of their Chalises and Crosses, and Images, and he hath five thousand Women or Whores in his Campe.' The following issue contained a hurried apology.

The printers had other problems, quite apart from censorship. Their sources of information were often contradictory – and conflicting reports were usually printed side by side, with the publisher accepting no responsibility. On one occasion (20 October 1631), however, an editorial opinion was voiced:

> Indifferent Reader, we promise you (in the front of our last Aviso) the Death and Interment of Monsieur Tilly, which wee now performe; notwithstanding the last Antwerpian Post hath reumoured the contrary, against which you may ballance each other, and accordingly beleeve: onely wee will propose one question unto all gaine-sayers, let them demonstate where Tilly is and that great formidable Army which he hath raised, and we will be of that Catholick faith.

Unfortunately, although Tilly had been wounded at the battle of Breitenfeld, he was far from being dead: whether the printer kept his rash promise is not known. Often readers had to be chided over their demand for exciting news, to be reminded that the lack of such news was not the printer's fault. 'In this time of cessation', announced the issue of 26 July 1622, 'you must not looke for fighting every day, nor taking of Townes; but as they happen, you shall know.' Further difficulties were emphasised in November 1625:

> I doubt not, but it is without doubt that it hath beene newes to most men, that they have beene so long without newes; but there is onely one supreme power, whom the Wind and Seas obey: as for man, he must purpose, but God determines, for howsoever it was was[*sic*] our desire to satisfie the desire of men, whose nature is *novitatis avida*, yet through the adversitie of the winds wee were frustrate a long time of our appetites, but wee were hindered by another unfortunate distaster [*sic*], for a Pinke, of which one *Blastoule* of Flushing a duchman was owner, in the which, the Post from *Holland* was a passenger, and was unhappily surprised and taken by the Dunkerkes, all the men in it captivated and carried to Ostend.

Such an attack by privateers must have been the last straw.

Despite such problems, the newsbooks thrived. In his pioneer work in this field, Dahl estimated their circulation as at least 400 copies; the more recent research of Frank puts it at an average of 500 in the 1620s, dropping to 250 in times of 'slow' news. But cold figures do not tell the whole story: more significant is the fact that contemporary writers recognised that a new and possibly dangerous force had emerged. In 1625 Abraham Holland published *A Continu'd Iust Inquisition of Paper-Persecuters*, making the obvious pun upon Butter's name:

To see such *Batter* evrie week besmeare
Each publike post, and Church dore, and to heare
These *shameful lies* would make a man in spight
Of Nature, turne *Satyrist*, and write
Revenging lines, against these shameless men,
Who thus torment both *Paper*, *Presse*, and *Pen*,
Th'Imposters that these *Trumperies* do utter
Are A, B, C, D, E, F, G, and . . .

In the following year Ben Jonson in *The Stable of News* denounced the newsmongers as dishonest swindlers; others joined in, with Christopher Foster in 1632 praying 'the Saviour to inspire the curranto-makers with the spirit of truth'. Most of the criticisms were aimed at the inaccuracy of the reports, for which the unhappy printers could often hardly be blamed: in fact, they regularly denied all personal responsibility. 'I have received three severall letters from Brussels', the author stated on 12 March 1624, 'a Soldiers, a townsmans, or burger of *Brussels*, and a merchants factor, of London. Now because you shall not say, that either out of my owne conceit I misliked a phrase, or presumptuously tooke upon me to reforme any thing amisse, I will truely set you downe their owne words.'

The very vigour of the steady flow of criticism suggests that the circulation of the newsbooks was by no means insignificant, and their influence considerable. Each copy would be read (or listened to) by a number of people, so that the actual circulation was far greater than the number of purchasers. A newspaper was still something of a novelty – and an expensive one: the price was probably twopence in the 1620s. And it seems unlikely that the newsbooks were quite as ephemeral as Richard Braithwait maintained in his assault upon 'a Corranto-coiner' in his *Whimzies: or, a New Caste of Characters* (again making the apparently irresistible puns):

Yet our best comfort is, his Chymera's live not long; a week is the longest in the Cities, and after their arrivall, a little longer in the Countrey, Which past, they melt like *Butter* or match a pipe and so *Burne*. But indeede, most commonly it is the height of their ambition, to expire to the imployment of stopping mustard-pots, or wrapping up pepper, pouder, stavesaker, Etc. which done, they expire.

Cautious as they were – 'I dare not write all that I know least trouble should ensue' said the writer on 18 January 1626 – the newsbooks never won the support of the government. Charles I probably disapproved of the public discussion of foreign affairs anyway, and he was becoming increasingly jealous of the flattering references to the Protestant hero, Gustavus Adolphus. Even the reading public was apparently wearying of the almost unbroken series of Protestant defeats, or of reports of victories which later proved to be completely unfounded. And on 17 October 1632 the newsbooks were suppressed. According to Butter, the news from the continent had been so bad that 'the lords would not have it known'. For the next six years, newsbooks disappeared. Repression was the order of the day, with the Star Chamber decree of 1637 laying down the most detailed rules yet for the regulation of the Press – partly, perhaps, as a result of the Archbishop's fury at the errors in the printing of the 1631 edition of the Bible, in which Exodus 20:14 read 'Thou shalt commit adultery', and Deuteronomy 5:24, 'The Lord hath shewed us his glory and his great asse'.

It was, however, becoming clear that a controlled news supply might be useful even to Authority. In 1638 the 'old firm' of Butter and Bourne once again petitioned the King for a renewal of their privilege to publish translations of foreign corantos. More enterprising was a petition put forward by one John Locke, a man who clearly appreciated that public interest was swinging away from foreign affairs, and who saw the advantages which the Crown might expect from a carefully supervised newsbook:

(1) To settle a way that when there shall be any revolt or backsliding in matters of religion or obedience (which commonly grows among the vulgar) to draw them in by the same lines that drew them out, by spreading amongst them such reports as may best make for that matter to which we would have them drawn.

(2) To establish a speedy and ready way whereby to disperse into the veins of the whole body of State such matter as may best temper it, and be most agreeable to the disposition of the Head and the principal members upon all occasions that shall be offered.

(3) To devise means to raise the spirits of the people and to quicken their conceits and understanding by giving them tastes of matters clear from the common mire of worldliness. It makes such apt to be drawn from the cold sotich humour of sloth [and] extends the sense by degrees to the conceit of the right rule of reason, whereby they are wrought easily to obey those by which these rules shall command them.

This interesting document is included among the *State Papers Domestic* of James I's reign,[1] although whether it was a petition to James or to his son is uncertain. Very definitely, it was ahead of its time. Much safer was the conservative approach of the old firm, which now received a licence

> for the imprintinge and publishing all matter of history of
> Newes of any forraine place or kingdome . . . And also for the
> translation, setting forth, imprinting and publishing in the
> English tongue all Newes, Novells, Gazettes, Currantos or
> Occurrences that concerne forreine parts for the term of xxi
> years. They paying yearly during the said terme towards the
> repayre of St. Pauls Church London the sum of 10 l.

But events at home were becoming too exciting for such a venture to have much chance of success. Foreign affairs were now very much in the background, and the air must have been alive with rumours as the so-called 'Eleven Years' Tyranny' ended with trouble in Ireland, an invasion by the Scots, the summoning of the Short Parliament, and an obviously growing cleavage between the King and important sections of his people. The Long Parliament met in November 1640 and proceeded to abolish the Star Chamber and the Court of High Commission – the main supports of the system of press control. The time was ripe for the appearance of newsbooks dealing with *English* affairs. Printers were understandably cautious, for there were still dangers involved. Few people in authority would have much sympathy with the idea of disseminating new of the weighty issues at stake among the general public. But, after some tentative experiments, the floodgates opened, and the period from late 1641 to the end of 1642 must surely rank as one of the most confusing in the whole history of the Press. Newsbooks appeared right and left; there was flagrant plagiarism, and titles were changed from week to week. Between June and December 1642 we are told that ten newsbooks included the words *Perfect Diurnall* in their title. Most lasted only for two or three issues. None was licensed or entered in the register of the Stationers' Company, and none was interfered with in any way.

Despite this practical freedom, the keynote remained one of caution. All the newsbooks were published in London, and London was largely under the control of Parliament. The news-writers naturally tended to support the Parliament: but great care was needed. Outright anti-royalism was out of the question, particularly in the early days of the civil war, when most people still hoped for a reconciliation. By and large, the newsbooks were dull. As the actual fighting developed, the Parliamentary bias of the newsbooks became more pronounced, and they began to refer to 'the malignant party', and even 'the bloody-minded cavaliers'. But what was really needed was a *challenge*: and this was provided in 1643 with the appearance at Oxford on 1 January of *Mercurius Aulicus*, the first royalist newsbook. Edited by John Berkenhead the paper was from the start violently partisan, with vicious but entertaining personal attacks on the Paliamentary leaders, atrocity stories, and human interest items about the King and the royal family. With its appearance there began one of the liveliest periods in the history of the Press. Hitherto, the newsbooks had largely avoided *comment*: but the gibes of *Aulicus* could not be ignored. To answer *Aulicus* appeared *Mercurius Britannicus*, edited by a Captain Audley with the assistance of Marchamont Needham, of whom more was to be heard later. Each week, *Aulicus* would begin with a section entitled 'London Lyes'. Each week *Britannicus*, equally tough and coarse, would reply – 'though', said its author on 14 December 1643, 'I think it beneath my pen to dip into the lies and follies and Calumnies of such an Oxford Pamphlet . . . this thing called *Mercurius Aulicus* . . . lies, forgeries, insolencies, impieties, prophanations, blasphemies and Poperie'. Typical of the exchanges was that sparked off by a report in *Aulicus* on 23 December 1643 that a prisoner of the royalists had been found committing buggery on a mare – and on a Sunday of all days, when 'His Majestie's Forces were at Church', thus 'telling the world what they [the Puritans] doe on Sundays'. *Britannicus* maintained that the soldier in question had in fact been trying to steal the horse in order to escape, and he very much doubted if any royalist soldiers had been to church 'since his Majestie first levied war against his Parliament'. If they had, it would have been to attend Mass!

The London newsbooks as a whole tended to keep out of this vigorous battle, and so lacked excitement. Nevertheless, cautious and dull though they were, they were not unsuccessful. By early 1644 a dozen appeared in London every week. Obviously in such exciting times news of any sort was very much in demand. According to Frank, the minimum circulation was about 200 copies, with the well-established newsbooks selling 500, and *A Perfect Diurnall* – reliable, if pedestrian – between 750 and 1,000 (the same estimate as for the far more lively *Mercurius Britannicus*). Such figures may well be exaggerated. However, with a dozen printed in London, and the growing royalist press outside, it is clear that the newsbooks must have reached a considerable proportion of the public.

The battle between *Aulicus* and *Britannicus* continued, to the obvious enjoyment of both. The effectiveness of *Aulicus* is suggested by the fact that other newsbooks felt obliged to come to the aid of its rival, including in October 1643 the curiously titled *The Scotish Dove, sent out and returning; bringing intelligence from the Armies, and makes some Relations of other observable Passages of both Kingdoms, for Information and Instruction. As an Antidote against the Poisonous Insinuations of Mercurius Aulicus and the errours of other Intelligencers.* In fact, *Britannicus* needed no assistance until the sudden collapse of his playmate left him at a loss. 'Not a word yet from *Aulicus*', he complained on 20 October 1645: and well might Needham mourn the disappearance of his rival, for his own newsbook had now lost its very *raison d'être*. Hitherto it had held a somewhat privileged position as the acknowledged answer to the royalist press; now it was simply one among a growing number of London newsbooks. Editing a newsbook in London was still a very ticklish task: pleasing Commons, Army, Lords and Presbyterians was no easy matter. And very soon Needham was in trouble for attacking the King:

> Where is King *Charles*? What's become of him? The strange
> variety of opinions leaves nothing certain: for some say, when
> he saw the Storm coming after him as far as *Bridgwater*, he ran
> away to his *dearly beloved* in Ireland; yes, they say he *ran away*
> out of his owne *Kingdome* very *Majestically*: Others will have his
> creating a new *Monarchy* in the Isle of *Anglesey*: A third sort
> there are which say he hath hid himselfe. I will not now
> determine the matter, because there is such a deale of
> uncertainty; and therefore (for the satisfaction of my
> Countrymen) it were best to send *Hue and Cry* after him.
> *If any man can bring any tale or tiding of a Wilfull King*
> *which hath gone astray these foure yeares from his Parliament,*
> *with a guilty Conscience, bloody Hands, a Heart full of broken*
> *Vowes and Protestations: If these marks be not sufficient, there*
> *is another in the mouth; for bid him speak, and you will soon know him:*
> *Then give notice to Britannicus, and you shall be well paid for your*
> *paines. So God save the Parliament.*[2]

This was powerful journalism. But its tone – and the references to
Charles's stutter – were somewhat tactless at this crucial period, when
negotiations were still possible, and Charles's future (and, indeed, that of
the monarchy as such) were undecided. The Lords protested, and
Needham retired (until 1647, when he made a comeback, but this time
on the royalist side). Other journalists approached the problem of the
King more discreetly; the author of *The Parliament's Post* managed in his
issue of 30 September 1645 to combine the political angle and the human
interest aspect and at the same time avoid the fate which had attended
Needham:

> Royall Sir, How doe you doe? What is the cause that maketh
> your Eye to melt, and the salt to runne downe so warme upon
> your cheeke? Why with your wet sorrowes doe you bedew the
> Earth, why with your sighes doe you increase the *cloudes*?
> *Gentlemen, This is my Lord the King.* Why with foulded Armes doe
> you stand musing of your selfe, why in the progress of your
> marche doe you turne so often and so distractedly from your
> Counsellors, why (as if all were lost in these parts) doe you
> sadly throw so many a Westerne looke? *Gentlemen, This is my*
> *Lorde the King.* Why do you refuse the comfort of your bedd?
> Why are you ashamed of the presence of your Bed-fellow, why
> doe you startle in your Chaire before the midnight feare, the
> first slumbers having scarce closed your eyes, as if your sleepe it
> is become your enemy? *Gentlemen, This my Lorde the King.*

Apart from a few such exceptions, it can hardly be said that the London
newsbooks really satisfied the demand for domestic news. The times were
far more exciting than the published news would suggest, for most

newsbooks contented themselves with a bald and superficial account of events, without comment or explanation of any kind. On the growing cleavage within the Parliamentary ranks, they maintained a discreet silence.

Very different were the royalist newsbooks, which flourished again with the publication of *Mercurius Pragmaticus* (edited by Needham, who was to become the most effective propagandist on the royalist side) and its various allies. Their authors led an exciting life, always on the run, but their newsbooks had all the glamour of forbidden fruit, and, by comparison, the licensed London newsbooks were dull and out-of-date, still crammed with foreign news. The royalist productions may have contained little real 'news', but they more than made up for this deficiency in invective and sensationalism. They were coarse and scurrilous, specialising in atrocity stories and in personal attacks on the Parliamentary leaders. And they were intensely *topical*. What the London newsbooks hesitated to mention, the royalists emphasised. Usually they began with a verse, not always of high literary merit, but often the sort of thing the reader might remember long after the actual event had been forgotten. Thus, *Mercurius Pragmaticus* on 20 October 1647 opened with a verse on the slogan 'No Bishop, No King':

A Scot and Jesuite, joyned in Hand,
First taught the World to say,
That Subjects ought to have Command,
And Princes to obey.
These both agreed to have no King,
The Scotch-man he cries further,
No Bishop; 'Tis a godly thing
States to reform by Murther.

More pithy, and perhaps more easily memorised, was the same newsbook's introduction to its issue of 9 May 1648:

Betwixt two Thieves our Saviour once
    Suffer'd for Us, and died;
So 'twixt two thievish Factions
    Our King is Crucifi'd.

Needham's success encouraged a whole host of imitators and replies. The royalist newsbooks indulged in personal attacks on all and sundry – Scots, Levellers, Presbyterians, the Army. Fairfax was 'King Tom', 'Black Tom'. or, less elegantly, 'Tom Turd'. Cromwell naturally came in for special attention, with the emphasis squarely placed upon his nose: he was, variously, 'Noll-Nose', 'His Nose-shippe', 'King Nose', 'Copper-nosed Noll', or, more elaborately, 'High and Mighty Cromwell, King of Cruelty, Lord of Misrule . . . and NOSE almighty'. But all the Parliament leaders were freely accused of wenching, unnatural acts, and of possessing every loathsome disease known.

The London newsbooks could not compete with this sort of thing.

But it is clear that there was a tremendous demand for news, even news that had been heavily censored and was, to say the least, colourless. It has been estimated that Pecke's *Perfect Diurnall* had at this time a weekly sale approaching 3,000. Yet, despite the extraordinary excitement of the time – with 1648 a particularly eventful year, witnessing the Scottish invasion, revolts in Wales and the navy, the second Civil War, Pride's Purge, and culminating in the trial and execution of Charles I in January 1649 – the London newsbooks had perforce to remain cautious. As always, there was the odd exception, as when Gilbert Mabbott, the official licenser, used his position to preach a Leveller programme in a newsbook misnamed *The Moderate*:

> The Law and Government of this land, being Tirannous and Arbitrary, and destructive to the freedome of the people, may be lawfully taken away by the people . . . and till that be done, the people of this nation are slaves, and not Free-men . . . All Power and Authorities, either by King or Parliament, acting against . . . the people are void by the Laws of God, man and Nature: the people . . . give these powers and Authorities, expecting they should not abuse their Trust in acting against the good of their Electees (their Lords and Masters), to whom they ought to give account, for breach of the Trust, because the servant cannot be above his master, nor the creature above his maker. (7 November 1648)

This was strong meat indeed for a London newsbook. But the execution of Charles was undoubtedly the greatest news event of the period. The royalist writers screamed in horror – and Authority was worried about the possible general reaction. The Army had already been goaded beyond endurance by the Levellers, one of whose main political platforms was freedom of the Press, and whose ideas were not merely ahead of their time, but were political dynamite. On 20 September 1649 it persuaded the Rump Parliament to pass the most detailed Press laws of the century, withdrawing official approval from all newsbooks then in being, enlarging the powers of the licenser, obliging all printers to post a bond of £300, and restricting printing to the City of London and the two Universities, with the exception of presses at York and Finsbury engaged in printing the Bible. But the old problem remained: news had become a recognised feature of social life – a complete ban was out of the question. Unfortunately, the sort of news approved by Authority was hardly likely to have much appeal to news-hungry citizens. *A Briefe Relation of some affaires and transactions, Civill and Military, both Foreign and Domestick*, duly licensed in 1649, could devote about three-quarters of its space to foreign affairs and dismiss domestic with the comment, calculated to make any professional journalist shudder, that 'through the goodness of God wee still can say we have not much Newes at home' (confirming this fact by leaving the last page and a half blank).

Such official offerings were no match for the royalist Press, which had taken on a new lease of life, and once again embarked on an extraordinary campaign of muck-raking. Its principal targets were Hugh Peters, one of Cromwell's right-hand men, and Hugh Martin, a known republican. *The Royal Diurnall* opened the assault on 11 March 1649:

> Hugh Peters is yet at Milford-haven, and is turn'd one of Venus Souldiers, for he hath got a Wench with Child there, and would have her to have laid it to her Master, but the Wench would not, but took it a great blessing to be with child by that man of God, and resolves if the Bastard proves a Boy, to make a Tub-Preacher of it!

A year later (still in *The Royal Diurnall*), the royalists were still harping on the same theme

> that right reverend Father in Rebellion, Lust and Lies, Hue Peters ... tickles up his Welch Buttocks at Milford-haven, levells his Petard, gives fire, and makes breaches between the Hamms of the Welsh Runts, reducing to the obedience of his Lust-y Masters at Westminister sometimes half a dozen in a day (3 April 1650).

Martin was

> a Saint of another Kidney, and discharges his Conscience at the Crosse-guns in Covent-garden twice or thrice a week, against the Butts of Venus, gives fire p——y fast, and Levells point blancke at the *Mark*; but if she recoyle through much foulness, the next day you may know what exercise he hath run at, by his wide stradling (23 April 1650).

As always, the mixture was well spiced with verse:

> Blush, shameless England, weep, drown'd in thy vile staine,
>   Of Blood with Teares: shall damn'd Rebellion reigne,
> Whilst CHARLS his sacred Blood doth cry
>   Aloud for Vengeance on the Blood-guilty? (4 March 1650).

But time was running out for the royalist journalists. They were hunted down with increasing efficiency, and by mid-1650 all had disappeared. However, the government was beginning to appreciate the effectiveness of propaganda, and a new London newsbook appeared, edited by the familiar figure of Needham, who had been arrested in 1649 for his activities on behalf of the royalist cause. He was experienced and a professional, and was paid the high salary of £100 a year to edit *Mercurius Politicus*. The newsbook was licensed by John Milton, about whose position as a licenser there has been considerable controversy, for in 1644 he had written *Areopagitica* – ever since regarded, to quote Siebert, as 'the most perfect literary expression of the ideal of freedom produced during the struggle of 1644. It gave to succeeding generations the benefit of an argument, the effect of which has expanded as the literary reputation of its author has increased.' The book actually had very little impact at the time of writing.

Mercurius Politicus made no secret of its purpose: it was to be 'in defence of the Common-wealth, and for the Information of the People'. As usual, the achievement of both aims proved impossible, and the 'information' provided was rarely exciting. Other newsbooks were licensed in the same spirit, but by and large the London Press continued to play the part of a kept Press, avoiding controversial issues. Some printers, however, found a solution to the problem: they avoided politics and theology, and instead concentrated upon the ribald and frankly pornographic. The lead was taken by John Crouch, who in 1652 produced a new paper, *Mercurius Democritus*, containing 'Wonderfull News out of the World in the Moon, The Antipodes, Tenebris, Faeryland, Egypt, Greenland, and the adjacent Countries'. His announced aim was, quite simply, 'to create laughter', and this he achieved by bawdry and smut – at the height of the Commonwealth, when public morality was an avowed concern of the government. Obviously, despite the Puritan dominance, a considerable section of the public craved for 'entertainment', and the success of the new venture is indicated by the fact that it immediately inspired a whole host of imitators: the *Laughing Mercury*; *Mercurius Infernus: or, News from the other World*; *Mercurius Jocosus, or the Merry Mercurie*; *Mercurius Cinicus, or, A True and Perfect Diurnall Intelligence, Communicating Admirable News out of the Air, in the Sun, the Sea, and the Earth, Published for the right Understanding of B--ds, Q--s, Wh--s, Small-coal-men, and Chimney-sweepers*; and several others. As their titles freely proclaimed, none made any attempt to present serious news. They vied with one another in smut: and again the indefatigable Crouch triumphed, with the production in 1654 of what must surely be one of the smuttiest papers in the history of the British Press – *Mercurius Fumigosus, or the Smoking Nocturnall*.

Mercurius Fumigosus was divided into two sections: the first, headed 'The Diurnall News', contained actual news items. It rarely took up more than half a page. The remaining seven-and-a-half pages were devoted to the 'Nocturnal News', and consisted of a masterly collection of stories of rapes, cuckolded husbands, drunken orgies and unnatural acts, all written up in a humorous style. Some were clearly based on actual events, but many fell into what can only be called the 'dirty joke' category, with the emphasis placed squarely on the genitals, pubic hair, breaking wind, excrement, and similar subjects. An idea of their general nature may be gained from a few examples. After a family quarrel, an irate husband dealt fittingly with his erring wife: he 'pulled her smock over her ears, and kick'd her before him in the open streets, she being so civill as to cover her Mustard-pott with one hand, and her Vinegar-bottle with the other, to keep out the flies'. (4 July 1655.) Then there was the report of the love play between a man and his girl-friend, the arrangement being that

she would put her wedding Ring upon his middle finger before, which she most willingly did; but his finger presently after swelled so bigge that he not onely lost his nails, but in all haste was forced to send for the Barber Chyrurgeon, who at first resolved it must be cut off, but applying some mollifying and assuaging Plaisters, he (as good luck was) got it off, to the great ease of the poor man whose precious thing he vowed should never more weare Wedding Ring. (6 September 1654.)

Another bright little story had to do with an encounter with one of the 'ladies of joy': 'She offered to lend the Taylors man as much haire from her Innocency as would make him a beard, and moreover, That if his Masters bald Crown did want Hairs to cover it, she would spare as much from the noddle of her Gate-house to make him a Night-cap against Winter' (15 August 1655). From time to time, the author would burst into verse – but always along the same lines:

The married man as much his wife doth wrong
In being hung too short, or too too long. (30 November 1654.)

Even the 'advertisements' bore the same stamp:

If any Man or Woman . . . can tell any Tale or Tidings of a Maidenhead of Two and Twenty years of age, lately lost at Placato between the Hamms in Bedfordshire, let them bring word to the figure of the Dildoe in Fucklesbury, or to the Divel over against Roague's Lane, not farr from Pintle Barr (5 September 1655).

It is amazing that in this period of Puritan domination such a paper was not instantly suppressed, but *Mercurius Fumigosus* was allowed to operate for over a year. At least its 'crimes' were reported humorously. That humorous note was missing from similar items in the more 'respectable' newsbooks, which then, as now, could always find room for a particularly atrocious crime and could report it in a minute and repelling detail which in these days of a 'free' Press is fortunately unknown. Thus, *A Perfect Account of the Daily Intelligence* of 24 January 1654 contained a particularly gruesome item:

At Cobham in Kent, a woman jealous of her husband, sent for the suspected female, and having drunk freely with her, she at last demanded of her, if she would have her nose cut off, or her bearing part; and immediately she and her maidservant fell to work, and exercised that part of her body which they thought had most offended. Not long after her husband came home, and demanding what there was to eat, she reply'd, that she had got him the best bit which he loved in the world, and so presented him with that most ungrateful object.

It is hardly surprising that the government finally intervened. The press was flourishing, with about fifteen newsbooks produced every week.

But too many of them were of the purely sensational type, and in August 1655 Cromwell ordered the laws regarding the Press to be strictly enforced. The results were drastic: within a month, only Needham's *Mercurius Politicus* remained, joined now by a Monday edition entitled *The Publick Intelligence*. These enjoyed a monopoly until 1657, when yet another Needham enterprise was permitted. This was *The Public Adviser*, a penny newsbook devoted entirely to advertisements, and including in its first issue the announcement that

> In Bartholomew Lane on the back side of the Old Exchange, the drink called Coffee (which is a very wholsom and physical drink, having many excellent vertues, closes the Orifice of the Stomack, fortifies the heat within, helpeth Digestion, quickneth the Spirits, maketh the heart lighten, is good against Eye-sores, Coughs, or Colds, Rhumes, Consumption, Head-ach, Dropsie, Gout, Scurvy, Kings Evil, and many others) is to be sold both in the morning, and at three o'clock in the afternoon.[3]

Cromwell was extremely successful in his final effort to control the Press, and his rigid system only broke down with his death, which produced another very confused situation. It had been an exciting period, and a formative one, with certain newsbooks going far beyond their coranto predecessors. The royalists had shown what could be achieved in the way of propaganda, while the 'humorous' newsbooks had indicated the possibilities in the way of entertainment. There had been tremendous expansion: the *Cambridge Bibliography of English Literature*, under the heading 'The News-Books 1641–59', lists no less than 350 titles. There had been considerable experimentation, particularly with newspaper titles, which had become increasingly exotic and original, including *Mercurius Psitacus or the Parroting Mercury*, *The Parliement's Scrich-Owle*, *Mercurius Radamanthus*, *Mercurius Phreneticus*, *The Wandring Whore*, and *Mercurius Insanus Insanissimus*. More significant for the future had been the steady expansion of advertising, from the occasional publishing notice to the appearance of a newsbook devoted entirely to advertisements. Equally indicative of the developing commercial life of the country, and of the value of newspapers in it, were the lists of shipping which appeared in most newsbooks of the 1650s. *The Perfect Proceedings of State Affairs* in 1655 regularly included such items as 'Ships this Week arrived in the Port of London', ships for sale, and 'Ships preparing to out from the River of Thames' (together with their name, burthen, captain, and whether or not they were taking on goods and passengers for their destination). Even *Mercurius Fumigosus* felt obliged to give its own version of such lists, though its ships bore such names as 'The Prepuce' and 'The Cock-boat' (19 September 1655). Undoubtedly, the printed news was reaching more and more of the population, and Authority had on several occasions, and however reluctantly, been forced to accept the fact that it had come to stay. According to *The Perfect Weekly Account* of 24 January 1649: 'In these our dayes the meanest sort of people are not only able to write Etc. but to argue and discourse on matters of highest concernment; and thereupon do desire that such things which are most remarkable may be truly committed to writing and made publique.' *How many* of 'the meanest sort of people' could read and argue intelligently was a question which was to plague Authority for centuries to come, and continues to baffle modern historians. But certainly, the undoubted advances the press had made were far from welcome to Authority, and one of the first actions of Charles II was to appoint Sir John Berkenhead (of *Mercurius Aulicus* fame) to supervise the newsbooks. Only two were permitted, both compiled by Henry Muddiman: the *Parliamentary Intelligencer*, soon renamed the *Kingdome's Intelligencer*, on Mondays, and *Mercurius Publicus* on Thursdays. Temporarily, the newsbook languished. But in its place there flourished that other direct ancestor of the modern newspaper, the *written* news-letter.

The news-letters had long existed as private sources of information among the wealthy and influential: they now assumed a far greater importance, partly because of the control exercised over printed news, and partly because of improvements in the postal services. In 1649 the original weekly post from London had been augmented by a second post, and a third was added in 1655, so that letters could be posted on Tuesdays, Thursdays and Saturdays to any sizeable town in the country. Again, it was Authority which first grasped the possibilities of the news-letter. From its very beginning printed news had been associated with the lower orders, and already there was the conviction that news was only safe as long as it was kept out of the hands of the general public (a conviction which was to remain until well into the nineteenth century). But the expense of the news-letter seemed to suggest that its circulation would be limited to the 'right' people. And the government proceeded to set up an elaborate intelligence system based upon the news-letter of Henry Muddiman.[4] It wished to disseminate news – news rigidly censored, of course; but it also wanted information. And Muddiman was given free postage for his news-letter in order that he might organise a network of correspondents to supply him with news. He charged the large sum of £5 a year for his news-letter: but most of his letters went to official recipients, who were expected to send in reports in return. Until 1663 he was virtually in control of all news, whether printed or written.

To tidy up the somewhat haphazard arrangements made since the King's return, the Printing Act was passed in 1662. It was a most stringent measure: not only was printing restricted to the master-printers of the Stationers' Company and to the two Universities and the Archbishop of York, but the number of master-printers and of the presses and apprentices to be kept by each was also rigidly controlled. At the time there were fifty-nine master-printers in London. No new ones were to be created until this number had been reduced by death or other causes to twenty – which was to be the grand total for the future. To enforce the Act an official Surveyor of the Press was appointed in 1663, with virtually unrestricted powers of search and seizure – Sir Roger

L'Estrange. And Sir Roger had very definite opinions about news:

> Supposing the Press in order, the people in their right wits, and news or no news to be the question, a Public Mercury should not have my Vote, because I think it makes the Multitude too familiar with the actions and counsels of their superiors, too pragmatical and censorious, and gives them not only an itch but a kind of colourable right and license to be meddling with the government.[5]

Nevertheless, he requested and was granted a patent for the exclusive publication of 'all narratives or relacons not exceeding two sheets of paper and all advertisements, mercuries, diurnals, and books of public intelligence'. Muddiman's newsbooks were replaced by *The Intelligencer Published for the Satisfaction and Information of the People* on Mondays and *The Newes* on Thursdays.

The government's control seemed complete. But now politics or personal ambition entered the picture. For some reason, one Williamson, under secretary to Lord Arlington and the employer of Muddiman in his official correspondence, was not satisfied with the arrangements. He began by refusing to supply L'Estrange with official information; then, when in 1665 the Court removed to Oxford to avoid the Plague, he invited Muddiman to edit a new publication, *The Oxford Gazette*, bi-weekly and in direct competition with L'Estrange's newsbooks. The first issue appeared on 16 November 1665, and the enterprise was an immediate success, for it contained all the official news. With the twenty-fourth issue, dated 5 February 1666, it became *The London Gazette*. L'Estrange's monopoly had been broken, though he remained Surveyor of the Press. In the field of news, the *London Gazette* now reigned supreme, though it was hardly an exciting publication and was frequently criticised on this ground.

The government's control of news could not last. Charles II's religious policy and his flirting with the national enemy, France, aroused all the old fears of Popery and Wooden Shoes. The growing interest in what was going on first manifested itself in a pronounced expansion of coffee-houses, mainly in London. From the very beginning, they had been centres of news and gossip. They now began to provide news-letters – and news-letters which were increasingly critical of the government, which became so irritated at their boldness and impudence that in 1676 it issued a proclamation 'for putting down and suppressing all coffee-houses, forbidding the selling coffee, chocolate, tea or sherbet, by retail after the 10th of January'. The real motive behind this obviously unenforceable edict was the clause permitting the sale of these various drinks on condition that the sellers took the Oaths of Allegiance and Supremacy and 'enter into recognizances not to print any libels or pamphlets against the government'. But the unofficial news-letters continued to flourish. Interest in politics was clearly growing, and that interest was by no means confined to the educated and privileged classes.

The Popish Plot could not have been so successfully exploited had it not been for this passionate and 'popular' interest. With the exposure of that plot, excitement rose to a peak, both inside and outside Parliament. The King was forced to prorogue his Parliament in May 1679, before the licensing regulations could be renewed. Temporarily, the Press was free – and it was to make the most of its freedom.

Already periodicals had appeared which were devoted simply and solely to religious propaganda. On 3 December 1678 was published *The Weekly Pacquet from Rome: or, The History of the Papacy*, duly licensed. Its purpose was clearly stated: 'to give an Historical Account gradually of the Usurpations, Cruelties, Etc. of the Bishops of Rome and their Creatures', to which cause it devoted its eight pages weekly. It was not a newspaper in any sense of the word. On 1 March 1679 it was joined by the *Catholic Intelligence: or, Infalliable News Published for the Education of Protestants*, full of sarcastic accounts of miracles, relics and superstition generally. Later in the year appeared *The Weekly Paquet of Advice from Germany: or, The History of the Reformation there*, a straight history of the Reformation. Nor was the market yet exhausted, with the appearance in 1681 of *The Weekly Visions of the Late Popish Plot*, written in essay form and in a literary style which defies understanding; and *The Popish Plot Displayed: Or, The Superstitions and Fopperies of the Romish Church Discover'd*, whose virulent anti-catholicism had at least the novelty that it was mainly in verse. The only comparable production on the other side was the *Weekly Discovery of the Mystery of Iniquity in the Rise, Growth, Methods and Ends of the late Unnatural Rebellion in England, Anno 1641*, a violently anti-Puritan history of the Civil War, and running from February to August 1681.

While the propagandists of both sides were happily ransacking history, other printers were concentrating upon rather more up-to-date news in this period of comparative freedom. Some sought to produce newsbooks in the old tradition, concentrating on foreign affairs and adopting an attitude of extreme caution towards domestic. But the intense excitement of the Popish Plot ensured that most newsbooks were primarily concerned with politics. Soon a vigorous newspaper war was in progress, with the various printers denouncing one another frequently and violently. Unfortunately, to the modern reader the difference between the 'Whig' and the 'Tory' parties is often obscure. It was, of course, often obscure to contemporaries, for the political party was still in the embryonic stage, lacking organisation, a coherent platform, and discipline. The position was further complicated by religion. Charles II was widely suspected of having Catholic sympathies; his brother, the Duke of York, was an avowed Catholic: but even the most ardent court (Tory) papers could not openly support Catholicism in the climate of opinion then prevailing. Equally, 'Whig' printers had to be even more careful, for they were decidedly unpopular at court. Both were fully aware that their freedom was likely to be exceedingly temporary. In fact, soon after the accidental expiry of the Licensing Act, the King had consulted the judges as to the possibilities of using his prerogative powers to renew the system of control. According to one account, 'they gave their opinion, that they knew not any way to prevent printing by law; because the Act for that purpose was expired. Upon which, some judges were put out [i.e. dismissed], and new ones put in; and then this opinion was given', that, 'to print or publish any news-books or pamphlets of news whatsoever is illegal; that it is a manifest intent to the breach of the peace'. And in May 1680 Charles issued a proclamation suppressing all newsbooks – a somewhat optimistic measure which proved impossible to enforce immediately. But the threat remained.

Some papers, particularly those on the court side, made no secret of their political sympathies. Thompson's *The Loyal Protestant, and True Domestick Intelligencer*, which first appeared on 9 March 1681, stated on 5 April that it was 'Published to prevent the many false and scandalous Seditious Reports . . . [which] do enflame the People against the Government'. It was to be very critical of what it called 'the parcel of Mechanical Statesmen' who had abused 'the Gentlemen (who are Persons of known Worth and Loyalty), calling them *Jesuits in Masquerade, Tories*, and *Church Papists*: Names which of late they have taken the boldness to brand his Majesty's best Subjects with'. And it revealed its political sympathies very clearly in its account of the trial of Colledge for high treason in London (a city notorious for its Whig sympathies). The accused was reported (9 July 1681) to have said

> that the Family of the Stuarts was a Cursed Family, That King
> James turn'd off his Wife, and Bugger'd the Duke of
> Buckingham; That the King designed to govern arbitrarily . . .
> and many other the most horrid Expressions . . . But
> (notwithstanding the Evidence was positive) the Grand Jury
> would not find the Bill . . . *This was a True Protestant Jury.*

Equally obvious in the Tory cause were L'Estrange's *Observator*, 1681, containing little news but much comment, and *Heraclitus Ridens; Or, a Discourse between Jest and Earnest, where many a True Word is spoken in opposition to all Libellers against the Government*, published by B. Tooke, also in 1681. Again, there was no news: the attack was on the Whig papers, with occasional tilts at Dissenters and the Commonwealth period in general. As usual, the printer relied heavily on sarcasm, with frequent references to 'true Protestants' and 'the Good Old Cause'. These effusions were answered in kind by such Whig publications as *Mercurius Bifrons: Or, The English Janus. The one side True and Serious, the other Jocular*, using humour as its main weapon, and specialising in incomprehensibility.

Most newsbooks ignored such flights of fancy, and claimed to provide *news*. They relied upon innuendo and sarcasm – and the modern reader often has difficulty in appreciating such subtleties, obvious as they may have been to the readers of the time. The situation is not made easier by the apparently distressing lack of originality displayed by the printers in their titles, a lack which was not always unintentional. On 7 July 1679,

Benjamin Harris (a man of pronounced Whig sympathies) produced his *Domestick Intelligence, or News from both City and Country. Published to Prevent false Reports.* But on 26 August there appeared a paper with the same title, but this time printed by N. Thompson (nicknamed 'Popish Nat') in the Tory interest. He numbered his first issue 'No. 16' (the same as his rival's paper for that week) in an obvious attempt to decoy his rival's readers away.[6] Harris changed his title to *The Protestant (Domestick) Intelligence* in January 1680 – as against yet another competitor, *The True Protestant (Domestick) Intelligence*, followed in 1681 by *The Domestick Intelligence*, published by T. Benskin. Later, Thompson's *Loyal Protestant and True Domestick Intelligence* was to add to the general confusion.

Most of these publications were single-leaf, often appearing twice a week: all were full of the Popish Plot. To modern eyes, they all say very much the same thing: but obviously contemporary readers read far more into the reports than is apparent today. Certainly, the printers accused each other of lies and deceit. The Tory *True Domestick Intelligence* of 24 February 1680 attacked 'the (falsely called) *Protestant Domestic Intelligence* (which rather deserves the name of the Heathen Commonwealth Intelligence)'. The Tory *Loyal Protestant, and True Domestick Intelligence* had its own black-list of Whig writers: Benjamin Harris – 'that common Broker of Faction'; Richard Janeway, hailed variously as 'simple Janeway, the Pimp to Fanaticks, and his scurrilous and scandalous Scribblers', 'this seditious Bog-House', and 'the Hackney of the crude Phanaticks'; and Smith, Care, Curtis, Mrs Benskin and Richard Baldwin. Both sides dropped gaily into the gutters from time to time. The Tory papers regaled their readers with stories of so-called Puritans getting wenches with child, or being found in brothels. For example, *The Loyal Protestant* of 2 September 1682 had an interesting report of a Dissenting minister who 'laid with two Wenches ten Nights at a Guinny a Night: That he exercised one whilst the other raised his Inclinations'. The Whig papers of course reported similar activities on the part of Popish priests. Otherwise, it was all a matter of careful selection of news items and of emphasis. According to the Whig papers, the Duke of York received a very cool reception in his various travels, while the Tory papers stressed the warmth of his welcome. The Whigs again stressed the tremendous welcome of the popular – and ostentatiously Protestant – Duke of Monmouth on *his* excursions, excursions which the Tory papers either ignored or dismissed very tersely indeed. Again, the Tory papers quoted at length from carefully selected loyal addresses from the counties, whereas the Whigs concentrted upon London, their main stronghold. In this way, the *Domestick Intelligence* of 16 September reproduced an address by 'several Hundreds of the Principal Citizens of London' to the Lord Mayor demanding 'what Advantages and Encouragement the Duke of *York*'s being a *Papist* gave to the Rise and Progress of this Horrid and Damnable *Plot*'. Always, the Whig papers stressed the disorders and uncertainties of the time, spreading what were later to be known as 'alarm and despondency' among their readers.

The Whig papers were clearly in the majority, and they had the tacit support of Parliament, if only temporarily. L'Estrange, in voluntary exile in Holland, wrote later:

> Every post . . . brought us over Gazettes, Touzers, Abhorrers and Printed Votes . . . What a deal of malicious humour, rather, has been contracted by the reading of them! For there never was so miserable a people; never so abandoned a nation; never so many false steps; oversights, miscarriages, neglects and oppressions in the administration of any government, if the least credit may be given to the insinuations of these minutes.

But journalism remained a dangerous profession. The *Currant Intelligence* of 14 February 1680 described the trial of Benjamin Harris for publishing a pamphlet, *Appeal from the Countrey to the City*, for which he was sentenced to the pillory, fined £500 and made to produce securities for good behaviour for three years. He was perhaps the leading Whig journalist: but Authority had had enough of newspapers in general, and if Whigs were prosecuted more frequently, the Tory journalists also had their difficulties. Nat Thompson found himself in gaol in March 1680 – to his obvious surprise.[7] One by one the Whig papers disappeared. Some Tory papers lingered on: the *Loyal Protestant* had displayed great glee at the misfortunes of its Whig rivals, but on 16 November 1682 its author had to announce that

> having continued the News-book for some time, and (as I thought) giving a *True Account* of such things as came to my knowledge, without offence to any, only those Plagues and Pests of the Nation, the Phanaticks . . . But being now informed, that Authority is displeased therewith, I am very willing to desist writing any more, in regard it would be most inexcusable for Me, who have ever writ in defence of *Them* and their *Authority*, now to continue in disobedience of their just Command.

In this brief period, from 1679 to 1682, the political papers dominated the scene – although some journalists still strove to avoid the obvious dangers involved in political comment, and the *London Mercury* of 10 April 1682 assured its readers of its intention 'not only to give a true, but an Impartial account of such matters as are reasonable fit for such Papers to intermeddle withall, always avoiding Reflections both on Church and State, public Transactions, and particular Persons'; but in that exciting time it was impossible for a newspaper to be neutral. Nevertheless, the main political battle had certainly not been fought in the news-sheets. In London, of course, the lower classes *were* important politically, and it was for this reason that the news-sheets were eventually silenced. Outside London their influence was probably negligible, and the real propaganda war had been conducted in the more private – and expensive – news-letters, aimed at the politically significant classes, the gentry, merchants, lawyers and so on. Again, the Whig news-writers had flourished. Best known was Giles Hancock, who charged from £4 to £6 per annum and rivalled Muddiman in the number of his correspondents. He was regularly the target of abuse of the Tory writers, under such endearments as 'the featest' little nangy fool'.

The situation became even worse with the accession of James II, whose pro-Catholic and pro-French policy strengthened all the old fears. As always, the centre of interest was London, for London absolutely dominated the country. The Exclusion Crisis had shown what might happen if the government lost control of the capital, and the lesson was not lost on James: every year witnessed major prosecutions of printers for seditious libel. But too much was at stake, and as popular excitement grew there was almost open defiance of Authority. The Queen was the main target of scurrilous abuse, and the King himself complained that 'pamphlets flew about fill'd with all the ribaldry and calumny that malice and wit were capable of inventing, where under the notice of novels and private relations of news that passed at Court, the horridest crimes were laid to the Queen's charge'.[8] James might be able to silence the occasional printers, but the news-writers were much more difficult to identify and suppress. They now flourished exceedingly, assisted by the growing popularity of coffee-houses. These coffee-houses provided a reasonably comfortable escape from the squalid and cramped living conditions of city life; they were convenient centres for social meetings and business discussions, and (very important indeed) they offered a selection of news-letters. Inevitably many were politically orientated right from the start. In effect, a whole propaganda machine had swung into action, with pamphlets and written news-letters being widely distributed, mainly through the coffee-houses but also through the post. In this campaign, however, the printed news-sheets played no part. A compliant Parliament had renewed the Printing Act, and newspapers were too vulnerable. But James himself became aware of the need for some sort of counter-attack. His proclamations against the circulation of seditious literature had proved unavailing, and, interestingly enough, he chose to revive the newspapers. On 21 February 1688 there appeared, duly licensed, *Publick Occurrences Truely Stated*, which, although printed by Henry Care, the former Whig propagandist, contained a strong defence of James's religious policy, stressing the value of toleration, liberty of conscience and the repeal of the Test Act. Care was perhaps, like Needham before him and Defoe and many others after, merely demonstrating the chameleon-like adaptability of the professional journalist.

William of Orange landed on 5 November, and the King had lost control of the capital. The whole machinery of Press regulation broke down, and, as in 1679, a flood of newspapers appeared, all on the Whig side. All had exciting stories to tell of local clashes with 'Papists', and, although the Revolution was virtually bloodless in the sense that there were no pitched battles, it is clear that many old grudges were settled.

Despite the almost desperate loyalty of these newspapers, William was quick to appoint a messenger and inspector of the printing press to enforce the Licensing Act, which was still valid. Obviously, anything in the nature of the 'Freedom of the Press' was hardly likely to commend itself to the very conservative revolutionaries of 1688, with their vivid memories of the Popish Plot: that crisis had demonstrated only too convincingly the dangers of the Press. Even the most diehard Whig could not look back with sympathy upon the activities of the Whig newsbooks during that hectic period; they had distorted, exaggerated and invented. The record of their Tory rivals had hardly been much better, and both had an unfortunate tendency to appeal to the lower classes which, ignorant, illiterate and voteless, found in rioting their only form of political self-expression. And so the Revolution Parliament – a Parliament perhaps dominated by the Whigs, but containing quite as many Tories – had no hesitation in renewing the Printing Act. One can but sympathise. The 'people' as a recognised force in politics simply did not exist: but its passions and prejudices did exist, and could very easily be played on.

From the point of view of printed news, the *London Gazette* once again reigned supreme. It was allowed few rivals. Indeed, the most important newspapers of this period from 1689 to 1694 were probably the monthly summaries from the continent, translations of the French-language originals published in Holland, with the deletion of passages which might offend English susceptibilities. Thus, the *Present State of Europe* omitted the comment of the *Mercure historique et politique* that England was a difficult nation to govern, and that if James had stayed longer he would have been executed, although it was prepared to repeat the rumour that James had sold Ireland to the King of France.[9] The decision must have been a somewhat delicate one. For a time Authority was prepared to license such journals of opinion as *The Pacquet of Advices from France: or, The French Intrigues towards the Enslaving of Europe* in 1691. This was not a newspaper but a propaganda sheet, and one which fitted in well with William's Grand Design against Louis XIV; its second issue, dated 9 April, regaled its readers with 'A late Character of the French King' and 'His Amorous Intrigues'. Nevertheless, it had only a short run.

The main interest of the period had undoubtedly been political: and the political papers had had their moments of triumph – and of disaster. But other types of journalism still existed. In 1676 there appeared *Poor Robin's Intelligence* – 'From the Beginning of the World to the Day of the Date hereof . . . price four fourths of a penny'. It contained no news, but concentrated upon humour and smut, and it was licensed by L'Estrange, who, although he objected to the public taking an interest in politics, apparently saw no harm in this sort of entertainment. In the issue dated, somewhat mysteriously, 'From St. Mark's Day, till the Morrow after Milk-Maid's-Holy-Day' there appeared an advertisement in the best Rabelaisian tradition of a quack:

> He understands Diseases by taking 3 Hairs from the Pole of the Patient, and perfectly cures 'em by cutting off the rest. If

therefore any young Widow, Wife, or Maid find herself over-burdened with the superfluous Excresences of the Pia Mater, be the Colour light-brown, or flaxen, she is most certainly troubled with Asthma's, Coughs, Cathars, or such-like Consumptive Distempers, and no way cureable but . . . by shaving the Pericranium, whose noxious Tresses he causes to be worn about the Streets as Trophies of his Skill and Ingenuity. Then (Madam) he applyes to your soft place a soverain Plaister.

Still following a familiar tradition, the paper on 10 April 1677 announced that 'At Madam Lena's House on Thursday next a rare Commodity call'd a Maidenhead . . . will be exposed for sale by the Inch of Candle'. Obviously there was still an appreciative market for this type of humour, and similar papers were permitted to appear throughout the period. *Momus Ridens: or, Comical Reports on the Publick Reports*, published in the early days of William's reign, relied heavily on verse and often verged on the obscene, as in its issue of 14 January 1691, an issue devoted largely to the problems of a bride on her wedding night, and ending with the couplet:

> The Virgin may weep and complain of the Knack,
> But there's nought but a May-pole can trouble the *Crack*.

None of these productions even approached the high standards set by their Commonwealth predecessors in smut or sheer humour. But no newsbook, however serious and politically-minded, could resist the temptation. *The Loyal Protestant* of 9 July 1681 reported a court case:

> Her Fellow-Servant Deposed, that taking Notice of this Wenchs caressing the great Mastiffe more than ordinary, she watched her into the Barn, where standing privily, she saw her Feed the Dog and Cherish him, and then pulling up her Coats, threw herself on her back, and with a peculiar Lascivious Meen, Invited him, but the Dog Essaying could not, which with Horror seeing, the Maid called her Mistress, who likewise came and beheld the Wench in another Posture, Beast-like upon all Four, with her Posteriours Bare, and the Dog effectually performing . . . Upon Examination she confessed, that she having been at Emsbury Fair, was overcome with Drink, and suffered three or four men to enjoy her, by which Coition she got the Venerial Disease, and supposing with herself that Copulation would help her Malady, and not having the Convenience of a Man, she betook herself to this Crime for Remedy.

The sort of item which would be certain of inclusion in the popular press of today was the report in the *London Mercury* of 1 September 1682 of a case before the justices of the peace in Pembroke:

> Mary Thomas of the Parish of Staynton, Widow, Maketh

Oath, That she is aged Eighty-four years and upwards; and that she is now pregnant with a bastard-Child; and that one John Sennett, Carpenter, is the Father of the same; and that the said John Sennett hath had frequent Carnal knowledge of her Body for the space of Four years last past.

More 'innocent', and certainly more learned, was the *Weekly Memorial: or, An Account of Books lately set forth; with other Accounts relating to Learning*, beginning on 19 January 1688 and published by authority. This may well have been the first periodical to devote each issue entirely to a review of one book. Then, in March 1690, John Dunton began his *Athenian Gazette*, a sort of seventeenth-century *Notes and Queries*, consisting of readers' questions and answers. The issue of 2 February 1692 contained such questions as 'Why the Owl is said of Old to be sacred to Minerva, and dear to the City of Athens' and 'What is the cause of Snow, Hail and Frost', together with queries regarding mathematics, science, Greek and Hebrew. Nor was the human interest angle ignored, and there were many questions on the lines of the 'correspondence columns' of modern magazines. Typical was the enquiry in the same issue: 'There are a Knot of Apprentices dwelling nigh each other, who are all concerned in keeping company with a Servant Maid of no good Repute . . . I desire your Advice whether I ought to make it known to their Master, or conceal it because it may occasion much Trouble.' The production won a considerable reputation, and was widely imitated. Interestingly enough, in view of John Dunton's considerable literary reputation, he also found time in 1696–97 to produce *The Night Walker: Or, Evening Rambles in search after Lewd Women*.

Equally harmless from the official point of view were the trade journals, now increasingly making their mark. Early in the field was *The City and Country Mercury: For the help of Trade and Dealing both in Country and City; and for the prosecuting all sorts of Felons and other Evil-doers, and preventing of Escapes; with the publication of Advertisments of all sorts, Etc.* Despite its impressive title, this consisted of a single leaf, with one side devoted to a dialogue between 'City' and 'Country' about crops, prices, and so on, and the other to advertisements. Also there was *The City Mercury: or, Advertisements concerning Trade*, which first appeared on 4 November 1675 as a single leaf quarto, packed with the advertisements. Most of these concerned property; but others had to do with various trades and occupations. An undertaker 'secureth the Corps of any dead Body from any ill Scent or Annoyance, without Embalming, Embowelling, or Wrapping'; there were notices from a country carrier, the Harwich coach, the inevitable quacks, a teacher, an exhibition of 'The Elephant', and 'a hot-house . . . where men may sweat'; and a ship was required 'fit for the *Virginia* Trade'. The main emphasis, as the paper itself stated, was 'For Buying and Selling of Estates and Places, for procuring of Money upon Real and Personal Security, and accomodating Persons of Quality and others with Servants'. Who, one wonders, were the 'others'? But soon papers became more enterprising. *The Currant Intelligence*, a bi-weekly beginning on 14 February 1680, laid its emphasis upon shipping, announcing that it would produce a list 'of all the Merchants Ships that either come or go out of any Port of the West of England'. Hitherto, what shipping news there was had been largely confined to the Port of London. *The Merchants Remembrancer* of 1681 presented a very detailed account of the prices of almost every conceivable commodity, 'Rising, Highest, Falling, or Standing'. Later in the same year, *A Collection of Letters, for the Improvement of Husbandry and Trade. By John Houghton, Fellow of the Royal Society*, made its appearance as a 22-page booklet, devoted to lengthy articles. Both were longlived. In 1694 Houghton's *Collection for Improvement of Husbandry and Trade* was thriving, it was now a two-leaf paper: most of the front page was taken up by an essay on such topics as the best way to grow wheat, the second contained an extremely detailed list of prices of various types of goods. The second leaf was headed 'Advertisements', and bore the editorial announcement: 'My Collection I shall carry on as usual. This part is to give away, and those who like it not, may omit the reading. I believe it will help on Trade, particularly encourage the Advertisers to increase the want of my Papers.' Also still flourishing was a later version of *The Merchants Remembrancer*, now entitled *Whitson's Merchants Weekly Remembrancer, of the Present-Money-Prices of their Goods Ashoar in London*.

But the government's control of actual 'news' could not last. The political conditions of the late seventeenth century made the existing system of repression increasingly futile. The great continental campaigns of William III against the national enemy aroused a demand for news that could not be satisfied by the meagre supply so grudgingly permitted by Authority. Not only did those campaigns promise all the excitement of blood and battle, but they also aroused quite genuine fears of invasion and of the possible restoration of the Stuarts, backed by French bayonets. And the thought of the introduction into England of those three abominations popularly associated with the national enemy, rape, popery and wooden shoes, was one which no Englishman could contemplate with equanimity. In fact, the atmosphere was charged with a sustained emotional tension, reflected at the top level by the savage political struggles at Westminster, but shared by everybody. News of any sort was at a premium: and the system of control became increasingly ineffective, as moonshine presses sprang up in the teeming warrens of London, defying discovery and suppression. Party politics eventually decided the issue, for when in 1695 the Printing Act came up for renewal, a predominantly Whig House of Commons demanded a new draft. So many objections were raised on matters of detail that the Act lapsed. Typically enough, the objections were based not on great questions of principle, but on such purely practical grounds as the difficulty of enforcement. Of the moral and philosophical issues involved, virtually nothing was said. Indeed, Authority had every intention of formulating new and more efficient measures, and on at least four occasions before the end of the century further Bills were introduced. But there was no agreement: and in this unheroic and rather disappointing way, England was to achieve the first major step towards the freedom of the Press.

2 Intelligence, instruction and entertainment 1695-1760

Once the Printing Act had lapsed, it became legally permissible to print and publish a newspaper without a licence; once again, despite the apparently temporary nature of the new freedom, newspapers sprang up almost overnight. Obviously a reading public was ready and waiting, and one large enough to promise quick returns on the very small capital outlay then required to produce a newspaper. Many of the new ventures were shortlived, but very soon there were experiments regarding the role and purpose of a newspaper.

Among the newspapers proper may be mentioned what Walker has named the 'Big Three': the tri-weekly papers, the *Post-Boy*, the *Flying Post*, and the *Post-Man*. There followed *The Foreign Post. And an Impartial and Particular Account of the Peace, with Domestick News*, the *Protestant Mercury*, and various others, some of which attempted to combine the cheapness of a newspaper with the appeal and intimacy of a news-letter. Baldwin's *Historical Account* addressed its reader as 'Sir', and ended with 'Yours etc.' *Dawk's News-Letter* went even further, being printed in a fine italic script. Significant for the future were the publication in 1701 of the first provincial newspaper, the *Norwich Post*, and of the first successful London daily paper, the *Daily Courant*, in 1702.

The *Daily Courant* appeared as a single leaf, with one side left blank. Its editor explained his policy at some length (30 April 1702): he would perform

what he takes to be the proper and only Business of a News-Writer; first, by giving the freshest Advices from all Quarters, which he will certainly be able to do (let the Post arrive when it will) by coming out Daily: and next, delivering Facts as they come related, and without inclining either to one side or the other: and this too he will be found to do, by representing the same Actions, according to the different Accounts which both Sides give of them . . . And thus having fairly related, What is done, When, Where, by which Side reported, and by what Ends transmitted hither, he thinks himself obliged not to launch out of his Province, to amuse People with any Comments or Reflections of his own; but leave every Reader to make such Remarks for himself as he is capable of.

He added, with reference to the blank side of the sheet, that 'This Courant is confin'd to half the Compass, to save the Publick at least half the Impertinences of ordinary Newspapers'. The appeal was thus to a reasonably educated and informed public. But many readers wanted more. Even in foreign news they wanted comment, or at least some explanation of the often contradictory reports lifted from the various official *Gazettes*: and they wanted domestic news. The wealthy could fall back on their news-letters, but few could afford such luxuries. The printers did their best, but it is clear that many were not as accurate or objective as the author of the *Daily Courant* claimed to be. Their foreign news they took from the continental *Gazettes* – although, as Addison was to point out (*Spectator*, no. 452), despite the fact that 'they all of them receive the same advices from abroad, and very often in the same words . . . their way of cooking it is so different, that there is no citizen, who has an eye to the public good, that can leave the coffee-house with peace of mind, before he has given every one of them a reading'.

The discrepancies and contradictions were even more apparent in the domestic news. A newspaper could hardly hope to survive on the official notices it could abstract from the *London Gazette*: its readers demanded excitement, entertainment, human interest stories, the latest reports – aspects hardly catered for by the *Gazette*. But there were no reporters, and no organised means of gathering the sort of news required, and the printers had to rely on highly unreliable sources: coffee-house gossip, tavern rumour, private tips, and eye-witness reports from soldiers and sailors returning from the war. The accounts could seldom be verified, and all too frequently they proved to be highly exaggerated, if not completely false. To make matters even more confusing, it seems that many newspapers were not above actually inventing 'news'. The charge was to be made again and again. Nevertheless the newspaper rapidly established itself. It has been estimated that in 1704 the circulation of the *London Gazette* was approximately 6,000, while that of the other main London newspapers was: *Daily Courant*, 800; *London Post*, 400; *English Post*, 400; *Post-Man*, 3,800; *Post-Boy*, 3,000; and *Flying Post*, 400.[1] Significantly, the *Post-Man* and *Post-Boy* were tri-weekly evening papers aimed at the country market.

At the same time, other types of periodical were developing in London, where the reading public was large enough to encourage printers to specialise. Very quickly indeed after the lapse of the Printing Act appeared trade papers, literary periodicals, and political papers. In 1695 *The London Mercury, Published for the Promoting of Trade* consisted solely of advertisements, which at first, and despite the paper's title, had to do only with 'Books newly Published' and quack remedies. Then in 1696 came *Lloyd's News*, a 'straight' newspaper but with a heavy emphasis on shipping reports. It was followed by such papers as *The General Remarks on Trade. Set forth by Mr. Povey, Undertaker of the Traders Exchange-House in Hatton-Gardens* in 1707, and *The British Mercury. Published by the Company of London-Insurance* in 1709. Both contained ordinary news, mainly foreign, but always with the stress on shipping, with tables of exchange rates, stocks, and the prices of various goods. And already new ideas were beginning to emerge. *The General Remarks on Trade* of 7 July 1707, for example, bore on its title-page two large woodcuts, one of a boy, the other of a large building, with the announcements:

> Favour our Undertaking so far, as to Promote the Sale of this Paper; because out of the Profits arising by the Sale of it, 20 Poor Boys, most Orphans, such as the Figure above represents, are Cloathed, Kept to School, allowed 2s.6d. a Week each, and at Two Years End, Five Pounds a Piece given, to put them out Apprentices.

and

> So be generous . . . for out of the Income of such Advertisements and other Business done at the Traders Exchange-House, 100 Decayed Men and Women are to be allowed 10 l. per Annum each, and a Room to Live in Rent-free, in such a College as is represented by the Figure above.

One hesitates to suggest that this warm appeal may have been an early anticipation of later press 'stunts'. But certainly the paper is interesting in other ways. Its earlier issues contained a good deal of foreign news; then the emphasis shifted to commercial advices, with lists of ships arriving at or departing from various ports, tables showing the direction of the wind, moneys advanced or paid off, and essays on some matter of trade interest, such as 'Fishing on the Coast of Great Britain and Ireland'. But gradually a completely new note appeared, and the essays began to have such titles as 'Instructions to Gentlemen to know whether a Picture be well Design'd, well Painted, and an Original'. And there was a series of questions and answers on John Dunton lines. This new approach marked the rising social status of the merchants and their increasing desire to acquire 'polish' and to feel at home in polite society.

This same emphasis was apparent in the 1690s, when a whole crop of periodicals appeared. In 1698 *The English Lucian: or, Weekly Discoveries of the Witty Intrigues, Comical Passages, and Remarkable Transactions in Town and Country: With Reflections on the Vices and Vanities of the Times* had a tendency towards smut, but it was an anticipation of *The Tatler*. There followed in 1699 *The Weekly Comedy, As it is Dayly Acted at Most Coffee-houses in London*, presented in the form of a discussion between members of a club: 'Snark, a Disbanded Captain. Truck, a Merchant. Scribble, a News-Writer. All-craft, a Turncoat. Cant, a Precisian. Snap, a Sharper. Squabble, a Lawyer. Whim, a Projector. Log, a Marriner. Scan-all, a Poet. Plush, a Quack. Prim, a Beau.' Again, this was an anticipation of the future, this time of Sir Roger de Coverley and the illustrious club of *The Spectator*. Also might be mentioned the *Gentlemen's Journal*, a monthly 'Letter to a Gentleman in the Country', with the same stress on the social graces and items about literature, history and philosophy. And there were the early political papers, such as Dunton's *Pegasus, With News, an Observator, and a Jacobite Courant* in 1696, a curious production, with some news, a political essay, and, in the 'Jacobite Courant', the technique of using a dialogue – in this case semi-humorous, but very definitely anti-Jacobite and anti-French.

Obviously printers were still feeling their way, uncertain of their market. This uncertainty is well illustrated in the story of Defoe's *A Weekly Review of the Affairs of France: Purg'd from the Errors and Partiality of News-Writers and Petty Statesmen, of all Sides*, which first appeared on 19 February 1704. It consisted of two sections. One was devoted to a lengthy essay on France under such titles as 'Of the French Nation' and 'Of French Greatness'. The other was more popular in its appeal. Entitled 'Mercure Scandale: Or Advice from the Scandalous Club. Translated out of French' (with, very soon, a subtitle, 'Being a Weekly History of Nonsense, Impertinence, Vice and Debauchery') it consisted of mock trials of newswriters, fully identified, being called on to explain such crimes as obscurity, misuse of English, ignorance and inaccuracy in facts. The emphasis was humorous: but at the same time, Defoe was undermining public confidence in many of his competitors. But he was experimenting. *The Review* was at first a weekly of eight pages; with its fifth issue, it became a four-page paper, published twice a week. The Scandalous Club no longer confined itself to the errors of rival journalists but began to deal with social comment generally. With the second volume, the title became *A Review of the Affairs of France, with some Observations on Transactions at Home*, and, with the third, *A Review of the State of the English Nation*. The Scandalous Club had now vanished, as also had the previous emphasis on humour, and the paper now consisted solely of serious essays, often on trade, but from time to time touching on morals, toleration, foreign affairs, conditions in prisons – essays often written with a strong social purpose, and publicising individual cases of injustice.

Many historians of the Press have regarded the *Review* as a vital stage in the history of journalism. Undoubtedly, Defoe possessed a remarkable talent for reporting. He has also been widely praised for his moderation and reason. However, in this respect his reputation has suffered a blow by the discovery that, while writing the *Review*, he was actually a secret agent for the Tory leader, Robert Harley, and was also accepting money from the Whigs. The key to this apparent ambivalence, according to Laurence Hanson, is that Defoe

> knew that he was a great writer who could write to more effect on most topics than any of his contemporaries, and that he saw no reason why the world should be deprived of the fine writing that he could give it. He could and did write on both sides in many controversies . . . His justification, if there were any need of it, would be that his pamphlets represent the best work on both sides.[2]

The argument is interesting, if not altogether convincing, and the essential problem of Defoe's journalistic morality must remain. But one gift he did not possess, the successful employment of satire. His satirical pamphlet, *The Shortest Way with Dissenters* (1702), had been taken at its face value by too many readers, had been publicly burned, and Defoe gaoled. He took the same risk in 1712 with a pamphlet intended to be a blast against the Jacobites, but widely taken to be a defence of them. He was again imprisoned, and his imprisonment ended the *Review*, which was already declining as the knowledge of its ministerial subsidy became known. But Defoe himself was far from finished. He was to remain an active journalist all his life, and was to continue his curiously murky political career.

Other essay-type periodicals had already appeared to challenge the *Review*. In the political field, the most powerful was *The Examiner. Or Remarks upon Papers and Occurrences*, which made its bow as a single-leaf paper on 3 August 1710. It too was Tory, and was apparently prompted by St John (later Lord Bolingbroke), the Secretary of State, who himself wrote some of the articles, indicating the growing awareness of leading politicians of the increasing importance of the periodical Press. The editor was Dr William King, and the chief writers were the poet, Matthew Prior, and Dr Atterbury (later sent to the Tower for his part in a Jacobite plot); its most notable contributor was Dean Swift, who in 1710 and 1711 made the *Examiner* the voice of the Tories.

The *Examiner* was a purely essay-type publication, containing no news items as such. Its effectiveness may be gauged by its devastating attack on the Whig claims that the Tory government had shown base 'ingratitude' to the Duke of Marlborough following his great victories in the war. On 23 November 1710 the paper compared the treatment of the Duke with that accorded its public heroes by Ancient Rome. 'We will', it announced, 'draw up two Accounts, the one of *Roman* Gratitude, and the other of *British* Ingratitude, and set them together in ballance.' There followed two columns, headed respectively 'A Bill of Roman Gratitude', and 'A Bill of British Ingratitude'. Under the first appeared:

For Franckincense and Earthen Pots to burn it in	4	10	0
A Bull for Sacrifice	8	0	0
An Embroidered Garment	50	0	0
A Crown of Laurel			2
A Statue	100	0	0
A Trophy	80	0	0
A thousand Copper Medals value halfpence a piece	2	1	8
A Triumphal Arch	500	0	0
A Triumphal Carr, valu'd as a modern Coach	100	0	0
Casual Charges at the Triumph	150	0	0
Sum Total	994	11	10

But the other column told a very different story:

Woodstock	40,000	0	0
Blenheim	200,000	0	0
Post-Office Grant	100,000	0	0
Mildenheim	30,000	0	0
Pictures, Jewels, Etc.	60,000	0	0
Pall-mall, grant, Etc.	10,000	0	0
Employments	100,000	0	0
Sum Total	540,000	0	0

The effect of the two columns side by side is shattering: it was a remarkable triumph in the field of political propaganda. In sheer self-defence, the Whigs started *The Whig Examiner* 'to give all persons a re-hearing who have suffered any unjust sentence of *The Examiner*'. Its chief contributor was Addison, but it lasted only four issues, when it was replaced by *The Medley*, aimed squarely at *The Examiner*, with Addison and Steele among its leading lights. Unfortunately for the Whigs, Addison and Steele did not possess the political acumen of Defoe: their talents lay elsewhere, as they were soon to prove.

Important developments had been taking place in the literary field. In 1708, another periodical of the questions and answers type had appeared, *The British Apollo, or Curious Amusements for the Ingenious . . . Perform'd by a Society of Gentlemen.* But such amateur enterprises were to be outclassed by a production which was to make both literary and journalistic history: *The Tatler* began in April 1709, mainly written by Steele, who was soon to be joined by Addison. Again, there was a period of experiment. The paper started as a tri-weekly, with news, advertisements, poetry and anecdotes. But it became a series of essays, one to each issue, on morals, manners and social behaviour generally. Its success was immediate, and when it came to an end in January 1711 it was not because of any falling-off of circulation, but because Steele and Addison planned an even more ambitious enterprise. Indeed, the popularity of *The Tatler* is indicated by its numerous imitators: *The Tory Tatler*, *The French Tatler*, *The Tatling Harlot* (1709), *Titt for Tatt* (1710), and *The Female Tatler. By Mrs. Crackenthorpe, a Lady that knows Everything* (and who gave the public the benefit of that knowledge three times a week from 8 July 1709 on).

The new enterprise was *The Spectator*, another purely essay-type periodical, but published daily. Mr Spectator was a country squire, but very much a man of the world, well-travelled, with a thirst for knowledge of any kind, and an inveterate *habitué* of the London coffee-houses:

Sometimes I am seen thrusting my head into a round of politicians at Will's and listening with great attention to the narratives that are made in these little circular audiences. Sometimes I smoke a pipe at Child's and while I seem attentive to nothing but the *Postman*, overhear the conversation of every table in the room. I appear on Sunday nights at St. James's coffee-house, and sometimes join the little committee of politics in the inner room, as one who comes there to hear and improve. My face is likewise very well known at the Grecian, the Cocoa Tree and in the theatres both of Drury Lane and the Haymarket. I have been taken for a merchant upon the exchange for about these ten years, and some times pass for a Jew in the assembly of stock-jobbers at Jonathan's.

This was the sort of world that the merchants and gentry wanted to hear about. But Mr Spectator widened his appeal by introducing his famous club: Sir Roger de Coverley, a Worcestershire squire; a member of the Inner Temple, 'but one who knows Aristotle and Longinus better than Littleton or Coke and is better known at the play than at the Courts'; Sir Andrew Freeport, merchant; Captain Sentry, a retired sailor; Will Honeycomb, an aged but still active gallant, 'who knows the history of every mode and can inform you from which of the French King's favourites our wives and daughters had this manner of curling their hair, that way of placing their hoods, whose frailty was covered by such a petticoat and whose vanity to show her feet made that part of the dress so short in such a year'; and, finally, a clergyman. The club thus represented the main classes and interests of eighteenth-century society, excepting only the political fanatic. In general, it sought to entertain and, at the same time, instruct. But it avoided the heavy moral and didactic approach, and its instruction was presented wittily, with polished essays on affectation, Ladies' Head-Dresses, Lottery Adventurers, Inconstancy, and Coffee-House Politicians. And its success was phenomenal for a paper which contained no blood or sex: Addison was soon claiming a sale of 3,000 copies a day, then 4,000, with particularly interesting issues selling far more. Its influence on the manners and social habits of the age was universally acknowledged. Unfortunately the perfection of art often entails the destruction of art, and when *The Spectator* died no one dared to try to fill the gap. Indeed, for many years to come, while the immortal paper was still being published in book form, and still being quoted by the society papers, every imitator felt obliged to apologise profusely for his temerity. But in this brief period the essay papers achieved a standard never to be attained again.

Such periodicals as *The Tatler* and *The Spectator* were, from the point of view of Authority, comparatively harmless. The same could not be said of the pamphlets, again written by some of the greatest literary figures of the age. Queen Anne, her ministers, and the clergy were scandalised by the flood of pamphlets meddling with the affairs of Church and State. As Chief Justice Holt explained in 1704, 'If people should not be called to account for possessing the people with an ill opinion of the government, no government can subsist. For it is very necessary for all governments that the people should have a good opinion of it.'[3] Anne herself made repeated efforts to persuade Parliament to take legislative action against this flood of seditious pamphlets and, to a lesser extent, of newspapers, which were beginning to shake off their early caution. She issued proclamations – without much effect, for she lacked the prerogative powers of her Stuart predecessors. By now, the so-called 'liberty of the Press' had become an accepted part of English freedom, and was a matter that required very delicate handling indeed, although few people in authority, whether Whig or Tory, would seriously have disagreed with Sir William Berkeley, Governor of Virginia, when in 1671 he thanked God that in Virginia 'we have not free schools nor printing; and I hope we shall not have these hundred years. For learning has brought disobedience and heresy and sects into the world; and printing has divulged them, and libels against the Government. God keep us from both.'[4] And not only was the Press suspect politically: it also lured the poorer classes away from their jobs, giving them ideas above their station in life. According to *The British Mercury* of 2 August 1712:

> Some Time before the Revolution, the Press was again set to Work: and such a furious Itch of Novelty has ever since been the epidemical Distemper, that it has prov'd fatal to many Families; the meanest of Shop-keepers and Handicrafts, spending whole Days in Coffee-houses, to hear News, and talk Politicks, whilst their Wives and Children wanted Bread at Home; and their Business being neglected, they were themselves at length thrown into Goals, or for'd to take Sanctuary in the Army. Hence sprang that Inundation of *Post-Men, Post-Boys, Evening Posts, Supplements, Daily Courants, Protestant Post-Boys*, amounting to 21 every week, besides many more which have not surviv'd to this Time.

Exaggerated the report might be. Certainly, the 'meanest of Shop-keepers and Handicrafts' could not afford to spend their days in coffee-houses. But the events of the recent past had shown the power of the newspaper press in arousing the dreaded London mob.

Much more dangerous was the political pamphlet aimed at the classes which really mattered. And the political pamphlet now entered upon one of its finest hours. Some 40,000 copies of Sacheverell's famous sermon were sold in a few days. Of his *Conduct of the Allies* Swift wrote exuberantly that 'they sold a thousand in two days, and eleven thousand were sold within a month'. And the vociferous outcries of the Whig pamphleteers had sorely embarrassed the Tory government's efforts in 1710 to conclude a peace with France – a peace which, according to the Whigs, was utterly dishonourable. Something would have to be done about the press – something more devious, less obvious, than a revival of the Printing Act, with all its associations with arbitrary government and Stuart 'tyranny'.

Queen Anne in her speech to Parliament on 17 January 1712 once again complained of the 'great license . . . taken in publishing false and scandalous Libels such as are a reproach to any government. This Evil seems too strong for the Laws now in force; it is therefore recommended to you to find a Remedy equal to the Mischief'. The remedy was the Stamp Act of 1712, which would both raise revenue and, according to an earlier proposal, reduce the circulation of newspapers (from 45,000 in 1710 to not above 30,000). The Act was primarily aimed at pamphlets. All pamphlets were to pay a stamp duty of two shillings on every sheet of a single specimen copy; a copy of every pamphlet was to be registered with the Stamp Office; and it was an offence to publish a pamphlet without the printer's name and address. The Act was thus a simple police measure. If the author of a pamphlet could rarely be identified, at least the printer could be suitably dealt with. As regards newspapers, a stamp duty was imposed of one halfpenny on every copy printed on paper of half-sheet size, and one penny on every copy 'larger than half a sheet and not exceeding one whole sheet'. This meant that a single-leaf would pay one halfpenny, and a four-page newspaper one penny. There was also a tax of one shilling on advertisements.

The immediate effects were drastic. News in printed form was still something of a novelty, and, moreover, that news seemed to be drying up, for the government was obviously determined upon peace. As Addison put it, in the *Spectator* (no. 445): 'I am afraid that few of our Weekly Historians, who are Men that above all others delight in War, will be able to subsist under the Weight of a Stamp, and an approaching Peace.' In fact, newspapers died right and left. 'All Grub-street is dead and gone last week', reported Swift, 'No more ghosts or Murders for love or money! . . . The *Observator* is fallen, the *Medleys* are jumbled together with the *Flying Post*, the *Examiner* is deadly sick.' But it was not long before ingenious minds discovered a loophole in the wording of the Act. If a newspaper were printed on a half-sheet of paper, it had to pay one halfpenny duty on every *copy*; if printed on a whole sheet, it paid one penny. But if it were printed on a sheet *and* a half it became technically a pamphlet, and so paid a duty of three shillings on every *edition* printed. The difference was considerable and, not surprisingly, most newspapers rapidly adopted a new format, and appeared as small booklets, either of twelve very small pages, or six larger ones, with the price generally three-halfpence.

In fact, the Stamp Act largely failed of its purpose. It had been aimed at the political pamphlet, and had the duty been levied upon every *copy* printed it might have succeeded. As it was, the pamphlet continued to flourish – as, after the initial confusion, did the newspaper. The daily newspapers, single-leaf, and unable to afford the cost of expanding to six pages (to say nothing of the impossibility of filling so much space every day) continued, paying the tax, and with their price increased. But the future belonged to those papers which could take advantage of the loophole: the evening papers, published three times a week and intended mainly for country distribution, and, above all, the weekly papers.

The essay-type papers strove to continue, without much success. The *Spectator* was suspended on 6 December 1712, being revived for seven months in 1714 before making its final bow. Its rivals and competitors –

such as *the Guardian,* the *Englishman, The Lover,* Defoe's *Mercator: or, Commerce Retrieved* – were hardly more successful. In fact, the death of the *Spectator* had marked the end of an era. Few readers were apparently prepared to spend their money on an essay-type paper, whether literary, political or commercial, when all those interests were now covered by the weekly newspaper, which had been forced by the Stamp Act to enlarge both its size and its appeal. Rarely indeed was there sufficient news to fill a six-or twelve-page newspaper. Space was embarrassingly abundant, and the printers were obliged to include material which was not strictly news at all. Some went in for commercial advices, and the *Weekly Journal* in 1714 devoted considerable space to shipping news, the course of exchange, and the prices of the more exotic foodstuffs. Typical of the last was a list in the issue of 30 April 1715, which included such goods as Malaga Lemons, Cheese Cheshire, Ditto Gloucestershire, Ginger, Raisins in the Sun, Malaga Raisins, Coffee Roasted, Coffee Raw, Currants, and Superfine Loaf Sugar.

Some printers turned to useful instruction, with the *British Mercury* presenting 'A Brief Historical and Chronological Account of all the Empires, Kingdoms, and States of the World . . . from the Creation to the present Time'. This mammoth enterprise occupied the printer from February 1713 to February 1714, when it was replaced by somewhat lighter fare. But the printer was still ambitious, and in October 1714 he launched upon yet another marathon series, 'An Abridgment of Geography', which he persisted in, despite protests from his readers. 'It is absolutely impossible to please all men', he complained on 11 June 1715: his geography lessons had been 'too heavy for such as seek for Entertainment'. This was not to be the last time that a newspaper imbued with a genuine desire to instruct its readers met with their solid resistance. Most readers wanted entertainment: and much more popular was the approach of *The Churchman's Last Shift,* whose printer, despite his strong Tory political views, evidently realised that his readers wanted more than a diet of politics, and gave them, in serial form, 'The Voyages of Sinbad the Sailor'.

Other printers scorned such concessions to human frailty, and turned to political essays to fill out their space, and here, perhaps, the growing influence of the newspaper was most pronounced. How influential the political newspapers were is uncertain: but, speaking of the Jacobite Fifteen, a government agent, Samuel Negus, who in 1724 compiled a *Compleat and Private List of all the Printing Houses,* was convinced that the freedom of the press had been 'the principal cause of the late rebellion and disturbances'.[5] As always, the initiative lay with the Opposition; and the Whig government soon felt in need of journalistic support: too many solid citizens, often with the vote, were gaining their knowledge of politics from newspapers. It adopted the desperate measure of employing Defoe, making use of his outward appearance as a Tory writer, but at the same time to reduce the sting of what he wrote in such Tory publications as *Dormer's News-Letter* and *Mist's Weekly Journal.* The experiment was not a success: indeed, the Whigs regarded Defoe with deep distrust, and suspected him of being the author of some of the more offensive essays.

Perhaps the first newspaper to reveal the possibilities of the brief weekly political essay was *The London Journal* during the South Sea Bubble crisis. Week after week, one 'Cato' denounced evil ministers, and it is reported that 10,000 copies of one particularly daring issue were sold. The ministry, goaded beyond endurance, replied: the printing office was raided and the presses smashed. Walpole's eventual solution was to buy the paper in 1722. But Cato was not alone in his attacks. The most outspoken – and notorious – of his allies was Nathaniel Mist, a diehard Tory if not an out-and-out Jacobite, who also found himself in trouble. In February 1721 he was condemned to stand twice in the pillory, pay a fine of £50, three months' imprisonment, and give securities for good behaviour, June found him again in Newgate. And there were many other prosecutions. As a further deterrent, the government in 1725 effectively removed the loophole in the wording of the Stamp Act. Henceforward, *every* sheet or half-sheet had to bear its appropriate stamp – the rather attractive red stamp which the very pro-government Exeter printer, Andrew Brice, was pleased to call 'The Blushing Blood-coloured Mark of the wholesome Severity lately stamp'd upon us'.[6] Again, the immediate effects were serious, with newspapers dying right and left, and few new ones being started.

This period of relative stagnation witnessed, however, the birth of what was undoubtedly one of the most significant political papers of the century: *The Craftsman. By Caleb D'Anvers of Gray's-Inn, Esq.*, begun in late 1726 as a bi-weekly single-leaf but in 1727 becoming *The Country Journal; Or, The Craftsman*, a four-page weekly, price twopence, with the emphasis upon the political essay. And these essays formed a steady, unrelenting attack upon Walpole, his 'corruption', his position as 'prime minister' (a term of abuse in the eighteenth century), and his whole system of government. The paper's strength lay in the contributions of its patrons, Bolingbroke and William Pulteney, men of considerable literary ability and leading politicians as well. Its attack had two levels. One was very serious indeed, comprising a consistent and watertight policy aimed at uniting Tories, dissident Whigs and all true patriots into an organised opposition party. Before each parliamentary session, the points to be raised by the opposition were aired in *The Craftsman* in an attempt to educate the reading public and form and guide public opinion. Bolingbroke's later book, *The Dissertation on Parties*, was based on the essays he had contributed to this newspaper. But the attack was not always so heavy, and the *Craftsman* could always be relied upon to entertain its readers. One of its most notorious essays was 'The First Vision of Camelick', which appeared on 27 January 1727. This purported to be a translation of a Persian manuscript. It was, in fact, a wicked satire on Walpole. It stressed the tremendous importance of 'The Sacred Covenant' – 'a solemn oath by the ruler to preserve the constitution inviolate and unchanged . . . accursed be he who layeth hands on the same; accursed be he who shall remove this writing from the people, or who shall hide the law thereof from the King'. Then followed the attack on Walpole personally, in his familiar role as the 'great corruptor':

> In the midst of these execrations enter'd a Man, dress'd in a plain habit, with a purse of gold in his hand. He threw himself forward into the room, in a bluff, ruffianly manner. A Smile, or rather a Snear, sat on his Countenance. His Face was bronz'd over with a glare of Confidence. An arch malignity leer'd in his eye. Nothing was so extraordinary as the effect of this person's appearance. They no sooner saw him, but they all turn'd their Faces from the Canopy, and fell prostrate before him. He trod over their backs without any Ceremony, and march'd directly up to the Throne. He open'd his Purse of Gold, which he took out in Handfulls, and scatter'd amongst the Assembly. While the greater Part were engag'd in scrambling for these Pieces, he seiz'd, to my inexpressible Surprize, without the least Fear, upon the sacred *Parchment* itself. He rumpled it rudely up, and cramm'd it into his Pocket. Some of the people began to murmur. He threw more Gold, and they were pacified. No sooner was the Parchment taken away, but in an instant I saw that august Assembly in Chains; nothing was heard through the whole Divan, but the Noise of Fetters and Clank of Irons.

This was brilliant journalism. Not surprisingly, Walpole prosecuted: but *The Craftsman* was not to be easily silenced. Its personal attacks on Walpole were particularly effective. They frequently took the form of advertisements - as in the issue of 27 May 1727:

> Notice is hereby given that a certain K——t of the Sh——e and another worthy M——r of P——t, not many Miles from this City having been for some Years afflicted with the most virulent Degree of the POLITICAL SPLEEN, which had emaciated their Constitution, and brought them into a very low and declining Condition . . . they at length apply'd themselves to Dr ROBERT KING . . . who with his GOLDEN SPECIFICK work'd so perfect a Cure in a few days.

These advertisements of Dr Robert King and his 'Golden Pills' had a double advantage: they brought the readers in - and they maddened Walpole.

The Craftsman undoubtedly represented Opposition journalism at its best in this period. But other papers were even more outspoken, although they lacked the wit and subtlety of Bolingbroke. Pre-eminent was *Mist's Weekly Journal*, a paper which well illustrated the trend of politicians in opposition to address themselves more and more to the lower classes. Indeed, the inflaming of popular opinion was almost the only weapon left to an Opposition facing a minister secure in the royal favour and operating the vast machine of patronage and 'corruption'. And a government informer complained with some justification that *Mist's* was 'written ad captum of the Common Pelple'.[7]

Mist's masterpiece was his famous 'Persian Letter' of 24 August 1728, a letter to the editor supposedly describing recent events in Persia. It began with an ironic reference to Mist's frequent spells in gaol: 'I observe that you have often been under Confinement for having disobliged the present Government, and I must say, that I hope for the future you will avoid all Occasion of giving Offence to the Ministry: A Ministry equally esteemed for their Abilities in Domestick, and their great Experience in Foreign Affairs.' This was heavy sarcasm indeed, for the Walpole ministry, according to the Opposition, governed by means of bribery and corruption, and was hopelessly inept in its foreign policy. The writer then turned to Persia. 'The old Usurper, Meryweis' had died, to be succeeded by Esreff thanks only to the latter's bribing of 'The Concubine'. The rightful heir was the Sophi, who, 'in his Persons and Deportment resembles his Father and Uncle', and who was highly moral, in contrast to Esreff, who 'is covetous to the Extreme of Avarice . . . he is despised by all that approach him, for the excessive Vanity that swells his Mind . . . has many Women in his Seraglio, but his first Sultana bears an absolute Sway over his weak Mind and disposes of the Empire at her Will.' The parallels were obvious. The 'old Usurper' was George I; Esreff George II; 'The Concubine' was George I's chief mistress, the Duchess of Kendal; the Sultana Queen Caroline; and the Sophi the Young Pretender. But worse was to follow. The 'great Director of Publick Affairs' was ' the Chief Scribe', who had reached his position by treachery to Meryweis, although

what added to his Power, was the immense Treasure he has bestow'd on the favourite Sultana, whose darling Passions, Vanity and Ambition were gratified, when she found herself possessed of Part of the Plunder of the unhappy Persians, and enjoying a greater Revenue than any Princess who hath filled the Arms of *Persian* Monarchs, before the Sceptre was wrested by Rebellion and Treachery from the Hands of those whose undoubted Right it was to sway it . . . You will naturally be surprised, that a Prince so unequal to Imperial Dignity, directed in all his Councils by a Minister who is as famed for Corruption as *Sejanus* and for Cruelty as *Nero*, should be able to maintain the Possession of the Empire, in Opposition to a lawful Sophi whose undoubted Right is supported by the Affection and Duty of the Generality of the People, by whom hourly Prayers are offered up for his Restoration.

Such an attack was outrageous – and once again Mist was on the run. The early eighteenth century was to witness a spate of press prosecutions. But the 'terror' proved surprisingly ineffective, despite the savagery of the penalties which could be inflicted. The weakness of the government's legal position was shown only too clearly in the prosecutions which followed Mist's 'Persian Letter'. Mist himself prudently disappeared: but two of his compositors were arrested. The government's legal experts went very carefully into the question of the responsibility for the printing and publishing of the libel: and they decided that the compositors could be charged only with a mis-demeanour. But the 'Letter' had been reprinted by Edward Farley, an Exeter printer, who had not followed Mist's example – and his case was very different: 'he is the Master of the Press at Exeter, there are two Witnesses of his reprinting the Libel at Exeter, and one of these speaks to his explaining it in the Criminal Sense at the Time it was so reprinted'.[8] The government went ahead: but the Attorney-General had to report that the prosecution's case rested absolutely upon two witnesses: one a 'Person of a loose Character', whose testimony would not have 'sufficient Weight with the Jury to convict', and the other Farley's own father-in-law, who was 'so far from being willing Witness, that nothing will come from him but what is forced'. In fact, he could not recommend even proceeding on the lesser charge of misdemeanour. There was only the consolation, that Farley had spent some twelve months in gaol – 'which is some Punishment, tho' by no means adequate'. Actually, Farley had died there during these lengthy investigations. But the case does illustrate the government's difficulties: witnesses were rarely forth-coming, and the legal position always uncertain. Moreover, such prosecutions provided the Opposition with first-class propaganda. As a writer to the ministry pointed out, 'there was never a Mist or any other Person taken up or tryed, but double the number of papers were sold upon it, besides ye irritating the people from ye false Notion of Persecution'.[9]

The obvious alternative to suppression was for the ministry to build up its own propaganda machine. At first, Walpole concentrated on the traditional weapon, the pamphlet, and into pamphlets went the most important writings in favour of the ministry. But the Opposition put its main efforts into newspapers: and soon Walpole was forced to build up a ministerial newspaper press. By 1731 he controlled, in varying degrees, the *Daily Courant, London Journal, Read's Journal, Free Briton, Flying Post,* and various others. Subsidisation usually took the form of free carriage through the Post Office, but hard cash was also involved. The highest-paid journalist in the ministry's employ was William Arnall ('Francis Walsingham, Esq.' of the weekly *Free Briton*), and the Secret Committee appointed to enquire into Walpole's financial management after his fall from power reported that Arnall had received almost £11,000 from the secret service funds over a period of only four years. According to the same report, Walpole had paid out more than £50,000 in the ten years from 1731 to 1741 – a fair sum, but not as large as had been suspected. At the same time, the Post Office was also used to block the distribution of the more dangerous Opposition papers: *Mist's Weekly Journal* and *The Craftsman* in 1728, and the *London Evening Post* in 1733. But such operations were hardly a success, at least according to the *London Evening Post* of 3 November 1733:

> Whole Piles of Pamphlets and Papers, sent *Gratis* by the Post-Office, lye neglected and unread, and in some Places the Packets are not yet open'd . . . the Waiters in several Places have been very near having their Heads broke for carrying *London Journals*, *Free Britons*, *Courants*, etc. to light the *Company's* Pipes, Gentlemen thinking it gives an ill-*Taste* to their *Tobacco*, and order'd them to the *Necessary-House*, as the most proper Place.

Walpole never managed to attract to his support the best writers and poets of the day. Against such giants as Bolingbroke, the two Pulteneys, Chesterfield, Swift, Pope and Gay, he could muster only pygmies. Indeed, his band of 'scribblers' was regularly the butt of Opposition satire, with some achieving the doubtful distinction of a mention in *The Dunciad*. Pope's description of Arnall was short and sharp:

> No crab more active in the dirty dance,
> Downward to climb, and backward to advance.
> (Book ii, 319–20)

'Francis Osborne' of the *London Journal* had promptly been nicknamed 'Mother Osborne' by *The Craftsman*, which found in his writing 'the strongest characteristics of feminine dotage'. And Pope wrote:

> Fast by, like Niobe (her children gone),
> Sits Mother Osborne, stupefy'd to stone!
> (Book ii, 311–12)

The London Evening Post took particular delight in exposing Walpole's propaganda system. This paper, a tri-weekly, had come rapidly to the fore in the Opposition press. *The Craftsman* probably remained the most influential, but it was too political for many readers, particularly those in the country, who wanted news as well as views. The *London Evening Post* never lost sight of the fact that it was primarily a *news*paper, although its reputation was increasingly to be based upon its political content, even here it avoided the lengthy and often tedious essay, preferring to make its point by terse and pungent comment and, later, by the brief but savage verses for which it was to become notorious. And it made politics not only interesting but amusing: there were few country papers which did not regularly reprint its comments and verses.[10]

In 1735 the ministry tried a new system, concentrating in one daily paper, *The Daily Gazetteer*, the talents of the writers hitherto dissipated in several. *The Craftsman* (12 July 1735) had its own explanation: 'Perhaps, he has a mind to try what a *Clubbing of Wits* would do, after They had all fail'd in their *separate State*; and as *nine Taylors* are generally allow'd to make a *Man*, He might suppose that *twenty or thirty Scribblers* would, at least, make one tolerable Writer'. Actually, Walpole had chosen his time well. Not only could the explanation and justification of the government's measures now be performed more efficiently, but the opposition had lost heart after its high hopes of the Excise Crisis and the General Election of 1734. It would seem that the new paper, despite the gibes of its opponents, was reasonably successful. Its average daily sale has been estimated at about 1,000, while the government purchased twice that number for free distribution.[11]

It was not until war with Spain began to loom on the political horizon that the newspapers got back their old fire. The main target of the opposition papers was always Walpole: and the *Daily Gazetteer* did its best to defend him. In its issue of 24 April 1738, nearly half of the front page was devoted to an ode to Walpole:

> This is the Sovereign Man, Compleat;
> Hero; Patriot; glorious; free;
> Rich, and wise; and fair, and great;
> Generous WALPOLE, Thou are He.

The trouble was that almost identical verses appeared frequently in the opposition papers, which relied heavily on sarcasm as a political weapon. Certainly, this ode would have been greeted with shrieks of mirth by all Walpole's opponents: and one can only wonder whether the proud poet did not have his tongue in his cheek when composing his eulogy. And such 'defences' counted for little against the vicious personal attacks upon Walpole – attacks which culminated in the *London Evening Post* of 16 February 1742:

> Should any Great m-n-st-r, after a blundering Administration
> of twenty years, be permitted at last to retire with the Spoils of
> his Country; and without mentioning the immense Sums he has
> in that time squander'd, enjoy at Ease the vast Fortunes he has
> rais'd, the stately Palaces he has built, the rich Furniture, fine
> Pictures, and other Curiosities he has purchas'd; and for his
> glorious Services be created a —— [Peer] of the Realm; –
> obtain for his *natural* Daughter the same Honour usually
> conferr'd on those of Kings; – possess, besides a pension of 4000
> l. a Year for Life, a *Patent-Place* in the Customs of 3000 l. a
> Year for Life; – obtain for his eldest Son a Patent-Place of
> 10,000 l. a Year – for his second Son 5000 l. a Year for Life, –
> for his third Son Places to the Value of 3000 l. a Year for Life;
> – for his Brother the Place of a Teller of the Exchequer, worth
> 3000 l. a Year, besides the *Patent* of Auditor of the West-Indies,
> which, under his Management, may be worth the D-v-l knows
> how many Thousands a Year; – besides several other Patent-
> Places among his Relations, amounting in the whole for himself

and his Family to upwards of *Thirty Thousand Pounds a Year . . .?*

The leaders in the political warfare were the pamphlet and the newspaper. But they had allies. One such was the theatre – not usually regarded as belonging to a history of the Press, but in the Walpole period (and for many years to come) part of an organised propaganda campaign. *The Beggar's Opera* of 1728 received much publicity in *The Craftsman*, although that paper probably read more political significance into it than Gay had ever intended. A play, *The Fate of Villainy*, produced in 1730, had a villain who engrossed and betrayed the King's favour. *The Fall of Essex* enacted on the stage the fate so earnestly desired for Walpole. In *The Fall of Mortimer*, the Opposition found a play ideal for its purposes. Not only was there a striking parallel between Mortimer and Walpole, but there was also the influence they had upon their respective queens:

Lord Mountacute.   'Tis full three years since *Mortimer* began
                           To Lord it o'er us by the Queen's vile Favour:
                           He stalks us as on a Mountain by himself,
                           Whilst we creep humbly in the Vale below . . .
Sir Rob. Holland.   In this short Space, he and his Brother-Devil
                           Have made, undone, new fram'd, shuffled
                             and tost
                           The Antient Customs of our native Soil
                           So very often, that the Kingdom staggers
                           Under the heavy Burthen of the Charge.

Every person in the audience could easily interpret passages like these. *The Craftsman* and *Fog's Weekly Journal* (*Mist's* under another name) were full of such 'parallels'.

Perhaps one of the most humorous reports was the description of a performance at the Southwark Fair in 1730. It appeared in *Fog's Weekly Journal* of 3 October. As Milton Percival says, Noodle will be readily recognised as Sir Robert Walpole, and Doodle as his brother, Horace. The writer was sitting beside a staunch ministerial supporter, who 'came there with some prejudice: for he told me he believed there was some roguery in this farce', and

> he began to take fire at the very first scene, for he started when these words were spoke: *We have gold to bribe, if bribery we need*; and, jogging me, asked me if these fellows did not deserve to be committed . . . There were at this time upon the stage two very grotesque figures, whom the author distinguished by the names of Noodle and Doodle, and it happened that another character, being in conversation with them, happens to call them a couple of *Norfolk Dumplings*; here, my neighbour had like to have lost all patience; for he would have it, that this was designed as a ridicule upon two particular persons, who, he said, were his best friends. As for my part, I could discover no more in it than

that the author designed to shew two foolish fellows, of a low country education, pretending to everything, and understanding nothing, thrusting themselves into all affairs, and outwitted by every one they have to deal with . . .

I say again, I could see no more than the author designed to make people laugh, at the expense of the two ridiculous characters; but my neighbour (whose head I take to be a little turned) took offence almost at every expression.

This was brilliant propaganda. Naturally, much of its impact is lost on a modern reader: but the contemporary audience had been carefully coached by the opposition press.

Another ally was the ballad, which enjoyed a lively revival. For many it remained the main source of news; for others, it filled a gap. Into ballads went the titbits of social and political gossip which the nesspapers did not dare to print, and many of these ballads were written by the leading wits and politicians of the time. They were certainly not intended only for 'street corners, and [to] appeal solely to the vulgar'. The tunes to which they were sung are now forgotten, so that the ballads seem more pedestrian than they really were. But no modern reader of *Britannia Excisa*, with its rousing chorus:

Horse, Foot, and Dragoons,
Battalions, Platoons,
Excise, Wooden Shoes, and no Jury;
Then Taxes increasing,
While Traffick is ceasing,
Would put all the Land in a Fury

could doubt its effectiveness.

Walpole's eventual fall in 1742 was hailed with a monstrous whoop of joy by the opposition press, which amused itself with gloating predictions of the fate in store for him. But very soon a note of disillusionment crept in and the main targets of the more outspoken papers became their former heroes, the so-called 'Patriots', who had betrayed the trust reposed in them by accepting office alongside Walpole's old cronies, and were helping to 'screen' him. The *London Evening Post* summed up the whole unhappy story on 1 January 1743:

With W——le's Politicks the Year *began*;
But soon th'indignant Patriots chang'd the Man;
With *Statesmen New* the Nation hop'd *New Schemes*,
Saw *Glorious Visions*, and dreamt *Golden Dreams*.
When from a Trance of Six Months they awoke,
They found *Truth* chang'd their fancy'd *Joy* to *Joke*.
Still the same Fate on *B--t--n's* Isle attends,
And wisely as the Year *began*, it *ends*.

Henceforward, the *London Evening Post* concentrated its attention on the 'Patriots' and their failure to live up to their announced ideals. But politics had lost much of its excitement. For a brief period the Forty-five rising took the centre of the stage. Otherwise, from the political point of view, it was a period of 'slow' news, enlivened only by the uproar over the 'Jew Bill' of 1753, in which the opposition press, led by the *London Evening Post*, conducted one of the most violent propaganda campaigns in the history of journalism.[12]

The Jewish Naturalisation Bill was a modest measure, which provided that individual Jews who had been resident in Great Britain or Ireland for three years might be naturalised by Act of Parliament without taking the sacrament. It certainly did not confer on all Jews the rights of British citizens, and would, in fact, have applied only to a very small number, for a private Act of Parliament was very expensive indeed. But it was seized on by the opposition as an attack on Christianity. At this point, the vicious little verses of the *London Evening Post* really came into their own, with its 'Call to the Jews' on 5 June 1753:

> Come, Abram's Sons, from ev'ry Quarter come,
> Britain now bids you call her Land your own . . .
> Revenge (your fav'rite Passion) you may hoist,
> And once more triumph o'er the Cross of Christ.

No item was too trivial – or too exaggerated – for the *Post* to print. The Jews were buying up the finest seats in the country; they were the receivers of most stolen property; they were parasites, engaged not in honest trade but in 'Stock Jobbs, Lotteries, and other iniquitous Arts of Exchange Alley'; and they would swamp the country.

At the same time, correspondents were busily engaged in raking up stories of Jewish cruelty and vice. 'In the Reign of Trajan', reported one (6 November, 1753), 'the Jews massacred Two Hundred and Fifty Thousand People in the Island of Cyprus, and besmear'd themselves with their Blood, saw'd them assunder, wore their Skins, ate their Flesh, and made them kill one another . . . this put an End to their Naturalisation Bill in that Country.' Despite this emphasis on sheer terror, the *London Evening Post* never lost sight of the humorous possibilities of the topic. Even the most bigoted of readers must have tired of the monotonous succession of letters denouncing 'those ravening Wolves, the devouring blaspheming Jews'. They wanted to be entertained as well. So the *Post* reprinted *The Craftsman's* 'News from One Hundred Years hence' – a clever parody of the *London Gazette*, but dealing with the year 1853, when, of course, England would be ruled by the Jews. Typical items were

> Last night the Bill for naturalising Christians was thrown out of the Sanhedrin by a very great Majority . . .
> Last Friday being the Anniversary of the Crucifixion, the same was observ'd throughout the Kingdom with the greatest Demonstrations of Joy . . .
> Last Sunday an Order came from the Lord C——b——n's Office, to the Managers of both Theatres, forbidding them,

under the severest Penalties, to exhibit a certain scandalous Piece, highly scandalous to our present happy Establishment, entitl'd, 'The Merchant of Venice' (14 July 1753).

In fact, the whole mixture was well spiced with humour, often in the form of announcements of the arrival in London of experts in circumcision, an operation which obviously fascinated the *Post*, and presented it with many opportunities to display its wit. According to the *Post*, those who supported the Bill were Jews at heart, and should become so in person as well. Thus the issue of 7 August 1753 stated that

> whereas many well-dispos'd Christian Jews in and about St. J——s's, Lambeth, the City, etc. are intimidated from fulfilling the Law, by an Apprehension of the Pain and Confinement attending the Mosaick Rite of Circumcision, as it is commonly perform'd in England and Berwick upon Tweed,
> This is to inform the Publick,
> That there is just arriv'd from Holland, Mr. Ishmael Levy, who had the Honour of being Circumciser to the Synagogue at Rotterdam upwards of Twenty Years. This Gentleman gives as little Pain in the Exercise of his Art as the Italian Tooth-drawer . . . All such Venerable PERSONAGES, N——n, M——s of P——t, etc., therefore, who are already circumcis'd in their Hearts, may now have an Opportunity of becoming Apostates from Christianity to all Intents and Purposes, without Hindrance of Business or the least uneasy Sensation'.

The motives behind this extraordinary campaign were purely political: and there was no doubting its success. Once again, the government banned the *Post*'s transmission through the post. But the damage had been done. From the beginning the opposition papers had taken their cue from the *London Evening Post*; and, as the campaign warmed up, newspapers all over the country reprinted its verses and comments. No paper could, in fact, afford to ignore them. So widespread and obviously popular an agitation on the eve of a general election could not be lightly dismissed, and the Bill was dropped.

In this way, political newspapers had flourished, particularly in times of unusual interest and excitement, and considerable progress had been made in the arts of presentation and propaganda. There remained the problem of parliamentary debates. The proceedings of Parliament were secret, and there existed a formidable machinery to keep them so. How many people were really interested remains a mystery, but clearly there was a demand. As early as 1711 Abel Boyer began his monthly *Political State of Great Britain* in which, during the recess of Parliament, he published cautious accounts of the speeches made in the previous session. His reports had two obvious defects: they were expensive, and they were out of date. But the London newspapers dared not even try to compete. Here, the written news-letter came into its own, defying the Resolution of

1694 that 'no news writers do in their letters or other papers that they may disperse, presume to intermeddle with the debates or other proceedings of this House', and providing their readers with up-to-date, if brief, details, often including the division figures and surprisingly well-informed comment. But the news-letter also had two defects: it too was expensive, and its parliamentary reports were necessarily short. The first objection was to some extent overcome, at least so far as country readers were concerned, by the fact that the country papers regularly printed excerpts from the news-letters, thus stealing a march over their more vulnerable London rivals. But the problem of brevity remained, until in 1731 Edward Cave made the debates the main attraction of his *Gentleman's Magazine*. Like Boyer, he postponed his reports until the recess, and then dealt with them with some caution. But so popular were his accounts that he was soon challenged by the *London Magazine*. Out of date as the reports were, they were clearly popular – so popular, in fact, that in 1738 the House once again resolved that

> It is a high Indignity to, and a notorious Breach of the Privilege of this House, for any News-Writer, in Letters, or other Papers . . . or for any Printer or Publisher of any News Papers, of any Denomination, to presume to insert in the said Letters or Papers, or to give therein any Account of the Debates, or other Proceedings of this House . . . as well during the Recess as the Sitting of Parliament.

The loophole seemed to have been closed. But neither magazine was prepared to give up its main feature so easily. In May 1738 the *London Magazine* hit on the idea of reporting the proceedings of a Roman Assembly, with speeches by Scipio Africanus, Tullius Cicero, and so on. A key was provided in a supplement, but it must have been an intriguing pastime for readers to try to guess in advance the real identity of the orators. More famous – perhaps largely because of the discovery, much later, that many of the 'speeches' had actually been composed by Dr Johnson – was the *Gentleman's Magazine* subterfuge in June 1738 of reporting the debates of the Parliament of Lilliput. The names of the speakers were somewhat familiar: Walelop (Walpole), Pulneb (Pulteney), Haxilaf (Halifax), although again a key was provided for those readers unable to work out these transparent disguises. Both magazines proved extremely popular, the *Gentleman's Magazine*'s circulation in 1741, when Walpole was under increasing attack, being reported as 15,000. Emboldened by this success the two became more reckless, until both were brought to account in 1747 for their accounts of the trial of Lord Lovat for his part in the Forty-five. At that point Cave gave up his Lilliput. The *London Magazine* continued, but far more cautiously, until 1757. The great battle over the reporting of parliamentary debates was still to be fought.

Not all readers were primarily interested in politics, however, although many journalists tended to assume they were. In 1728 'Henry

Stonecastle' endeavoured to revive the old tradition of the *Spectator* with a periodical entitled *The Universal Spectator*. Typically, he felt obliged to apologise for his temerity:

> Let no Man envy us the celebrated Title we have assum'd, or charge us with Arrogance, as if we bid the World expect great Things from us: must we have no Power to please, unless we come up to the full Height of these inimitable Performances? Is there no Wit or Humour left, because they are gone? Is the Spirit of the SPECTATOR all lost, and their Mantle fallen upon no Body? Have they said all that can be said?

The argument was sound enough, though the new venture was a very poor imitation of its model. But it was a start, and prepared the way for the literary periodicals of the 1750s. And there were various other experiments, such as *The Friendly Writer and Register of Truth*, begun in September 1732 as a monthly magazine written for women by a woman. Its first issue ran, perhaps typically, to forty-four pages, and opened with the defiant announcement:

> It needeth, I tell thee, what Means have moved me to an Undertaking of this Manner . . . Truly thy Sister hath, for long Times past, beheld, with much Grief and Sorrow at Heart, the abominable Deceits which wicked and regardless Men do *Daily*, *Weekly* and *Monthly* send abroad into the World . . . I shall despise those who take Occasion to scoff at my Manner of Writing, and scorn the Work of a weak Woman.

The style was chatty, setting out the events of the month day by day, but including 'The Black Catalogue: or, List of Lies, Blunders and idle Tales, set forth by the Sons of Satan'. How successful this spirited anticipation of future feminist movements was is unknown. But the *Grub-Street Journal* had already hit upon this idea of a black list, as indeed had Defoe many years earlier in his *Review*. From time to time, the author of the *Grub-Street Journal* amused himself by printing news items selected from various papers, commenting humorously on their obvious discrepancies. Thus, he reprinted a report of a murder: 'Last night, John Ferguson, an alehouse keeper . . . was killed by some ruffians that were drinking in his house, who calling for his reckoning at their absconding, was stabb'd and hack'd by the said ruffians with butchers knives, and made off.' According to the *Journal* (10 September 1730), 'This article contains several surprising particulars. First, this alehouse keeper was killed by some ruffians; next, he called for his reckoning; then was stabb'd, and hack'd by the said ruffians, after their absconding; and after all this, he at last made off. The *Grub-Street Journal* could hardly be called a true literary periodical, although it did from time to time include verse. This was usually reasonably serious, but the Rabelaisian note occasionally made itself heard, as in the issue of 9 July 1730:

> Cupic once having robb'd a Hive,

He lik'd the trade, and hop'd to thrive:
At length the filching knave was stung;
Mad with the pain, he stamp'd, he flung;
His clammy fingers oft he blew
And to his Mother straight he flew.
Mama, he cries, this cursed Bee,
How it has wounded me, you see.
How big the swelling! yet the sting
Was but a tiny little thing.
Quoth Venus, Precious Son of mine,
Just such a tiny thing is thine;
And yet how much 'twill make 'em swell,
After stol'n sweets, the Girls can tell.

The real development of the literary magazine did not take place until the 1750s. In November 1753 *The Spectator*, a bi-weekly, made the customary apology: it made no claim to equal its predecessor. But another periodical did make such a claim: *The Tatler. By William Bickerstaff, Esq., Nephew to the late Isaac*, begun in December 1753 as a weekly. It was a barefaced forgery, based on the assertion that its author had been left 'an invaluable old Trunk', crammed with manuscripts by his renowned uncle. It did not last. One of the best-known periodicals of this period was *The Gray's Inn Journal. By Charles Ranger, Esq.*, begun on 29 September 1753 as a weekly, price twopence. Its author was actually Arthur Murphy, previously one of the leading lights of *The Craftsman*. This venture was to be very different, according to the introduction:

> I never could conceive, what kind of Advantage can redound to a rational Creature, who can neither receive Instruction or Entertainment, by reading that Mr *Such-a-one* died at his Country House, when perhaps the Gentleman is in perfect good Health; and if *Squire Rent-Roll* is arrived in Town with a grand Retinue, I apprehend it in no way interesting to any Man breathing, except his Taylor. As this Kind of Information was neverly properly co-incident with my Plan, I am pleased to be disengaged from it . . . The *Gray's-Inn Journal* was commenced to promote useful Mirth and good Humour.

The paper laid great emphasis on essays discussing such topics as 'the British Fair', pride, ambition, and so on. The main emphasis was upon humour – usually 'polite', although it could be broad, as in the extraordinary 'advertisement' which appeared on 20 October 1753:

> Lately arrived in this Town, Abraham Grotesque, Stay-maker, who ingages with the Ladies to shew more of their Charms, and much lower than has hithero been done by any of the Trade: He also makes them appear so big about the Waist, that they have all the Pleasure of appearing with Child, without the Burden of being so; and the most Innocent, by his means, seems to be within a Month of her Time!

The Entertainer of 1754, a weekly periodical price three-halfpence, specialised in gossip and scandal – with such 'advertisements' as that of 17 September:

> Whereas Miss Fitz-Gay had the misfortune to lose her Virtue and Reputation at Vaux-Hall t'other night; this is to give notice, that whoever will bring the same to *Mrs Helpwell*, at the *Naked Woman* in *Russel-street*, *Covent-Garden*, shall receive the full reward of half-a-crown, to be paid by *Miss Fitz-Gay* herself, at her lodgings in *Catherine-street*.

One suspects that some of these 'advertisements' were barbed, and had particular references. And there were many similar publications. But already periodicals were appearing which were to achieve lasting fame – such as *The Rambler* of 20 March 1750, a bi-weekly with no news and no advertisements, price twopence, written by Dr Johnson; and his essays, under the title 'The Idler', which appeared in *Payne's Universal Chronicle* from 1758 to 1760. Both were somewhat 'heavy' in their approach; more 'popular' were *The World* and the *Covent Garden Journal*. In general, the aim was to improve the morals and manners of the readers – and particularly the female readers – whose fashions, extravagance and gallantry were described and denounced in essay after essay. But the emphasis was on passion and sex, and the highly-coloured accounts of romance and seduction tend to make one doubt the sincerity of the declared moral aim. However, there is no doubting that many readers preferred this sort of 'instruction' to the heavier moral essay, and the popularity of these journals was not seriously challenged until the outbreak of war with France in 1757 introduced a more serious note into all newspapers.

Once again, therefore, newspapers were beginning to specialise. Perhaps the most important development was the trade paper. Virtually every paper devoted some space to trade announcements, with 'Remarks on Trade', lists of goods imported and exported at the 'Bear Key' (the Bear Quay, off Thomas Street, London), lists of bankrupts, prices of stocks, and the 'Course of Exchange'. Advertisements were increasing steadily in number and importance, despite the duty of one shilling upon every advertisement imposed by the Stamp Act of 1712 – a duty doubled by the Stamp Act of 1757. Most advertisements still concerned quack cures and publishing notices – a brief glance at any eighteenth-century newspaper will explain why that century has been called 'the Golden Age of the Quack'. The main point of interest about the publishing notices is their extraordinary variety: religious works were regularly advertised in this age of the flesh, together with ponderous tomes on history and philosophy. Unfortunately, the effect of these solid works was often diminished by the company they found themselves in – notices of somewhat dubious medical works and of books that were quite frankly pornographic. *The Craftsman* on 30 June 1744 announced the publication

of a book on the cure of venereal diseases. The purchaser was also entitled
to a free copy of

> The Treatise of *Unfortunate Women*. Being the PRESENT STATE
> as is NOW at *this Time* of the COMMON WOMEN *of the Town*,
> and KEPT WOMEN in *London*, 15 Miles round, Considered. It
> being *Always* BAD with them at this SEASON of the Year.
> With the *Prints*, (from the Life) Finely Engraved, of the more
> NOTED of *These* Ladies, that their Persons may be, *At First
> Sight* Known. Also, Their NAMES – and *Where* they *Live.*

This advertisement can only be classed as a classic example of cause and
effect. But if many of the books thus advertised were calculated to arouse
the baser appetites of their readers, other advertisers were quick to offer
remedies for the consequences of over-indulgence or of a careless choice of
partners – either in the way of aphrodisiacs or of 'cures'. On 17 January
1719 *The Orphan Reviv'd: or, Powell's Weekly Journal* extolled the virtues of

> Wright's Diuretick or cleansing Tincture, which Urinally
> discharges all the Faeces or putrid Relicks of the Lues
> Alamode, or Veneral Infection, and chases its Concomitants,
> the wretched Retinue of that complicated Distemper, and
> carries off all Mucous, filthy Senious Matter lodg'd in the
> Reins, and elsewhere, by ill Curses, which either cause a
> Sharpness in the Urine, or too frequently provokes it. This
> Relick is discoverable partly by the subsequent Symptoms; by a
> Debility or Weakness of the Back; a foetid or nauseous Smell of
> the Urine, with a purulent Matter or seculant Sordes residing
> at the Bottom.

> The papers of this period were preoccupied with venereal diseases,
but their advertisements covered every disease known to modern medical
science – and many unknown to it. One preparation would remove 'all
Deformities, such as Tetters, Ringworm, Morphew, Sunburn, Scurf,
Pimples, Pits, or Redness of the Small-Pox'. It would also, somewhat
unexpectedly, give 'a more exquisite Edge to the Razor'. There were
'cures' for 'frightful Drams, confus'd Ideas, Failure of Memory, and the
Horrors'. And there were worm powders by the score, whose proud
manufacturers often went into the most frightful details of the
effectiveness of their products. *The British Weekly Mercury* of 29 January
1715 informed its readers that

> This Day a Young Gentlewoman had a Worm brought away
> 16 Foot and odd Inches long . . . This, with several others of a
> prodigious Size, are to be seen at the said Mr Moore's, viz.
> One of thirty Foot long, another 5 and a half, being part of one
> of 16 Yards odd Inches; another 6 Yards and a half, another 50
> Foot, and another in the form of a Bird, but very small.

A universal panacea, and one which was advertised in practically every newspaper in the country, was Daffey's Elixer. An example comes from the *Newcastle Courant* of 29 August 1724:

a certain Cure (under God) in most Distempers, viz. The Gout and Rheumatism, with all those torturing Pains attending them; it takes away the Scurvy, Root and Branch, and gives immediate Ease in the most Racking Pains of the Cholick. It's a Sovereign and never failing Remedy against Fluxes, spitting of Blood, Consumption, Agues, Small-Pox, and Meazles; it carries off the most violent Fevers; it eases After-pains, and prevents Miscarriages; cures the Rickets in Children; Is wonderful in the Stone, and Gravel in the Kidneys, Bladder or Ureter, and brings away Slime, Gravel, and oftentimes Stones of a Great Bigness. For Stoppage or Pains in the Stomach, Shortness of Breath, Pains in the Head and Heart, a better Remedy in the World cannot be. It perfectly destroys Worms, tho' you are almost overgrown with them; cureth the black or yellow Jaundice, King's Evil, and those who are stopp'd with Flegm, restoring a languishing Body to perfect Health, strengthening the Vessels of both Sexes, and changeth the whole Mass of Blood, being a noble Cordial after hard Drinking.

Otherwise, the main emphasis was on trade and property, and in the growth of advertising can be traced significant developments in the society the newspapers served. In the early years of the century, advertisements had been little more than incidental items in most papers. But on 3 February 1731 there appeared the *Daily Advertiser*, a single leaf intended 'to consist wholly of Advertisements, together with the Prices of Stocks, Course of Exchange, and Names and Descriptions of Persons becoming Bankrupts'. It was ahead of its time: a daily paper could not yet succeed on advertisements alone. And soon it became a standard newspaper of four pages, although still with a heavy emphasis upon trade. But the age of the 'Advertiser' had begun, with more and more papers adopting the word in their subtitle, and ever-increasing space being given up to advertisements.

The period had thus witnessed significant developments. Despite stamp taxes and advertisement taxes, all the traditional forms had been renewed, and there were once again political papers, literary and society papers, and trade papers. Perhaps the one tradition missing was the primarily bawdy one. But all papers could find room for items of this nature. *The British Mercury* was a political sheet, but on 17 June 1727 it was pleased to include an eminently non-political poem:

It was my sad Mishap
To meet a Round-Ear'd Cap,
Who gave my Heart a Rap
     Sincerely.
With her I took a Nap;
I wanton'd in her Trap,

And got a swinging Clap
  Severely.
If e'er it can be my Hap
To meet this Round-ear'd Cap,
I'll give her such a Rap,
  Sincerely:
For suff'ring me to nap
Before she'd clean'd her Trap
By which I got my Clap
  Severely.

Throughout the period as a whole, the circulation of newspapers was growing. Unfortunately, the relevant records of the Stamp Office have been destroyed, and the newspapers themselves showed a remarkable reticence on a subject which their modern counterparts are inclined to over-emphasise. Indeed, the *Newcastle Courant* of 7 April 1739 could dismiss the whole sordid subject with the comment: 'It would be Vanity in us to print the Number of our Subscribers'. It was widely rumoured that the more outrageous issues of *The Craftsman* sold as many as 10,000. Haig (the historian of *The Gazetteer*) concludes that a claim of 1,000 would be accepted as a reasonable figure for a daily paper in 1737, while the more successful might have a sale of 2,000. Official figures of the *gross* number of stamps sold to London, provincial and Scottish papers cover only the years from 1750 to 1756. They indicate a steady growth from 7,313,766 stamps in 1750 to 10,746,146 in 1756.[13] There followed a distinct falling-off, due to the Stamp Act of 1757, which imposed a duty of one penny on all newspapers, whether printed on a half-sheet or a full sheet, and doubled the advertisement duty to two shillings. In contrast to the relative apathy with which the 1725 Stamp Act had been received, this Act was greeted with shrieks of protest and despair. According to the *London Evening Post* (as quoted by the *Ipswich Journal* of 9 July 1757), 'it is certain that many of the News Papers in Town, and most, if not all, in the Country, would be dropt'. Other papers denounced the new Act as an attack on the liberty of the Press. But the newspaper Press as a whole soon recovered. Now that the tax on a full sheet of paper was the same as that on a half sheet, the size of a daily newspaper could be doubled. Admittedly, the price had to go up, and it now became $2\frac{1}{2}d$ for a newspaper of four pages. And very soon, new papers appeared. Competition was becoming increasingly intense: and the newspapers were soon to strive to outdo one another by reporting the proceedings of Parliament.

3 Liberty, licentiousness and venality

With the accession of George III, the Press was about to enter one of its most exciting periods: rarely in the eighteenth century had popular interest in politics and public affairs been greater. The Seven Years War continued to promise an abundant supply of what Defoe had termed 'those dear Things call'd Blood and Battle', but our domestic affairs also promised to be more than usually interesting. George III was something of a contrast to his predecessors. They had preferred 'harlots and Hanover': but George 'gloried in the name of Briton'; he was moral to the point of priggishness; and he detested the political corruption he saw about him. Whether or not he was determined to follow his mother's advice, 'George, be a King!' he was certainly determined to end the rule of the Whig magnates and to end the war.

The first task involved the ousting of the Duke of Newcastle, Walpole's Grand Elector, and master of the whole system of machine politics and patronage. The second involved the more difficult problem of getting rid of the popular hero, Pitt the Elder. The obvious weapon was the Press. Court propaganda had two main points: against Newcastle, the denunciation of 'corruption' and the call to all true patriots to rally round the King; against Pitt, the condemnation of his war as bloody and expensive, and the attempt to diminish his reputation. In both aims the King was remarkably successful, although Pitt cooperated in his own downfall. And the news that he, who had always denounced patronage and pensions, had accepted a pension and a title for his wife (henceforth known to the press as Lady Cheat'em) aroused the same sort of outcry as had followed the fall of Walpole, when the 'Patriots' had similarly betrayed the trust reposed in them. As the *Public Advertiser* put it (6 July 1764), with particular reference to the Earl of Bute – a Scot, the King's former tutor, and now the power behind the throne, and a man who was soon to become the centre of a remarkably dirty newspaper war:

Deluded Britain, see thy *Patriot Friend*,
To B——, so late his Scorn, now condescend:
To thy Regard or Praise, he's no Pretension,
See him first roar at Jobs, then take a Pension;
And unembaress'd, as if 'twere forgot,
Hear him damn Scotchmen, see him court a Scot'.

Unfortunately, George III did not live up the high hopes that had been held of him. He was very much under the influence of his mother, and notoriously under the spell of Bute, with whom the young King seems to have been utterly infatuated. Bute's Scottish ancestry was unfortunate at a time when memories of the Forty-five were still fresh in many people's minds, and it became the main theme in the opposition's campaign. The court's hired writers faced a growing and increasingly scurrilous attack, one centred more and more not on the pamphlet but on the weekly political newspaper. A new stage was reached with the publication on 5 June 1762 of the *North Briton*, a weekly paper of six pages, price 2½d. This was the work of John Wilkes, who achieved standards of invective which his opponents could not possibly match. Week after week he attacked Bute and the Scottish influence at court: his attacks ranged from the notice in the issue of 17 July 1762 of the death of 'Mr John Bull, a very worthy, plain, honest, old gentleman of Saxon descent; he was choaked inadvertently by swallowing a thistle' to 'the perfect Description of the People and Country of Scotland', which appeared on 28 August 1762:

> Their beasts be generally small, women only excepted, of which
> sort there are none greater in the whole world. There is great
> store of fowl too, as foul houses, foul sheets, foul linnen, foul
> dishes and pots, foul trenchers and napkins . . . The ladies are
> of opinion that Susanna could not be chast, because she bathed
> so often. Pride is a thing bred in their bones, and their flesh
> naturally abhors cleanliness; their breath commonly stinks of
> pottage, their linnen of p——ss, their hands of pigs t——ds,
> their body of sweat.

This pleasant topic took up the whole issue. Always Wilkes attacked Bute, whose alleged intimacy with the King's mother was the subject of regular comment. But there was danger in all this, for the government was watching the press very carefully indeed, and he was lucky to get away with his issue of 19 February 1763, with its supposed letter from 'J.R.' (the Pretender) to his 'Dear Cousin' (George III) expressing his 'infinite satisfaction' at 'the most promising state of affairs . . . the check you have given to that wicked revolution spirit' and looking forward to his own early restoration to the throne. Finally, on 23 April, came Wilkes's crowning achievement, and one which was to give him a leading place in all future histories of journalism: the famous Number 45, discussing the King's speech at the opening of Parliament. This speech, said Wilkes,

> has always been considered by the legislature, and by the
> public at large as the *Speech of the Minister* . . . This week has
> given the Public the most abandoned instance of ministerial
> effrontery ever attempted to be imposed on mankind . . . Every
> friend of his country must lament that a prince of so many
> great and amiable qualities, whom England truly reveres, can

be brought to give the sanction of his sacred name to the most
odious measures, and to the most unjustifiable public
declaration, from a throne ever renouned for truth, honour,
and unsullied virtue.

After this sarcastic opening there followed a powerful attack upon the
betrayal of the King of Prussia and the peace as a whole, with a slashing
condemnation of Bute and 'the foul dregs of his power, the tools of
corruption and despotism'.

The *Stuart* line [he continued] has ever been intoxicated with
the slavish doctrines of the *absolute, independent, unlimited* power of
the crown. Some of that line were so weakly advised, as to
endeavour to reduce them into practise: but the English nation
was too spirited to suffer the least encroachment on the ancient
liberties of this Kingdom. The *King* of *England* is only the first
magistrate of this country: but is invested by law with the
whole executive power. He is, however, responsible to his
people for the due execution of the royal functions, in the
choice of his ministers, and equally with the meanest of his
subjects in his particular duty. The personal character of our
present amiable sovereign makes us easy and happy that so
great a power is lodged in his hands: but the *favourite* [Bute] has
given too just cause for him to escape the general odium. The
prerogative of the crown is to exert the constitutional powers
entrusted to it in a way, not of blind favour and partiality, but
of wisdom and judgment. This is the spirit of our constitution.
The people too have their *prerogative*.

The ministry had to take action. Already, there had been considerable
disquiet over the excesses of the press. 'Are the people . . . all gone mad? I
never read such shocking stuff in my life as the political papers . . . they
are even a disgrace to Grub-Street', was a typical comment. Number 45
was brought to the attention of the Earl of Halifax, the Secretary of State,
who referred it to the Attorney-General and the Solicitor-General for
their opinions. In the meantime, he issued a general warrant ordering the
arrest of 'the Authors, Printers and Publishers of a Seditious and
Treasonable Paper, entitled *The North Briton*, Number 45'. The name of
the author was an open secret, but Wilkes was a Member of Parliament,
and parliamentary privilege was a ticklish matter. The law officers duly
reported that the paper was libellous, and that the plea of privilege did
not extend to cases of treason, felony or breach of the peace. And the
arrests began – forty-eight in all, including Wilkes, who promptly sued
out a writ of Habeas Corpus, not in the Court of King's Bench, where his
case would normally have been heard, but in the court of Common Pleas.
The reason for this technical move was that the King's Bench was
presided over by Chief Justice Mansfield, who as a Scot was hardly likely
to be sympathetic; but Chief Justice Pratt in the Court of Common Pleas

was a friend of Pitt and Temple, whose faction Wilkes supported. Wilkes apparently presented his case in a masterly fashion, using expressions calculated to appeal to the public who crowded the Court and its approaches:

> My Lords, the liberty of all peers and gentlemen, and, what touches me more sensibly, that of all the middling and inferior set of people, who stand most in need of protection, is in my case this day to be finally decided upon a question of such importance as to determine at once whether English liberty shall be a reality or a shadow.

Pratt upheld the plea of privilege, and Wilkes was released, amid loud cheers: the London mob had found its champion. He demanded the return of his seized papers, and within a month suits were brought by many of the forty-eight persons originally arrested under the general warrant.

The real point at issue was the legality of the general warrant, which merely specified the offence, but did not name the persons charged with it, and allowed widespread arrests and the seizure of personal papers. For many years, the Secretaries of State had been issuing such warrants in the case of people suspected of seditious libel, and the validity of those warrants had not been challenged. Now that challenge developed, and from one point of view it might be said that Wilkes was striking at one of the most formidable and frequently invoked weapons of press intimidation. The suits were brought by men who could hardly afford the cost of legal proceedings, but behind them was Wilkes, who made sure that public sympathy and support were kept alive. And behind him stood Lord Temple, leader of one of the most powerful Whig groups. What emerged very strongly was the attitude of London, with its long tradition of opposition to the national government. Walpole had had his difficulties with London juries, and now once again it was a London jury which decided the cases and awarded damages out of all keeping with the various plaintiffs' station in life, but which reflected the opinion of the City itself.

Then the House of Lords entered the performance. Wilkes had written an *Essay on Woman* – a parody of Pope's *Essay on Man*, but with notes attributed to a member of the Upper House. It was, to say the least, pornographic. It had presumably been found in the ransacking of Wilkes's house and had certainly never been printed for public consumption. But now it was read out to the House – with great gusto – by the Earl of Sandwich, one of the greatest rakes of the time, and the House, having (according to some reports) listened appreciatively, resolved that the *Essay* was 'a most scandalous, obscene and impious libel'. Hereafter, Sandwich was nicknamed 'Jemmy Twitcher', after the character in *The Beggar's Opera*, for having thus turned on his fellow libertine.

The ministry now pushed through the Commons a motion that the privilege of Parliament did not extend to writing or publishing seditious libels, and Wilkes was formally expelled. The legal proceedings could now go forward, and inevitably he was found guilty of republishing the *North Briton* and of publishing the *Essay*. In the meantime he had been wounded in a duel, and decided to depart to France (to the great relief of all, his friends included). As he did not attend to receive his sentence he was declared an outlaw; but he was now the darling of the mob, which very nearly rescued the *North Briton* from its public burning, and burned instead a jackboot and a petticoat (symbols of Bute and the King's mother). The cry was increasingly: 'Wilkes and Liberty'.

The practical effect of all this excitement was to end the use of general warrants, although they were not formally condemned, and the threat remained. There also remained the problem of the power of the jury in libel actions. Hitherto, it had been accepted that the law officers' *ex officio* statement that a paper was libellous was, if supported by the presiding Justice, held to provide complete legal establishment of the actionable character of the paper, and such terms as 'false', 'malicious', 'scandalous' and 'seditious' did not have to be proved. In defending John Williams in 1763 for reprinting the *North Briton*, the counsel for the defence, John Glyn, had tried to tell the jury that in matters of libel they were not merely judges of the *fact* of publishing alone – an argument denied by Chief Justice Mansfield, who gave a precise and accurate statement of the law: the jury were judges of the fact of publishing only. Thus on the legal side Wilkes had challenged the validity of general warrants, and the vital issue of the role of juries had been raised. At the same time, the privilege of Parliament had been questioned, for, with the steadily increasing competition among newspapers, it was inevitable that printers would encroach on the forbidden ground of parliamentary debates, particularly as interest in those debates had never been keener.

As early as 1760 the *London Chronicle* had, on 31 January, printed 'The Thanks of the Hon. House of Commons . . . to Sir Edward Hawke, by their Right Hon. Speaker', together with Hawke's reply. The thanks were for Hawke's victory at Quiberon Bay. Both addresses were flowery in the extreme, and contained nothing to which exception could be taken, but they were clearly verbatim reports, and the House was not so much concerned about the character of such reports as the fact that they had appeared at all. And the publisher of the paper, together with those of the *Daily Advertiser*, *Public Advertiser* and *Gazatteer*, who had all copied the offending paragraph the following day, were called to the bar of the House, where they were 'upon their Knees, reprimanded by the Speaker; and discharged, paying their Fees'. The standard fine seems to have been £100 with confinement in Newgate until paid. After numerous complaints, the House in 1762 again resolved that it was a 'high indignity to, and a notorious breach of the privilege of this House' to print any account of its proceedings. An extremely important issue was involved: the question of sovereignty, always a delicate issue in the English constitution. Originally, the right of Members of Parliament to express themselves without fear of reprisals from the Crown had been a healthy privilege and one necessary for the freedom of discussion. But now the situation was vastly different. The claim was being made by what seemed to many to be a corrupt assembly voting under the instructions of its political managers; it seemed to isolate Parliament from the very people it was supposed to represent, and to protect it from publicity and criticism. The Radicals were soon to make much of this very question: did sovereignty lie with Parliament – or with the People?

So popular were reports of the debates that printers were prepared to take the risk. In 1765 there were three victims: Samuel Woodfall of the *Public Advertiser*, who swore that he had copied an item about the House of Lords from the *St James's Chronicle*; Baldwin of that paper, who maintained that he had taken it from the *Gazetteer*; and Say of the *Gazetteer*, who could only plead for mercy on the somewhat irrelevant grounds that he had a family of six children. All received the standard sentence. In 1767 it was the turn of Say again, and then of Wilkie of the *London Chronicle*. Reporting Parliament was obviously a hazardous business, for the claims of privilege were wide and undefined. In 1764 it was held that a letter written by Wilkes in the *London Evening Post* was a reflection upon a member of the House of Lords. The printer, Meres, was duly fined, as also was Say of the *Gazetteer*, who had copied the letter. Say – who seems to have acquired a taste for martyrdom – was once again in trouble in 1768, this time over a sarcastic 'advertisement' in his *Gazetteer* of 4 February. The item was certainly not prominently displayed, but it read 'An ESTATE for seven years to be SOLD. To prevent trouble, none need apply who cannot deposit four thousand pounds, five hundred of which to be advanced on making out the title, which is a very good one, and the remainder not to be paid till the deeds are executed.' The 'estate' was, of course, a seat in the House of Commons at the forthcoming general election, but that so harmless an item should have called down the displeasure of the House shows how sensitive that body was becoming to criticism of any sort.

In 1768 Wilkes returned, and the hitherto scattered and disorganised elements of protest were drawn together. Wilkes was incorrigible. Although still technically an outlaw, he stood for the City of London in the election. He came at the bottom of the poll, but he obtained 1,000 votes, enough to show how dangerous he could be and how weak the ministry was to allow him to stand. London had, of course, its long tradition of opposition to the government generally. It was easy for ministerial writers to dismiss Wilkes's support with contempt, as Smollett in the *Briton* in 1762 had done:

> *Canaille*, forlorn grubs and gazetteers, desperate gamblers,
> tradesmen thrice bankrupt, prentices to journey men,
> understrappers to porters, hungry pettifoggers, bailiffs followers,
> discarded draymen, hostlers out of place, and felons returned
> from transportation. These are the people who proclaim

themselves free born *Englishmen*, and transported by a laudable spirit of patriotism, insist upon having a spoke in the wheel of government.

George III heartily agreed: 'What time do we live in when a parcell of low shopkeepers pretend to direct the whole legislature?'. Undoubtedly, Wilkes owed his immediate support to such classes in London, which was the scene of considerable industrial disturbance, with strikes and machine-breaking. But he was soon to gain more significant support. He now stood for Middlesex, and was elected – only to be refused his seat by the House of Commons. This was the first of the notorious 'Middlesex elections'. Again he stood, with the same result. The third time, the ministry put up its own candidate, one Colonel Luttrell, who was declared elected although he had polled far fewer votes. Throughout all the excitement, Wilkes was in gaol – probably the safest place to be in, with rioting the order of the day. His popularity with the mob, and his control over that mob, were amazing. As Burke was shrewd enough to observe, 'the crowd always want to draw themselves from abstract principles to personal attachments . . . Since the fall of Ld. Chatham, there has been no man of the Mob but Wilkes.'[1] But the decision of the House that Colonel Luttrell was elected – although decisively beaten on the votes, and despite the fact that Middlesex did not *want* him – was a threat to voters everywhere. Elections would mean *nothing* if such decisions could be taken by a House which seemed more and more to consist of placemen who had got there by corruption and voted according to orders. There was now a link-up between Wilkes's mobs and people who had the vote.

The excitement in London continued, culminating in the 'Massacre of St George's Fields', where on 10 May 1768 a dozen rioters were killed by the military. It then died down, until it was deliberately revived by Wilkes, who published in the *St James's Chronicle* of 10 December a copy of a most indiscreet letter sent by Lord Weymouth to the local magistrates *before* the now notorious massacre, urging them to call on troops 'when the Civil power is trifled with and insulted, nor can a military Force ever be employed to a more constitutional Purpose, than in Support of the Authority and Dignity of Magistracy'. This was provocation indeed, and Wilkes made the most of it in his introductory statement which showed 'how long the horrid Massacre in St George's Fields had been planned and determined upon, and how long a hellish Project can be brooded over by some infernal Spirits without one Moment's Remorse'.

More and more the newspapers were becoming the vehicles of political controversy – and not the weekly newspapers, but the dailies. Pamphlets were still important and could make their point at greater length, as in the *Speech of Oliver Cromwell at the Dissolution of the Long Parliament*: 'Ye are a factious crew, and enemies to all good government. Ye are a pack of mercenary wretches, and would . . . sell your country for a mess of potage'. *The Public Advertiser*, despite its title, still devoted more space to news and letters than it did to advertisements, and this space was increasingly taken up by politics. It was obviously swamped by letters, usually reflecting opposition opinions; it printed as many as possible, often six, acknowledging receipt of many more, and refusing others. Often it summarised letters, with cutting comments. Thus, on 11 August 1764 it remarked that

> 'We cannot see much Wit in the Advertisement of the Life and Opinions of Lord Chief Justice Jeffreys . . . and therefore must decline publishing it. The Ode to Mary . . . is too juvenile a Performance for the publick Inspection. A.Z. will excuse out not inserting his Letter, however true it may be, when he considers that the Printer, by publishing it, would in all Probability be deprived of that precious Jewel of an Englishman, his Liberty; and though the bearing Persecution is deemed laudable among the Quakers, yet he not being of that Sect, declines depriving them of any of their Praiseworthy Acts'.

Just as writing to *The Times* was later to become a popular sport, so already the habit of writing to newspapers had become firmly established. The same trend was obvious in all the London papers: there were more advertisements, but the emphasis was on politics, which brought the customers in and could be both spirited and entertaining. The *St James's Chronicle* of 11 May 1765 printed two verses on the same topic. The first was entitled 'An occasional Song, on Lord Hinchinbrook's coming of Age, Son of Lord Sandwich, April 8, 1765'. Sandwich was now one of the Secretaries of State, but his name was always connected with the Navy. The song therefore stressed that aspect of his career:

> Come cheer up my Lads, Let's be merry and gay,
> And joyfully revel this grand Holiday;
> For Hinchinbrook now in full Splendour does shine,
> And gives a new Lustre to Sandwich's Line.
> > Heart of Oak is the Sire, Heart of Oak is the Son,
> > They always are ready, steady, Boys, steady,
> > And will add to the Glories their Ancestors won.
> While Sandwich presides at the Helm of the State,
> He'll guard us from Dangers, though ever so great.
> His Countrymen too on this Truth may depend,
> To this Country and Town he will prove a staunch Friend.
> > Hearts of Oak . . . etc.
> Then charge high your Glasses, and fill up your Bowls,
> Let Joy and Good Humour enliven your Souls;
> Let your Hearts glow with Pleasure, with Friendship and Mirth,
> And hail the great Day that gave Hinchinbrook Birth.

The effect of this eulogy was somewhat marred by the second set of verses, for Sandwich was even better known as a rake and as 'Jeremy

Twitcher', the nickname he had earned by his base desertion of his fellow-rake, Wilkes. The next effusion was entitled 'An Occasional Song on the Birth-Day of little Master H——, son and Heir to Jeremy Twitcher', and it struck a different note:

> Come on, jolly Dogs, let's get drunk and be mad,
> Make Beasts of ourselves while there's Booze to be had,
> For young Master H——'s Twenty-one,
> The fam'd Jeremy Twitcher's belov'd hopeful Son.
> Hollow Oak is Papa, Hollow Oak is his Heir,
> They are always ready, steady, Boys, steady,
> And will add to those *Deeds* which make all Europe stare.
> While *Twitcher* the Helm of the State does direct
> Our *Wives* and our *Daughters* he'll surely protect;
> His Countrymen too on his Word may depend,
> To *Wilkes* he already has prov'd a staunch Friend.
> Hollow Oak . . . etc.
> Then Fill up your Glasses, let Bumpers go round,
> Ley *Bawdy* and *Blasphemy* freely abound;
> *Religion* and *Virtue* let's laugh too to Scorn,
> And hail the *great* Day *little* Master was born.

This sort of thing was relatively harmless. But soon a far more destructive character was to appear upon the scene: Junius, whose first letter appeared in the *Public Advertiser* of 21 January 1769. For sheer invective he had few rivals. Other writers might be more brutal, but Junius had style, and was vastly admired by contemporaries. His personal attacks on ministers were characterised by their inside information and their daring. Then, on 19 December 1769, he made journalistic history, in a letter to the King: 'Sire – it is the misfortune of your life . . . that you should never have been acquainted with the language of truth, until you heard it in the complaints of your people. It is not, however, too late to correct the error.' The King had two courses open to him: either he could 'support the very ministry who have reduced your affairs to this deplorable situation . . . shelter yourself under the forms of a parliament, and set your people at defiance', or he could take the honourable course:

> Discard those little, personal resentments which have too long directed your public conduct . . . Come forward to your people . . . speak to your subjects with the spirit of a man, and in the language of a gentleman . . . Tell them you are determined to remove every cause of complaint against your government; that you will give your confidence to no man who does not possess the confidence of your subjects.

And he reminded George of the fate of the Stuarts; 'The prince who imitates their conduct, should be warned by their example; and while he plumes himself upon the security of his title to the crown, should remember that as it was acquired by one revolution, it may be lost by another.'

The letter was an instant success. The *Public Advertiser*'s daily circulation had risen from 2,800 to 3,400 as a result of the earlier letters: it now jumped to over 5,000. Moreover, every newspaper not under ministerial influence reprinted it. The ministry reacted swiftly, starting prosecutions against Woodfall, John Almon of the *London Museum*, Miller of the *London Evening Post*, Robinson of the *Independent Chronicle*, Say (inevitably) of the *Gazetteer*, and Baldwin of the *St James's Chronicle* – a very impressive round-up. The first to be tried was Almon, not Woodfall – in the hope, presumably, that a verdict against one who only reprinted the letter, and who would be tried in Westminster, which was amenable to government control, would ease the case of the crown lawyers against the original publisher in the opposition-minded City of London. The jury, directed by Mansfield, produced the required verdict of guilty, and the ministry then proceeded against Woodfall, Baldwin and Miller. Again, Mansfield gave strong directions to the jury: in an action for libel, the court alone had the power to judge whether or not an offending publication was libellous, and the jury had only to decide whether the defendant was the publisher. 'As for the liberty of the press', he continued, 'I will tell you what it is; the liberty of the press is, that a man may print what he pleases without a licence: as long as it remains so, the liberty of the press is not restrained.' But the City of London jury was not satisfied with this narrow interpretation. In the case of Woodfall it brought in the ambiguous verdict, 'guilty of printing and publishing only', and it acquitted the other two. The ministry seems to have been, temporarily at least, discouraged, and it may also have been alarmed at the excitement the various crises had aroused. As Chatham, now in opposition, put it, 'the late doctrines . . . concerning the rights of juries to judge of *Law* and *Fact*, have spread universal alarm, and raised the justest indignation. This is laying the axe to the root with a vengeance! Jurors who may not judge, electors who may not elect.'

Despite all Parliament's efforts, reports of its proceedings continued to appear – to the fury of Colonel Onslow, nicknamed 'Little Cocking George' by the Press. The leading journalist in this war was now Roger Thompson, who had formerly been employed as a compositor by Charles Say on the *Gazetteer* and the weekly *Craftsman*. Say, when threatened with prosecution over the Junius letter, had a stroke of palsy and was for a long time – or so he said – 'in great danger'. Thompson took over both papers, receiving in return a salary of two guineas a week plus one-eighth of the profits of the *Gazetteer* and a one-eighth share of the *Craftsman*. Later a more personal arrangement was made: Thompson was to have one of Say's daughters in marriage (provided he could win her consent), and was to succeed to his master's business. And in 1770 he found himself in charge of three London papers, the daily *Gazetteer*, the weekly *Craftsman*, and the tri-weekly evening paper, the *General Evening Post*. Say retired into the background, probably with a sigh of relief, for he had had a lively but expensive journalistic career which included a reprimand and a fine of £100 by the Commons in 1760, three fines of £100 by the Lords, and a very narrow escape over the Junius letter. Under Thompson the reporting of debates not only continued but became more regular and accurate. Other papers followed suit. But on 5 February 1771, on the motion of Colonel Onslow, the House's resolution of 1738 prohibiting the publication of its proceedings was reaffirmed. The Colonel then took direct action, entering complaints against the *Gazetteer* and John Wheble's *Middlesex Journal*, both for their report of his motion. The offending paragraph read as follows.

> It was reported that a scheme was at last hit upon by the ministry, to prevent the public from being informed of their iniquity; accordingly, on Tuesday last, little *cocking* George Onslow made a motion, that an order against printing Debates should be read . . . Mr Charles Turner opposed the motion with great spirit; he said, that not only the debates ought to be published, but a list of the divisions likewise; and he affirmed, that no man would object to it, unless he was ashamed of the vote he gave.

This provocatively worded account had first appeared in the *Middlesex Journal* of 7 February; it had been reprinted in the *Gazetteer* the following day, though omitting the reference to 'little cocking George'. It seems possible that the provocation was deliberate, for neither printer obeyed the order of the House to appear before it: they knew they were not alone, and had the backing of Wilkes, now an alderman, and of the City. A royal proclamation was issued for their apprehension, with a reward of £50. Onslow now widened his attack to include Woodfall's *Morning Chronicle*, Baldwin's *St James's Chronicle*, Thomas Evans's *London Packet*, Wright's *Whitehall Evening Post*, Samuel Bladon's *General Evening Post*, and Miller's *London Evening Post*.

Four of Onslow's second string made their appearance. Two, Baldwin and Wright, knelt in penance – the last ever to do so – and, after being reprimanded by the Speaker, were discharged upon paying their fees; Bladon was immediately discharged; and Evans withdrew before he was called, giving as his excuse the fact that his wife had broken her leg. When later ordered to attend, he refused to do so until the legal authority of the House had been determined and 'it is universally known whether a British subject has, or has not, a right to be tried by a jury'. And he got away with it. Woodfall could not attend, for he was in process of being punished by the Lords for a similar offence. He was fined £100 plus a month in Newgate – a sentence he did not serve, being released on humanitarian grounds: the only accommodation available was among debtors and criminals, and 'the petitioner has the most fatal Consequences to dread from the noxious Effluvia occasioned by a Number of Bodies (many of them very uncleanly)'. Meanwhile, Wheble and Thompson remained at large, together with Miller. They were apparently in close touch with Wilkes. After a month of open defiance, the City and the printers took the initiative, in a move planned by Wilkes. Wheble allowed himself to be arrested by a fellow-printer, and was taken before the 'sitting Alderman' at the Guildhall, who happened to be Wilkes. By what authority had Wheble been brought before him, Wilkes demanded. By the authority of the proclamation was the answer. Thereupon, said Wilkes, 'As you are not a peace officer, nor constable, and you accuse not the party of any crime, I know not what right you have to take his person; it is contrary to the chartered rights of this city, and of Englishmen'. Later the same day the comedy was repeated over Thompson, this time before another of Wilkes's cronies, Richard Oliver.

These actions demonstrated the City's opinion of a royal proclamation. They did not strike directly at the House of Commons. That clash was now to come. Again, there can be little doubt that Wilkes organised the whole affair. This time, the leading character was Miller: when he failed to attend the House, a messenger was sent to apprehend him on the authority of a warrant signed by the Speaker. Miller was well prepared to meet the messenger, who found himself charged by a City constable with assault and false arrest, and taken before Wilkes, Oliver and the Lord Mayor, Brass Crosby. By what authority, they demanded, could a citizen of London be arrested within the jurisdiction of its magistrates? The warrant of the Speaker was illegal, if not backed by an order of a City magistrate. The matter had now become a direct confrontation between the City and the Commons, with the City assuming the role of protector of English liberties and enemy of privilege and corruption. There was popular ferment in the City following the arrest of the Lord Mayor and Oliver (but not, significantly, Wilkes). The ministry took the obvious line that the honour and dignity of the House were at stake. The controversy had reached a high constitutional plane. Brass Crosby and Oliver were found guilty of breach of privilege of the House in releasing Miller and detaining the messenger, and were sent to the Tower. At the end of the session, they were released, to the roar of a twenty-one gun salute, and escorted to the Mansion House by over fifty carriages. As the courts subsequently upheld the action of the Commons, the result was really a victory for the ministry.

Parliament's right to suppress the publication of its debates had not been questioned and had certainly not been surrendered. But to the people it seemed that a great victory had been won, and there was something to be said for this interpretation. Rather than risk another clash with the City, Parliament delayed further action until it was too late. Accounts of its debates rapidly became the very lifeblood of the newspapers, and after 1771 no consistent effort was made to prohibit such reports. Again, almost accidentally, an important principle had been won, for the printing of debates implied a certain responsibility of Parliament to the people.

The stars had been Wilkes and Junius. But other political papers of the time were far more outspoken – often outrageously so. On 21

November 1769 *The Parliamentary Spy* began its career as a six-page weekly, price 2½*d*. It started well, with as its main feature 'A depraved House of Commons destructive to a Free Nation: a debilitated nobility, a *self-created* house of representatives, and clergy bowing to the altar of *Baal*, have brought on *us* that load of evils under which *we now* groan. An *exotic clan* basks in the sunshine of court-favour. A *standing army* threatens us with immediate destruction.' The author amused himself by writing nasty letters to various ministers. And, on 10 April 1770, he wrote 'To the Third George':

> From your childhood you betrayed a tincture of *pride*,
> unqualified by decency . . . Without a *genius* equal to the
> weight, you pored over folios, and by the most studious
> application acquired a knowledge as quickly shook off as it was
> slowly gained . . . Inspired by your tutor [i.e. Bute] with an
> affection for arbitrary and despotic power, you became its first
> victim by suffering him to hold your mind in a subjection
> intolerable to thought . . . Passive obedience and non-resistance
> were pleasing ideas to a weak mind . . . As every action of your
> life manifests your unfitness for governing; and as the
> misconduct or villany of your ministers threatens you with a
> catastrophe dreadful even in thought, I would advise you either
> to resign the reins which tremble in your hands, or consult
> some of those whom you take to be your enemies.

This was strong meat indeed. But already it had a rival, *The Whisperer*, begun in 1770. For sheer violence this paper would be hard to beat, and one wonders that it did not attract more attention. Its opening issue set the pattern:

> In the reign of *Charles* the first, the people were not afraid to
> declare their sentiments upon public measures, they were not
> afraid to declare their disapprobation of the King's arbitrary
> proceedings . . . And shall it be recorded of this enlightened
> age, that Englishmen were so degenerate and regardless of their
> freedom; as to prefer ease and pleasure, to a bold and glorious
> defence of their liberty and property, against the designs of a
> self-willed p——e, and a corrupt h——e of c——ns. . . . If it is
> just to oppose the despotic proceedings of *Charles* the first, it
> must be equally just to oppose the like proceedings in G——
> the t——. *The Whisperer* is therefore determined, unawed by
> fear of prosecution, to lay before the public some of the
> arbitrary measures of this r——n, that fall little short of those
> which brought *Charles* to the block.

The author was as good as his word. The issue of 3 March 1770 was not only libellous and scurrilous, but came very close to treason:

> Are we to be deceived, abandoned and enslaved, by a German

> w——[i.e. the King's mother] and a prostituted Earl of the
> House of Stuart . . . Are we so degenerate, so dastardly as
> tamely to submit, to the yoke of slavery, under a P——e of the
> house of B——k [Brunswick]. Britons, rouse, rouse, from that
> state of Lethargy . . . Is the name of *George* more terrible than
> *Charles* or *James* . . . Is the tyranny of G——e the t——d easier
> to be borne . . . The K—— ought to remember his family
> came to the crown of these Kingdoms by one revolution, and
> that it is possible they may lose it by another.

The paper continued until January 1772, when the author announced
the launching of a new paper, *The Scotchman*, which would be published
'with more Spirit than any Paper which has yet appeared in Print'. This
appeared on 21 January 1772, with the mixture very much as before, but
certainly with more 'spirit':

> Englishmen . . . seem now to have lost all sense of national
> honour and are ready to yield up the greatest of all civil
> blessings to the will of a ty——t, bred in Gothic ignorance, and
> guided by a banditti of SCOTCHMEN . . . Nero is recorded as
> the most infamous of all the Roman emperors, for cruelty,
> rapine, injustice, extravagance, and to comprehend all other
> crimes, *Ingratitude*. What shall I say of G—— the t——? If he is
> the worst of all the *Brunswicks*, it will be allowed me, he is as
> *gentle*, as *just*, and as *grateful* as *Nero* was; proofs of this are
> recorded in St George's Fields, the Kalendar of Newgate.

The fearlessness – and the scurrility – reached their peak on 8 February
1772 with a vicious attack upon the Queen Mother and Bute (still
regarded as the power behind the throne) in their familiar roles as Hecate
and the thane. Under the heading 'Murders Committed – Poisoned',
there followed:

> Question Who poisoned her Husband?
> Answer   HECATE and the THANE
> Question Who poisoned the late D—— of C——d at the very
>   juncture when he would have destroyed their
>   CURSED influence?
> Answer   The same infernal wretches
> Question Who sent away the late D—— of Y—— giving him a
>   slow poison, because he discovered several of their
>   amours to the late K——, and disapproved all the
>   infamous measures of Lord B——?
> Answer   The same hellish crew.

What impact such publications had is impossible to say. But one may well
sympathise with Lord North when he complained that 'the first thing we
lay our hands on in the morning is a libel; the last thing we lay out of our
hands in the evening is a libel'. One may also sympathise with those who

opposed the whole idea of a free press. Gone were the days of innuendo and implication – when the Duke of Newcastle could remark that 'I am too dull to taste them, and if they are not deciphered for me, I could not in the least guess, very often, what they mean . . . I detest the whole thing'. Now the facts were stated, often with brutal frankness and bias. At the same time newspapers were able to publish, with a fair degree of immunity, the debates in Parliament. Advertising was becoming steadily more important with the expansion of commerce and industry. A truly independent press seemed to be in the offing: but this was not to be. What *was* in the offing was the scandal sheet and unprecedented venality and corruption.

For this development, the *Morning Post* must take much of the blame. It began on 2 November 1772, and was run by a group of proprietors which included John Bell, of typographical fame, James Christie, founder of Christie's, the Rev. John Trusler, and Richard Tattersall, founder of Tattersall's. But the leading light, the man whose personality was to make an indelible mark on the new paper, was the editor, the Rev. Henry Bate, whose salary was four guineas a week.[2] The *Post* was founded strictly in the 'advertiser' tradition, with more than half its space taken up by advertisements. But it differed from its daily competitors in very significant way. They assumed that their readers wished to be informed, particularly regarding politics. Bate revived the other great tradition of journalism, that of *entertainment*, in the form of Society gossip, amusing, witty, and usually malicious. The formula was apparently popular and the paper flourished; it was very definitely an organ of the leisured classes, but the lower classes have always been very ready to read about the activities of their betters, particularly when served up in a titillating way. Money could be made out of this, and it would seem that from the very beginning the *Post* was selling 'puffs', and that by 1780 there was scarcely a paragraph in it which had not been paid for by someone. Equally profitable was the charging of suppression fees, either to suppress some embarrassing item altogether or to contradict a story which had already been published. Nor could politics be completely ignored. By 1776 the Opposition had acquired a new cause: America. The miserable mismanagement of that war was condemned by almost the entire Press, with particular reference to the Admiralty, and during 1778 and 1779 demands for the removal of the Earl of Sandwich as First Lord outnumbered demands for peace. The ministry replied by filling paragraphs in the *Morning Post* in his defence, and the paper was popularly known as *Lord Sandwich's Morning Post*.

The profit made from these somewhat dubious sources is perhaps indicated by the fact that a share in the paper (there were twenty-five shares) was valued at £350, but, according to the *Post* of 26 September 1780, individual shares were being bought and sold at 'near 800l'. And then the competition became even worse, for in 1780 Bate quarrelled with the proprietors and started the *Morning Herald,* a paper modelled on the *Post* but destined to outlive it. By 15 December 1780 it was claiming that its circulation 'is already increased to the very extensive sale of 3000 copies daily', and it doubted if the *Post* sold more than 1000. The *Post* felt obliged to answer, and on 1 January 1781 declared that 'our weekly distribution at this time amounts to twenty-one thousand three hundred' – a figure promptly challenged by Bate. However accurate the claims might be, it is clear that this type of journalism was profitable. And at this point the resistance of the 'old school' collapsed, and all papers included anecdotes and personalities, together with such items as 'Bon Mots', 'Theatricals', 'Poetical Beauties' and 'Literature and Music'.

Obviously, the influence of the *Morning Post* was not wholly bad. It meant a tremendous widening of the scope of a newspaper. At the same time, increased attention was paid to a feature which had been somewhat neglected in the past: presentation and aesthetic appearance. This emphasis on elegance culminated in 1787 with the appearance of the *World, and Fashionable Advertiser*, hailed as 'The Paper of Poetry' and selling 2,600 copies by October.[3] Undoubtedly, previous papers had laid too much stress on politics. The subject could not, of course, be ignored; very soon practically every London paper was turning this, too, to financial advantage, and accepting political subsidies. But the emphasis was increasingly upon entertainment and amusement in the form of personalities and anecdotes, focused mainly on people of wealth and status. They must often have provoked considerable speculation. On 11 April 1781 the *Morning Herald* informed its readers that

> Lord Cholm——y's intended departure for the continent, is not, it seems to revive the languid flame of love, in a personal visit to Miss Dal——ble, that affair having been long at an end and the Lady perfectly happy in the arms of a new *inamorato*: his Lordship's tour however is not to be of a very solitary nature, as one of the most accomplished women of this island has actually consented to accompany him!

The wording was sometimes obscure: but the general tone was menacing, with the implied threat that more specific details would be published if the victim did not pay up. In 1780 Bate had been a little too specific, when on 25 February he printed 'Queries Addressed to his Grace, the Duke of R——'. Lest any reader should be uncertain as to his target, he added a quotation:

> . . . All the treasons
> Complotting and contriving in this Land
> Fetch from false *Richmond* their first head and spring.
>   Shakespeare.

The queries accused the Duke of opposing every proposed measure for national security, and of providing the French with a plan of the Sussex coast. The quick-tempered Duke refused to regard this attack by such a rogue as Bate as a matter of honour, and instead of a duel – which Bate, a skilled swordsman, had probably hoped for – began legal proceedings, and won. Soon after this unhappy affair the *Morning Post* went into temporary decline, although its daily sale in late 1783 when it was bought by John Benjafield was estimated at 1,650, and its shares sold at 'about 400 l. each'.

The new editor was the Rev. William Jackson, apparently a worthy successor to Bate, and popularly known as 'Doctor Viper' because of what a contemporary called 'the acrimony of his pen . . . the extreme and unexampled virulence of his invectives . . . like darts of the savage, barbed and poisoned with the most refined art and rankest venom'. Under Jackson and Benjafield the *Morning Post* revived – largely on extortion, a practice which Benjafield systematised until it became the principal source of income. An obvious target was the Prince of Wales, who had added to his other follies by secretly marrying Mrs Fitzherbert, a widow several years his senior, and a Roman Catholic. For the Prince to marry at all without the royal consent was contrary to the Royal Marriage Act, and marriage to a Catholic was a violation of the Act of Settlement, on which the Hanoverian title depended. To do the Prince justice, he did not originally have marriage in mind, but the lady was adamant. He was, to say the least, vulnerable, and he needed only two 'paragraphs'. The first, on 8 February 1786, merely remarked that 'Mrs *Fitzherbert* pays a hundred guineas for her box at the Opera House, from which it may be presumed, that the connections and suite of that Lady have increased, are increasing, and not likely to be diminished' – a rather neat reference to Dunning's famous motion in 1780 that 'the influence of the Crown has increased, is increasing, and ought to be diminished'. The second 'paragraph' on 18 February was more pointed: 'It is confidently reported, that a certain marriage has been solemnized by a *Romish Priest*, who immediately quitted the kingdom.' The Prince paid up. But not all the victims were of so exalted a rank, and well might the *Gazetteer and New Daily Advertiser* of 7 December 1789 protest that

> The abuse of the liberty of the press has of late years become so great, that no character is safe . . . Such was not the case with the papers some years ago: the change took place when some needy adventurers thought that a fashionable Paper, that is, a record of private and public scandal, would suit the taste of the Public, and fill *their* Pockets better than a periodical detail of political information . . . The public *have been* to blame by encouraging such Papers. Many like the tale of a scandal, which does not affect themselves – and the man of middling rank chuckled to read the amours and intrigues of Lords and Ladies, little thinking that his turn would one day come, his harmless actions be misrepresented, and his character blasted in a paragraph.

This was a remarkably acute forecast of the future, up to and including the present day.

One of the 'needy adventurers' referred to was undoubtedly Major Topham of the *World and Fashionable Advertiser*, yet another of the flamboyant personalities so frequently thrown up by the eighteenth century. Educated at Eton and Cambridge, he had served in the Horse Guards, possessed a fine property, a wide acquaintance in fashionable and theatrical circles, and a succession of glamorous mistresses, notably the actress Mary Wells. According to a contemporary account,

> He drove a curricle (constructed after a plan of his own), with *four* black horses, splendidly caparaisoned, and followed by two grooms in conspicuous livery . . . His dress consisted of a short scarlet coat, with large steel buttons; a very short white waistcoat, top-boots, and leather breeches, so long in their upper quarters, as almost to reach his chin . . . [It] must be remembered that, at that time, every other person wore very long coats, and very long waistcoats; and breeches so very *short*, that *half* the day, and one *whole* hand were entirely employed in raising them *en derriere*, to avoid any declension, en avant.

Obviously, there had been significant changes in the social status of newspaper editors. *The World* regarded itself as the infallible authority on all matters of taste and fashion – and, according to a hostile critic, was 'perfectly unintelligible, and therefore much read'. One of its main attractions was Robert Merry, who, under the name of Della Crusca, founded a whole school of poetry – poetry of the most mawkish kind, but amazingly popular. By 1 January 1788 Topham was claiming a daily sale of between three and four thousand. But he had other interests besides poetry. The theatre was one. The relationship between the Press and the theatre had always been close: but Topham's interest was perhaps even closer, in that his mistress was one of the leading actresses of the day. But there were other reasons. Theatre managers were willing to pay for the suppression of hostile criticism; Francis Williams records a pleasant story of Mrs Wells (Topham's former mistress) and her second husband finding the interest of *The Times* in her activities too embarassing. The husband invited Finney, the main conductor of that paper, to his house, and handed him a packet of bank notes, with the simple enquiry: 'Will that be enough?' According to the account, 'Finney devoutly replied, "Give me a few more and by St Patrick I'll knock out the brains of anyone in an office who dare even whisper your name."'

Like all the editors of the time, Topham specialised in personalities. His most lucrative target was the Prince of Wales. In 1788, with the worsening of the King's health, the Regency crisis developed. Topham chose the side of the Prince, but seems to have felt that he might need a little encouragement. On 6 September he published, without comment:

MRS. F——TZH——T
To the Remembrance of one

> Who was ——, Wife and no Wife, Princess
> and no Princess, sought, yet shunn'd,
> courted, yet disclaimed; the Queen of all
> Parties, yet the Grace of none . . .

The Prince took the hint, and offered £4,000 cash and a lifetime annuity of £400 for the outright purchase of the *World*. The offer was refused, in favour of a subsidy. Journalism was becoming a very profitable business, if a somewhat degrading one.

All papers accepted political subsidies. Needless to say, actual details are most difficult to ascertain, varying as they did from flat annual subsidies to payment for the insertion of an occasional paragraph. The general election of 1784 and the triumph of William Pitt probably marked a critical point in the story of the political control of the Press. Despite the enormous popularity with which he has been credited, Pitt had neither the confidence of the people nor of the Commons. He was certainly subjected to unprecedented abuse from the Press, despite his efforts to buy newspaper support. Pitt's victory was due to George III, the Treasury, and golden guineas. The press in general had been against him: and this problem he was determined to overcome. He had at his disposal the Secret Service funds; and the government had various other means of intimidating or discouraging uncooperative newspapers, by denying them inside news and official advertisements; it could also devise 'trouble at the Stamp Office'. What all this amounted to was suggested in the general election of 1788, in particular the key Westminster election, which must rank as one of the most scandalous in English history. By the time it began the Treasury is estimated to have controlled seven of the ten morning papers: the *Daily Advertiser*, *Morning Chronicle*, *Morning Post*, *Public Advertiser*, *Public Ledger*, *The Times*, and the *World*. It also controlled most of the evening papers. The opposition had only three major papers – the *Daily Gazetteer*, *General Advertiser*, and the *Morning Herald*. But this election raises again the whole problem of the real influence of the Press, for, despite the formidable array of ministerial papers, the Whig candidate won.

In the next great domestic crisis, the agitation over the Regency Bill in 1789, the numbers were more even, with seven papers each. How much money was involved is again largely unknown, particularly in the case of the Opposition newspapers. The *General Advertiser* received £200 annually, with the promise of another £100 later; the *Morning Chronicle* had £300 annually; and the Whigs are reported as having deposited 'SEVERAL THOUSAND POUNDS' to buy a paper which can only be called the spurious *Star and Evening Advertiser*, set up in deliberate imitation of the original paper of that name (see below p. 77). The Prince of Wales is said to have paid a quite exorbitant price for the *Morning Post*: a thousand guineas for Benjafield's two one-twenty-fourth shares, plus an annuity of £350, at a time when the paper was selling fewer than 500 copies a day. But the Prince needed support badly. Of the ministerial papers, *The Times* and the *World* were probably the most influential. In 1787 the government had appointed John Walter, the proprietor and conductor of *The Times*, to the post of Printer to the Customs; at the beginning of 1789 it added a subsidy of £300. Even more important was the *World*, which received a £600 subsidy, the highest the ministry ever offered.

The Opposition made the spurious *Star* its main organ, and that paper certainly did its best, with vicious but clever attacks on Pitt, who was freely accused of deliberately sacrificing the King's health in order to preserve his own power. Intermingled with extravagant praise of the Prince were burlesque medical bulletins of the King's health, as in the issue of 18 February 1789:

> Dr LANE yesterday *walked* JOHN MURRAY [the King] round St. Dunstan's. The MANIAC knocked down a *dustman*, bit the finger of a *sweep*, and overturned some mad oxen in *Fleet-market*. Dr LANE was obliged to put on the *strait-jacket* as soon as he became more tame, his friends being very apprehensive of their *personal safety*.

But Pitt was the main target. Typical was the comment on 10 June 1789:

> The number of *appellations* given to Mr PITT must surely cause just surprise to foreigners. Previous to his being called *Pope* Pitt, *Emperor* Pitt, *Prince* Pitt, or Premier, he was styled the *immaculate* boy, the *miraculous* Minister, the *pattern of virtue*, the *picture of chastity*, and the *Minister of the Crown*. – It is a wonder that he has not yet been called, the *Grand Turk*; but there is one title which he can never attain, and that is, the *Minister of the People*.

The comment is interesting, in view of the traditional image of the Younger Pitt.

The Opposition had chosen the spurious *Star*. It was not a good choice – but the paper's history was an interesting one. *The Star and Evening Advertiser* had made its bow on 3 May 1788, with the announcement that it would appear at 3 p.m. each day: 'The news received by the Post cannot be inserted in the other Papers till the next day: whereas the intelligence received by the Proprietors of the STAR will be published on the day it arrives.' The new venture was conducted by Peter Stuart, who was also one of the proprietors, investing £1,000 in the paper. The concept was promising. No one expected an evening paper to be anything more than a digest of the daily papers, and the *Noon Gazette, and Daily Spy*, in existence as early as 1781, presented only 'the actual News . . . of the Morning Papers'. The *Star* aimed to do something more.

At first, the new paper was politically neutral, but by mid-November 1788 it was coming out strongly in favour of the Prince of Wales, adding to its staff a medical expert on insanity. Its circulation was now 2,000. But the new approach was not to the liking of the other proprietors, and Peter

Stuart was dismissed. He promptly began another paper, and at 3 p.m. on 13 February two *Stars and Evening Advertisers* made their appearance. For the sake of convenience, the second paper will be referred to as the 'spurious' *Star*. Peter apparently took with him most of the key staff of his former paper – pressmen, compositors, clerks and 'all the literary talents and connections', amounting to 'sixteen or eighteen persons in all' (a far cry from the days when newspapers were run on a family basis). The cost of setting up the new venture was estimated at £6,000 at the least, and where the money came from remains a mystery. Almost certainly some came from the Whigs. But Stuart had to look elsewhere for his real income. He adopted the usual methods, and his first issue suggested that 'Mr B——n and Miss J——s should not shew their affection so much in public', and that 'Mr V——s should ogle less frequently from the boxes, and think more of the world of which he must soon be an inhabitant'. But to Peter must go the credit for a new development of this system of blackmail, for very soon there appeared a volley directed at Bath and then Bristol – a series of 'portraits' of prominent people (who were tacitly invited to buy themselves out of the lists). The other papers had confined their extortionary activities to London: this new market was entirely unexploited.

The spurious *Star* at first seemed far ahead of its namesake. It was the first evening paper to offer 'Original Information' as against a simple collection of items copied from the dailies. Also, it was one of the first papers to present a well-developed editorial: hitherto, newspapers had largely confined their opinions to brief paragraphs, or had given them in the form of letters from correspondents, but the *Star* emphasised the subject which was of most interest to its readers – 'THE KING' – and located it where it would attract most attention. Unfortunately, this promising beginning was not maintained; its original information became less original, and its entertainment was often in the worst possible taste. It was efectively boycotted in Bristol. And it expired suddenly on 16 June 1789. But it had made its mark.

Much more complicated was the question of political subsidies. Professor Aspinall has shown that the government's expenditure on the press during the early years of the French Revolution was not far short of £5,000 a year – not a large sum when one considers that the propagation of revolutionary doctrines, the outbreak of war on the continent, and the existence of considerable popular discontent at home made the influencing of public opinion a matter of extreme urgency. Early in 1789 the Under-Secretary of State for Foreign Affairs declared that it was high time something was done about the Press, since almost all the newspapers were 'in the pay of the Jacobins'. He was exaggerating: almost all the newspapers were certainly *not*, for something had already been done about the Press. The government was paying out regular subsidies to the *Diary, or Woodfall's Register* (£400 a year), the *London Evening Post* (£200), the *St. James's Chronicle* (£200), *Public Ledger* (£100), *Whitehall Evening Post* (£200), *Morning Herald* (£600), *Oracle* (£200) and

The Times (£300). It also had 'interests' in other papers. But the picture is horribly obscure. Secret Service funds, if they are to be effective, must be secret: and the eighteenth century at least achieved this goal. Aspinall remarks on the 'devious means' by which payments were made, and on the lack of accurate accounts. How *effective* the system was, both from the government point of view and that of the Opposition, remains controversial, for newspapers rose and fell in popularity.

By the beginning of 1793, the government controlled nine daily papers: the *Diary*; *The Times*; the *Morning Herald* (the most powerful of all, with an estimated circulation of between 4,000 and 5,000 a day); the *Sun*, an evening paper; *Oracle*; *World*; *Public Advertiser*; *Public Ledger*; and the *True Briton*. The Opposition had only four: the *Morning Chronicle*, easily the most influential, thanks to James Perry, with a circulation of several thousand, and reputedly clearing some £6,000 a year; the *Morning Post*; *Gazetteer*; and the *Star*. Apart from the *Chronicle*, all were in financial difficulties, and could expect still further difficulties with the government. Eighteenth-century newspapermen were not generally noted for integrity, much less stupidity: and it might well have seemed that the opposition Press would virtually cease to exist. Instead, it flourished partly because of the sheer excitement of the times, and partly because of the attraction of papers prepared to play the dangerous but profitable game of attacking the government.

The enthusiasm with which the French Revolution was greeted in England, notably by poets and dissenters, was naturally reflected in the press. When the Jacobin excesses turned English public opinion against the Revolution, those papers which continued to support the 'ideas of 1789' were accused by their rivals of being in French pay. As Canning wrote,

> *Couriers* and *Stars*, Sedition's Evening Host,
> Thou *Morning Chronicle* and *Morning Post*,
> Whether ye make the Rights of Man your theme,
> Your country libel, and your god blaspheme,
> Or dirt on private worth and virtue throw,
> Still blasphemous or blackguard, praise Lepaux.[3]

Undoubtedly the Revolution made a deep and abiding impression on English journalism, with political parties sharply split over vital issues that people could feel deeply about, and wild accusations of treason. The *Morning Post* was singled out for special attention as it moved steadily towards the Left. It regularly denounced Pitt's 'arrogance and obstinacy', and in 1797, after the King had attended the Thanksgiving Service for the victories of St Vincent and Camperdown, its new proprietor, Daniel Stuart, wrote: 'The result of the procession to St Paul's was that one man returned thanks to Almighty God and one woman was kicked to death.'

The flippancy which had made such papers as the *World* and the *Oracle* fashionable was coming to an end. But despite its new stress upon politics, the *Morning Post* did not forget the entertainment role of a newspaper – although Stuart did try to play down the scandal and spicy gossip for which it had become notorious. His announced aim was 'with poetry and light paragraphs. . . to make the Paper cheerfully entertaining, not entirely filled with ferocious politics'. The Lake Poets were perhaps his most notable acquisitions. Southey's famous character, Father William, first appeared in the *Post* of 17 January 1799, while 'Old Kaspar' and little Peterkin made their bow in August 1798. The paper also first published no less than seven of Wordsworth's sonnets. At a somewhat lower literary level, Charles Lamb acted as society reporter, drama critic – and punster, with the task of providing daily a number of 'witty' paragraphs at sixpence a time. By some standards, he was grossly overpaid. Typical examples were:

> It is not astonishing that the daughters of Eve should slip, when they are attracted by the *Serpentine* River!
> Two disputents made up to a soldier on guard the other day in the Park, and asked him, when shall we arrive at the *next century?*
> Before you come to Buckingham Gate, was the answer!
> Formerly thieves first *robbed*, and then *stript*, the passengers:
> Ladies nowadays are willing to spare them the trouble of the *latter ceremony.*

> (4 January 1800; 14 January 1803)

Thanks to its star contributors, the *Morning Post* was once again in the ascendant. When Stuart took over the paper its circulation had been down to 350: it now climbed steadily and by 1803 (according to Hindle) reached the remarkable figure of 4,500 a day. The *Morning Chronicle* with 3,000 came next, with the other papers far behind. These figures, incidentally, do not agree with those in the *Annual Register* of 1822 for the year 1801, with *The Times* having a daily sale of between 2,500 and 3,000; the *Morning Herald* between 2,000 and 1,500; the *Morning Advertiser* nearly 2,500; the *True Briton, Oracle* and *Morning Chronicle* between 1,500 and 2,000; and the *Morning Post* and *Public Ledger* about 1,000.[4] But much could happen in two years, and when Stuart in 1803 sold the *Post* (a property he had originally bought for a mere £600) it was for £25,000; unfortunately, he now proceeded to concentrate upon *The Courier*, raising the circulation of that paper from 1,500 to 7,000, but in the process severely damaging his former paper. Under his control, the *Post* had boasted contributions from some of the most distinguished writers of the day, but much of the talent accompanied him when he left. The *Post* still had pretensions to literature, but its new heading, 'Literary Chit Chat' was perhaps indicative of the change. It was an age when the fortunes of newspapers rose and fell, and when political allegiances changed with the seasons.

The *Morning Post* had supported the Prince of Wales during the whole Regency crisis. Its adulation of the Prince reached its climax on 15 August 1811:

While wrapt in gloom BRITANNIA lay,
Broke not one bright, one cheering ray?
Some promise of a fairer day?
Yes, PRINCE belov'd, from thee she saw
Hope's brightest emanation flow,
She saw the filial drop divine ‾
Hang glist'ning in thine eye;
She saw the feeling heart was thine
And bless'd the happy augury,
And cried, 'A duteous son will prove
A Parent to his People's love.

The *Post* followed this outrageous effort with an even more extravagant poem in honour of the Prince in March 1812, a poem which provoked an answer from Leigh Hunt in the Sunday *Examiner* of 22 March. Hunt opened with a savage attack on the *Post* generally – 'a bye word for its cant and bad writing, and which has rioted in a doggrel, an adulation, and a ribaldry, that none but the most prostituted pens would consent to use'. As examples, he quoted some of the more sickening passages from the poem in question, ending with:

Thus gifted with each grace of mind,
Born to delight and bless mankind;
Wisdom with Pleasure in her train,
Great Prince! shall signalize thy reign; –
To Honour, Virtue, Truth, allied –
The Nation's safeguard and its pride.

'What person', [he demanded], 'acquainted with the true state of the case, would imagine, on reading these astonishing eulogies, that the *Glory of the People* was the subject of millions of shrugs and reproaches! That the *Protector of the Arts* had named a wretched Foreigner his Historical Painter in disparagement or in ignorance of the merits of his own countrymen! That this *Mecaenas of the Arts* patronised not a single deserving writer! That this *Breather of Eloquence* could not say a few decent, extempore words . . . That this *Conqueror of Hearts* was the Disappointment of Hopes! That this *Exciter of Desire* (bravo, Messieurs of the *Post*!) – this *Adonis in Loveliness* was a corpulent gentleman of fifty! In short, that this delightful, blissful, wise, pleasurable, honourable, virtuous, true and immortal PRINCE, is a violator of his word, a libertine over head and heels in debt and disgrace, a despiser of domestic ties, the companion of gamblers and demireps, a man who has just closed half a century without one single claim on the gratitude of his country or the respect of posterity.'

This was perhaps going too far. Hunt and his brother were each sentenced to two years' imprisonment and a fine of £500. The *Morning Post* continued unabashed. Its adulation was now extended to all members of the royal family (save only Caroline, wife of George IV) and to all foreign royalty (with the exception of Napoleon). It reached rock-bottom in its issue of 22 July 1824, with its 'Original Poetry on the Death of the King and Queen of the Sandwich Islands':

> . . . 'Twas Majesty, though not in pomp array'd,
> Of Ermin'd Robe, nor jewell'd princely diadem.
> 'Twas Majesty: though wrong'd, and basely made
> The jest of worthless fools, and idly mock'd by them.

The Leigh Hunt episode was important. It showed that, despite the venality and corruption of the period, advances had been made, particularly in the field of political reporting. Goldsmith's comment in the *Citizen of the World* in the mid-eighteenth century that

> The universal passion for politics is gratified by daily gazettes . . .
> You must not, however, imagine that they who compile
> these papers have any actual knowledge of the policies or the
> government of a state; they only collect their materials from the
> oracle of some coffee-house, which oracle has himself gathered
> them the night before from a beau at a gaming-table, who has
> pillaged his knowledge from a great man's porter, who had his
> information from the great man's gentleman, who has invented
> the whole story for his own amusement.

was no longer acceptable. William Windham in 1795 could still describe journalists as a set of 'bankrupts, lottery-office keepers, footmen and decayed tradesmen'; but, flamboyant and eccentric as many of the *Morning Post*'s staff may have been, they could hardly be described in such terms. The Press as a whole was in fact becoming increasingly well informed – and daring – in its political reports. Naturally, the ministerial papers could afford to be more outspoken, but the same maturity was apparent. Thus, on 30 October 1795 the *Tomahawk! or, Censor General* presented a very witty account of 'Opposition Arrangements':

> Mr Fox to reprobate the war, condemn the whole system of
> administration, and deplore the exhausted state of our
> resources; but not to be so lavish of his praise in reviewing the
> *blessed* effects of the French Revolution. Mr Sheridan to attack
> the minister on the subject of finance, and substitute *wit* and
> *humour* on every occasion for *sense* and *argument*. N.B. Not to
> forget to *bore* the House, at the end of the session, with a
> proposition for the reform of the Royal Boroughs of Scotland,
> that he *knows* can never be acceded to. Mr Courtenay . . . to be
> *jocose* and *ludicrous* on all serious subjects . . . Mr Curwen to
> prove there are no seditious meetings.

Occasionally, this new paper really excelled itself, with such parodies as this (2 November 1795):

> The Weird Jacobins
> Scene, Palace Yard. Thunder and Lightning.
> Enter F——x, Th——lw——ll [Thelwall], and Sh——n [Sheridan]

> Th——lw——ll
> When shall we three meet again?
> In Plunder, Murder, or in Slain?
> F——x
> When the Jacobin's are done.
> When th'Address is lost and won!
> & All
> F——x is foul, and foul is F——x!
> Keep clear of GUILLOTINES and BLOCKS.

Fox was the main target, although the paper made the most of what it termed 'French Atrocities'. Its excessive loyalty was proved on 31 October, when it reported an attempt on the life of the King. Each page was printed in red, with a red band all around it. And the issue of 5 November was printed throughout in red:

> This being the ANNIVERSARY of the KING and
> PARLIAMENT of England having escaped from being blown
> up with GUNPOWDER, by the RELIGIOUS JACOBINS of
> old; as it is a memorable RED-LETTER day, and a day of
> Patriotic Festivity, we have printed THE TOMAHAWK in a
> SUITABLE CHARACTER.

Opposition papers were similarly outspoken. The *Morning Post*, when in opposition, had not hesitated to savage Pitt, although, when it changed sides, its treatment of Fox was even more vicious, culminating in his obituary on 31 March 1807:

> BRITANNIA'S boast, her Glory and her Pride,
> PITT! in his Country's service liv'd, and died –
> Fully resol'vd, at last, with PITT to vie,
> For *once* to serve his country – FOX – *did die.*

Newspapers might change sides in this way, but political backing seems to have encouraged the Press to new standards, both of abuse and of approach. In the reports of Parliament, important speeches were given full coverage, but the trend was towards brief synopses – often well informed, but somewhat biased. Thus, the *Morning Post* of 10 March 1780 reported:

> Mr Jenkinson followed Mr Townshend, and made one of the
> most laboured and intelligent, heavy and scientific speeches we
> ever remember to have heard . . . Mr Burke replied in one of
> the ablest speeches ever pronounced in parliament . . . Mr
> Dunning spoke in favour of the question with infinite subtlety
> and ingenuity. He untwisted every argument that had been
> advanced on the side of Administration, and after separating
> their component Ingredients, shewd the weakness and fallacy of
> every individual part . . . This was by far the best political
> speech he ever made, and contained such peculiar connection

of argument, that no abstract, as the present is, could do anything like justice to it.

In fact, political subsidies had their advantages. The basic factor, as always, was finance. Newspapers might achieve quite large circulations, but increasingly heavy taxation made the actual returns small. The future lay with advertising: it was by advertising alone that independence could be won. Much of the success of the *Morning Post* after it had been taken over by Daniel Stuart had been due to his realisation of this – and to his recognition that there were advertisements and advertisements, and that some paid more in the long run than in the short. Said Stuart,

> I encouraged the small and miscellaneous advertisements in the front page, preferring them to any others, upon the rule that the more numerous the customers, the more permanent and independent the custom. Besides, numerous and various advertisements interest numerous and various readers, looking out for employment, servants, sales, and purchasers, etc. etc. Advertisements act and react. They attract readers, promote circulation, and circulation attracts advertisements.

In this way, he largely anticipated the later policy of *The Times*. The *Morning Chronicle* in 1815 stated that a sale of 4,000 copies a day would not pay half the cost of production, and that but for the advertisements the paper would have had to be sold at a shilling instead of $6\frac{1}{2}d$ ($7d$ after the subsequent increase of the stamp duty from $3\frac{1}{2}d$ to $4d$ in that same year). Cobbett agreed: his *Register* had to be sold at a high price because it had no income from advertisements. He explained on 4 March why he had been compelled to raise the price from $10d$ to one shilling. Of the $10d$, $3\frac{1}{2}d$ had gone on the stamp; the actual cost of the paper as a raw material was more than a penny an issue; and the newsmen received twopence. This left $3\frac{1}{2}d$ to cover printing, wasted paper, unsold copies, salaries, and so on. The main concern of John Walter was the cost of printing *The Times*, estimated in 1805 as £3,500 a year.

How heavy production costs could be is revealed by a very detailed estimate of *The Times* in the late eighteenth century, based on an average sale of 2,000 – a figure claimed by that paper in 1794.[5] The costs include six days' paper at £4.4s0d a day – a total of £25.4s0d; six days' stamps at £16 a day, making £96; and the wages of compositors, pressmen and readers, £35.6s10d. So it cost £156.6s10d to produce the paper for one week. If all 12,000 copies were sold to hawkers at $3\frac{1}{2}d$ each, the income would be £175. But against this had to be set publishing charges of £3.3s and overhead expenses on plant and premises. The final 'surplus' was £11.6s2d, but even this did not represent clear profit – other staff had to be paid, such as messengers, clerks, translators and parliamentary reporters. It was for this reason that Walter experimented with methods of reducing printing costs. Nevertheless, profits *were* being made. In late

1784 the *Morning Post* declared a dividind of £1,500; and the *Oracle* could make a profit on a daily sale of 1,700. The profits came from puffs and contradiction fees, political subsidies, and, increasingly, from advertising. Figures of advertising revenue are exceedingly difficult to estimate, for the price varied according to the standing of the newspaper, the length of the advertisement, and its position: it could range from four shillings to as many pounds. The government had laid a heavy hand on this source of income, raising the duty to 3s in 1789 and to 3s6d in 1815. But it would seem that the more successful papers could make as much as £40 or £50 a day from advertisements. The income from the more dubious sources can only be guessed at.

The period had thus witnessed significant developments. Not least, of course, was the rise of *The Times*. In its early years, that newspaper had been in no way outstanding. Only when John Walter II took over in 1803 did it begin to forge ahead. His aim was independence. He was soon involved in a war with the Post Office, whose clerks held the profitable monopoly of translating foreign news. They were known as 'guinea men', and it cost a newspaper proprietor at least one hundred guineas a year to buy their summaries. John Walter decided to buy his own foreign journals and use his own correspondents and translators. But Authority considered that no individual had any right to receive foreign newspapers except through the medium of the Post Office – an attitude perhaps understandable in time of war or threat of war. Walter's letters were received either late or not at all, but even at the height of hostilities, he still managed to make arrangements with blockade runners. His success is indicated by the fact that *The Times* published the first news of the Battle of Trafalgar, and on 6 November 1806 Plumer Ward wrote to Lord Lowther: 'I am almost ashamed to send your Lordship a newspaper as the latest news from the Continent, but I assure you *The Times* publishes, seemingly from authority, more than can have been officially received, from the state of the packet boats and the winds.' And a letter from the Foreign Office dated 18 September 1813 stated that 'Mr Hamilton presents his compliments to Mr Walter, and is directed by Lord Castlereagh to request that he will have the goodness to tell him if he has received any Intelligence of the reported defeat of the French near Dresden which is now in circulation'.[6] *The Times* was already on its way to establishing its extraordinary dominance in the years to come. But other papers were also flourishing. The *Morning Post* (which changed hands in 1801, at a price, it was rumoured, of £25,000 – a remarkable recovery for a paper which only a few short years before had been practically worthless) boasted that it accepted no favours; and in 1803, according to Daniel Stuart, an official 'came to me with a message of thanks from the prime minister, Mr Addington, offering me anything I wished. I declined the offer.' In fact, the commercial situation now allowed independence if it were desired.

There had also been attempts to launch purely literary journals. *The Traiteur*, begun on 18 November 1780 as a six-page paper, price 3d, made the usual apology:

> Those who imagine that they are going to feast on politics . . .
> will most inevitably experience being 'sent empty away!'
> Neither will *they* be more grateful, whose vitiated tastes are
> pampered into the sole enjoyment of highly seasoned
> SCANDAL . . . The Editor . . . is so far sensible that he must
> fall infinitely short of his excellent predecessors, that he resolves
> to make *no* apology where the best would be insufficient. He is
> prepared for the whole army of Critics to exclaim that any
> successor of the *Tatler* and *Spectator* must fail.

In fact, most did fail, and quickly. But developments in other fields were
more important. The first *regular* daily evening paper was *The Star* in
1788; it had a circulation of 2,000. It was followed by *The Courier in 1792*
which reached 7,000 at its height. Even more significant was the
appearance of Sunday newspapers, the first of which seems to have been
Mrs. E. Johnson's Sunday Monitor and British Gazette of 1779. There were
soon rivals. Most contained a moral essay of some sort; otherwise, the
emphasis was squarely upon news – with a certain amount of 'instruction
and entertainment'. Few could compete with the elegant appeal of one of
the best-known of all the early Sunday newspapers, *Bell's Weekly
Messenger* on 3 January 1802:

> The Messenger stands on a particular ground . . . Discumbered
> from advertisements, our Publication is entirely devoted to
> useful instruction . . . From the originality of the leading
> articles . . . the variety of topics the multiplicity of important
> events, and the number of interesting occasional remarks
> relative to the Sciences and the Fine Arts, our Journal is
> calculated to help the pen of the historian, to assist the artist, to
> entertain the curious, the grave and the volatile, to gratify the
> politician, the courtier, and the mechanic, the soldier and the
> churchman, the lawyer and the doctor; and, above all, to afford
> an innocent amusement to the fair sex, and to improve their
> knowledge.

The Sunday newspapers were obviously experimenting, and, after
a slow start, they caught on. *Bell's Weekly Messenger* was selling over 6,000
a week in 1803, and breaking all records for certain issues: that on
Nelson's funeral sold 14,405 copies.[7] By 1812 at least eighteen Sunday
newspapers were published in London, with sales ranging from 1,000 to
12,000. But this growth had not been achieved without opposition. The
sale of everything except milk and mackerel on Sunday was against the
law. Not only did Sunday newspapers compel the people actually
engaged in their production and sale to profane the Sabbath, but their
very content was calculated to injure and deprave public morals. The
question was raised in Parliament in 1799, when a Bill was introduced
'for the suppression . . . of newspapers on the Lord's Day'. It was defeated.

One opponent pointed out that in order to prevent the employment of people on Sundays, Monday newspapers would have to be banned as well. Mr Sheridan asked whether stale news was any more palatable than stale mackerel? But the attack was to be renewed many times. Already, however, the Sunday newspapers had become firmly established, with tremendous consequences for the future.

Perhaps not surprisingly, this period had also witnessed the revival of yet another journalistic tradition, the pornographic, displayed in such publications as *The Rambler's Magazine; Or, The Annals of Gallantry, Glee, Pleasure and the Bon Ton* of 1783-1790 (described by a modern writer as containing informative, do-it-yourself articles on sexual techniques, health, flagellation, and so on); and *The Bon Ton Magazine* of 1791-96 – the first of many specialising on what was to become known as 'the Victorian Vice', the birching of girls. One quotation will suffice: '. . . and after a few words of lecture, during which the snowy prominences lie quivering in sad suspense, she applies the rod with such vigour and dexterity to poor Bett's backside that in less than a couple of minutes, her bouncing bum is "all one red".'[8]

The future was wide open!

4 The early Radical Press and the Sunday newspaper

A new voice had been added to the general turmoil – that of the Radicals, the product of the steady development, in the background, of the so-called Industrial Revolution. That involved the rise of *individuals*, whose status can only be described as 'middle-class' – enterprising, making their own way in life, very poorly represented in Parliament, but increasingly wealthy; not by nature or temperament conservative, but rather inclined to a root-and-branch reform of the whole political and parliamentary system. In its early days, Radicalism was a somewhat dilettante movement, led by middle-class highbrows, very sedate and very respectable. They relied on pamphlets for their influence, and perhaps no one would have been more alarmed or bewildered if the radical causes they urged in their elegantly written pamphlets – such as universal manhood suffrage and annual elections – had suddenly come about. Their temporary linking-up with Wilkes and his City mobs had shown some of the dangers apparent in the movement as a whole. Now those dangers became even more apparent. The French Revolution added a touch of fire to the Radical movement. It was closer to home than the American Revolution, and obviously far more explosive. The effect on British Radicalism, with all its abstract theories about natural rights and the equality of man, was similar to that of the Russian Revolution of 1917 on Communism. Here, it seemed, was a country actually trying to put those theories into practice, into hard political *fact*. It all seemed to suggest that the theories were not as abstract and idealistic as their opponents' thoughts. And, for the first time, the Radicals began to make real contact with 'the people'.

As before, their main weapon was the pamphlet – with particular emphasis on the writing of Tom Paine. They answered Burke's *Reflections on the Revolution in France* in 1790 (the classical Tory and conservative denunciation of that Revolution, which sold 30,000 copies) with Paine's counterblast of 1791, *The Rights of Man*, Part I, which, though costing three shillings, sold 30,000 copies within a few weeks. Its sale was powerfully assisted by the London Corresponding Society, and it was quoted at every meeting of the various Radical societies. Paine was urged to bring out a cheaper edition, and Part II, which appeared in 1792, was issued not only as a three shilling pamphlet but also in a sixpenny edition.

Within a month 32,000 were sold, and the cheap edition continued to sell strongly. It reached a new level of the population, the 'Jacobin societies', composed of middle-class enthusiasts and the aristocracy of the workers. At the same time, the sheer excitement of the period made the opposition newspapers increasingly bold, and attracted a far wider audience.

Undoubtedly the government was alarmed at this upsurge of the reading habit. Lord Granville considered that the Press was the most powerful of the agencies which had produced the French Revolution; Windham was equally convinced that it was mainly responsible for the naval mutinies of 1797. There was a widespread fear that 'incendiary' writers were capable of setting the masses at war with their rulers. The government took swift action: the newspaper stamp was raised to 2d in 1789, and to 3½d in 1797 (4d in 1815); the advertisement duty was increased to 3s in 1789, and to 3s6d in 1815; and the Attorney-General could proudly claim in 1795 that 'there had been more prosecutions for libel during the last two years than there had been for twenty years before'. But the repression seems to have been ineffective, for, according to Windham in 1797, newspapers were still circulating their poison every twenty-four hours, and spread their venom through out the kingdom; they were to be found everywhere in common ale-houses and similar places frequented mainly by the most ignorant and unthinking section of the community, and he never saw anyone of low condition with a newspaper in his hand without comparing him to a man who has swallowed poison in the hope of improving his health. Wilberforce also stressed the danger involved in the increasing circulation of newspapers. 'In general', he declared, 'those persons who were for ever improperly busying themselves in politics were the least useful and least worthy members of the community'. There was in fact general agreement among the ruling classes that too many of the poor were reading newspapers and learning subversive ideas from them.

How justified such fears were will never be known. Few people could afford to buy a newspaper outright: the ever-increasing stamp duty meant that a paper cost 6d by 1800, and 7d by 1815 – prices prohibitive to all but the wealthy; but coffee-houses took in large numbers of papers, as did clubs. Of course, few working-class people frequented such establishments, but their needs were also catered for. Public houses took in newspapers, which could be read aloud to those customers who could not read. As Cobbett asked, when he was still a young Tory and not yet converted to the cause of Reform:

> Where was one to find an ale-house without a newspaper? Ask any landlord why he takes the newspapers; he'll tell you that it attracts people to his house; and in many ways its attractions are much stronger than those of the liquor there drunk, thousands upon thousands of men having become sots through the attraction of these vehicles of novelty and falsehood.

Barbers' shops served a similar function. This spread of the newspaper public produced a pronounced reaction against popular education – which had always been suspect to those who demanded of the working man an honest day's work for a very modest day's pay, and who were afraid that education might well give him ideas above his station in life. As the early Cobbett put it, in 1807:

> I appeal to any commanding officer who has continued long settled with his regiment, or to any captain of a man-of-war, whether your 'scholars', as they are called, are not in general the worst of soldiers and sailors. The conceit makes them saucy; they take the lead in all matters of mischief; they are generally dirty and drunkards, and the lash drives them to desert.

In fact, to the horror of those well-intentioned people who had supported charity schools and Sunday schools, and to the sardonic amusement of those who had warned against such foolhardy ventures, 'the chickens hatched in the schools had come to roost wearing liberty caps'.

It seems probable that the common Englishman's revulsion at the events in France and the Napoleonic peril made much of the repression unnecessary. Certainly, when the government took the final step of suppressing the Radical societies altogether, they fell virtually without a blow. The immediate danger seemed to be over. It would appear that the Jacobin bogey was vastly exaggerated, and that the Press had as yet little popular influence, although during the Luddite troubles of 1811 to 1813 a writer in the *Quarterly Review* complained about 'anarchist journalists' who dominated the weekly papers and had infiltrated the dailies, 'inflaming the turbulent temper of the manufacturer, and disturbing the quiet attachment of the peasant to those institutions under which he and his fathers have dwelt in peace'.

But real trouble was to come with the peace of 1815. The war boom was followed by a slump, there was the problem of demobilisation, and, in the background, the frightening social and economic changes of the Industrial Revolution. How close to revolution Britain was is still a matter of some controversy. Certainly, there was widespread unemployment and even starvation, and a sudden revival of radical journalism aimed at the artisans and labourers. This journalism took the form of a weekly paper of political comment – in effect, a weekly pamphlet. It aimed at moulding events rather than recording them. The newspaper of this period was primarily a commercial concern, financed by advertisements, and not as yet venturing on extended political comment. The new political weekly contained few or no advertisements; and it was the work of a single individual, virtually unassisted.

The story of the Radical Press at this stage is largely the story of William Cobbett, who had begun his journalistic career as a true blue Tory but had later seen the light; and who, after 1815, was generally regarded by the Tories as the incarnation of the devil. His *Political Register* was now firmly on the side of 'the people'. But its price (1s0½d for sixteen small quarto pages) put it far beyond the reach of its intended audience, although working-men clubbed together to buy it and read it aloud in ale-houses. Here was a new type of journalism. The whole emphasis was on the 'editorial' essay, with its spirited attacks on domestic affairs and its proposed remedies for the desperate plight of the economically oppressed. It was a type of journalism which struck home as none had done since the days of Tom Paine. But even Paine had been too abstract and doctrinaire to have much popular appeal: he had to be 'translated' into language the working-man could understand. And this Cobbett proceeded to do.

The *Register* displayed a particular interest in America, with a whole series of letters in which the conditions of that new, free and lightly taxed country were sharply contrasted with the suffering and heavy taxes of Britain. On 13 January 1816 Cobbett asked:

> As to the Americans being in *rude* state, on what is this notion founded? Their dress, their amusements, their manner of eating and drinking, are so much like ours, that, were it not for the absence of beggary, misery, and filthy streets, a man dropped down in an American town would imagine himself still in England.

Closer to home were his demands for parliamentary reform. But Cobbett had no sympathy with the Whig Opposition in this respect: 'It is the *country* that is now stirring. But, does it stir for the OUTS? No; nor would it have stirred an inch for them if they had bawled 'till Midsummer' (*Register*, 2 March 1816). His idea of reform was far more radical.

> What GOOD would a reform of Parliament do now? [He demanded in his issue of 12 October 1816.] It would do away with the profligacy, bribery and perjury of elections, and would thereby, in one single cut, do more for the morals of the people, than has, since the system has existed, been done by all the Bible Societies and all the schools that have ever been set on foot, and all the sermons that ever have been preached.

It would put an end to 'that accursed thing, called Parliamentary interest. Promotions and honours in the army, the navy, the Church, the law, and in all other departments would follow *merit*'. And

> A Reformed Parliament would not forget to enquire *why* Mr Ponsonby and Lord Erskine receive four thousand a year each, and are to receive it for life; *why* Mr Huskisson is always to receive twelve hundred pounds a year when he is not in an office which brings in more than that sum; *why* Mrs Mallet du Pan and William Gifford are kept by the public; *why* the Seymours receive such immense sums, and the Somersets; *why* Lady Luisa Paget and numerous other dames of quality receive incomes out of the public taxes.

This was lively stuff indeed, if somewhat ahead of its time. And it was backed by vague hints of physical force. Said the *Register* of 23 March 1816:

> It is impossible to make *millions* of men submit to ruin and starvation . . . It would be presumptious even to guess at what may be resorted to . . . Shall we endure all this misery without *calling to account* those who had the management of our affairs? Shall we submit ***********?

His main desire, however, was to impress on the people that the root cause of their distress was political, and not due primarily to machinery – to rally them behind the cause of true reform instead of dissipating their strength in machine-breaking and sporadic outbursts of direct action and violence. In the *Register* of 26 October 1816 he explained his policy:

> The newspapers which are notoriously devoted to corruption are continually endeavouring to rouse and direct the rage of the people against bakers, brewers, and butchers. The corrupt men know very well what is the real cause of the people's suffering: but their object is, first, to turn their eyes away from that real cause; and, next, to stir them up to acts of violence against tradesmen who are fellow-sufferers with themselves: because by so stirring them up an excuse is offered for quelling them by force of arms.

There followed the announcement of one of the most significant innovations of this period:

> I am, for my part, so deeply impressed with the magnitude of this evil, that I propose to address, in my next *Register, a Letter to the Labourers and Journeymen of this Kingdom*, calculated to lay before them a perfect knowledge of the real causes of their sufferings, and to preserve the tranquillity and to restore the happiness of that country. That this letter may have as wide a circulation as possible, it is my intention to cause it *to be published afterwards on a single open sheet of paper*, and to cause it *to be sold at a very low price*.

In fact, Cobbett had seen the way to a far wider circulation and influence; he had found another loophole in the wording of the Stamp Act:

> Still, however, there is one way left which these Argus-eyed laws have left us to circulate our observations in a cheap form without exposing ourselves to penalties, other than those which the Attorney-General and a special jury may think proper to inflict. *Open Sheets*; that is to say, a sheet of paper, *not folded up*, nor printed with an intention to be folded up, requires no stamp.

In its new form, the *Register* appeared as one sheet of paper, of broad foolscap size, with four wide columns. It omitted the news contained in the expensive edition (which continued) – news which subjected the latter to the stamp tax – and contained only the essay. And it cost only twopence. The traditional date for this innovation is 2 November, with its rousing appeal 'To the Journeymen and Labourers'. But the Newspaper Library at Colindale has an issue of 19 October in this form, and it is possible that the experiment started a week before that. Presumably Cobbett was trying out his newly discovered loophole in the law.

He was now making contact with a completely new public. As he put it, on 16 November 1816:

> Two or three journeymen or labourers cannot spare a shilling
> and a halfpenny a week; but they can spare a halfpenny or
> three-farthings each, which is not much more than the tax
> which they pay upon a good large quid of tobacco. And besides
> the expense of the thing itself thus becomes less than the
> expense of going to a public house to hear it read. – Then there
> is the time for reflection, and opportunity of reading over
> again, and of referring to interesting facts. The *children* will also
> have an opportunity of reading it . . . The wife can sometimes
> read, if her husband cannot. The women will understand the
> causes of their starvation and raggedness as well as the men and
> will lend their aid in endeavouring to effect the proper remedy.
> Many a father will, thus, I hope, be induced to spend his
> evenings at home, in instructing his children in the history of
> their misery, and in warning them into acts of patriotism.

The picture so warmly painted of whole families devoting themselves to what could only be described as sedition was not one calculated to warm Tory hearts!

Cobbett's success was remarkable. On 16 November he remarked that 'the spies have, I dare say, found that twenty thousand copies of the *Register*, no. 18, have already been sold'. He followed this up on 30 November with the triumphant statement that 44,000 copies of the first cheap issue had been sold, adding 'Let Corruption *rub that out* if she can'. His claims were not seriously challenged: if anything, contemporaries added to them. In 1817 Bentham said that the circulation was 60,000, while the *New Times*, a paper set up against Cobbett, reminded its readers on 1 January 1818 that

> this paper was established in a moment of alarm, and even of
> tumult; amidst internal dangers and distresses more formidable
> than those of foreign hostility . . . Cobbett was upon the spot.
> He had organised a system by which he was enabled to throw
> from 60 to 70,000 of his Twopenny Pamphlets into circulation
> weekly, among the lowest and most uninformed classes of the
> manufacturing population, at that time struggling with unusual

misery, from the temporary stagnation of trade. Thus was the venom of the most poisonous doctrines diffused with the most malignant efficiency.

There was no doubting Cobbett's business efficiency. He set up an effective system of distribution throughout the country, sending bundles of the *Register* by coach to agents in every town. Shopkeepers in towns and villages were invited to act as agents, and were requested to send a regular weekly order giving very plain directions as to the coach by which their parcel might be dispatched. As a further inducement the *Register* announced on 7 December that

> any person *in the country* who takes in a *thousand* copies a week *regularly*, will be supplied at 11s. a hundred [a considerable saving]. – The Author recommends to the friends of freedom and the propagation of useful political knowledge *not* to purchase to *give away*. The best way is to let the thing take its natural course. That which is not worth buying for twopence is not worth reading . . . If a man sell but a hundred in a week, it gives him a profit of 4s.2d. – I have heard of one man who lives in a cottage by the side of a common, who has sold *1800* of these *Registers*, by which he had cleared *three pounds fifteen shillings*. He goes to all the Market Towns and Villages.

Actually, it took no tremendous sales ability to sell the *Register*, for Cobbett quickly mastered the art of writing for the working classes, and of identifying himself with them. Even his enemies had to admire his style. They might object to his coarseness and invective, but such objections overlooked the problems of the audience Cobbett was aiming at, one which could only understand a direct, simple and concrete approach. The earlier Radicals had talked above people's heads when they held forth so eloquently about 'natural rights'. But people could understand Cobbett when he denounced the wealth of the aristocracy and upper clergy; they could understand him when he denounced specific taxes, as he did on 2 November 1816:

> You have been represented by the *Times* newspaper, by the *Courier*, by the *Morning Post*, by the *Morning Herald*, and others, as the *Scum* of Society . . . There are few articles which you use in the purchase of which you do not pay a *tax*. On your Shoes, Salt, Beer, Malt, Hops, Tea, Sugar, Candle, Soap, Paper, Coffee, Spirits, Glass of your Windows, Bricks and Tiles, Tobacco.

And they could appreciate his coarseness, for it was part of their lives.

Cobbett's importance was as a pioneer, appealing to an audience wider than any political writer had ever known before. His weakness was one of character, perhaps a lack of moral fibre. He was never a man of violence, despite the tone of many of his articles; and when, in 1817, following the suspension of Habeas Corpus, the government threatened him with arrest, he chose to flee to America. But he left behind him a legend, and already rivals appearing in this new journalism of protest. One of the first was *The Black Dwarf*, started by T. J. Wooler on 29 January 1817, price 4*d*. The issue of 5 February 1817 may be taken as typical:

> Who are the seditious? The lower orders of Englishmen, in many of our manufacturing towns, are nearly as bare as the savages of Africa. The scanty produce of their toil will neither enable them to feed, not cloathe *themselves*; and yet they must be taxed, to find the most sumptuous fare, the most magnificent equipages, for those who impose upon their patience the most unrelenting oppression; and if the feelings of humanity should produce the complaint of misery, they are branded with sedition and threatened with the coercion of military force. A nation cannot be seditious against itself. The *general* will is the predominant law. The richest man in the country has no greater right in it than the meanest.

Here again was an example of the abstract theories of the French *philosophes* and their English imitators being 'translated' into concrete terms which working-men could understand.

The main weapon of the *Black Dwarf* was sarcasm:

> Give Lord Castlereagh a couple of bad potatoes and a little cold water for his daily sustenance, and see what STUFF his LOYALTY could be made of. Put George Canning in the workhouse of Bethnal Green, and allow him half-a-crown a week (and that is more than he is worth to the state) and hear then what beautiful tropes and similes he would find for the Constitution. (26 February 1817)

In similar vein was its stinging paragraph in the same issue on 'the State of Ireland':

> The people of England have long been in error, it seems, upon the subject of the condition of the *Irish peasantry*; and Lord Castlereagh and Mr Curwen have stepped forward to set them right. It is not true, they say, that Ireland is the most debased and degraded and unhappy country in the world. They are a contented, a *high-spirited* and a happy race of mortals . . . True it is, that they are almost in a state of nature, as it respects cloathing and habitation: true it is, that their wretched cabins, built of mud, and destitute of cleanliness and convenience, are the very images of the abode of misery and desolation, – that the inhabitants of these horrid looking receptacles, which a hottentot would disdain to dwell in, look forth from them in rags and tatters, staring like an unhappy bedlamite looking

after some visionary beam of comfort; true it is, that their appearance only excites disgust; yet notwithstanding all this, they are *contented* and *cheerful* and *happy*.

The *Black Dwarf* was far bolder than Cobbett, and it became increasingly critical of his timidity, accusing him on 2 April 1817 of 'running away' and giving sarcastic quotations from his writings. 'Such men', it concluded, 'are indeed better *out of the ship*: but it is provoking to see them pack up their stores and leave their ship-mates half-starving upon the wreck.' And the following issue saw a five-page article devoted to a 'Farewell to Mr Cobbett': 'Oh! what a falling off was there! . . . [He] carries with him the contempt and scorn of every manly mind in England . . . silly old man!' At the same time, Wooler proudly announced that 'the *Black Dwarf* is now said to be the greatest object of *ministerial* hatred'. He may well have been justified in his claim, for his editorial on 9 May, under the heading 'Danger of Public Writers. Arrest of the Editor' described his arrest on the comprehensive charge of 'Libel upon King John, King Charles the First, King James the Second, and King William the Third, besides the common house of Parliament, and the *whole people of England*'. He was to remain in gaol for two months.

The *Black Dwarf* specialised in vicious personal attacks – at first on Castlereagh, Canning and the Prince Regent, but later on Lord Sidmouth. It excelled itself on 18 December 1818 with a huge head-line 'MURDER!!!' and an editorial accusing Sidmouth of this crime for having condemned three forgers to death: 'Lord Sidmouth has dared to take upon himself the responsibility of life or death – he dared to assume the power of the monarch . . . We must therefore bow with reverence to King Sidmouth! We must prostrate ourselves before *King Sidmouth*! We must supplicate the mercy of King Sidmouth!' According to the ministerial *New Times* of the following day, 'the article was the most audacious and libellous, perhaps, ever committed to the Press'.

The impact of the *Black Dwarf* was assisted by the placards which advertised each issue. Unfortunately it is impossible in cold print to give an adequate impression of the glaring headlines and sensational layout employed. 'Just Published, no. 7, Price 4d., of THE BLACK DWARF' included a large woodcut of a black coffin on which, in white, were the letters H.C. Should readers fail to understand the allusion a motto was added: 'Alas, alas, Poor Habeas' (for the suspension of Habeas Corpus had already been denounced in the *Black Dwarf* (3 March 1817) as 'a declaration of war against the liberties of the people, and the cause of reform'). The placard continued:

This Number contains Reasons for TURNING OUT THE MINISTERS
And endeavouring to recover the Constitution.
Caterpillars no part of the Gooseberry Bushes they eat, nor
Earwigs of the walls they live in
Monkies not made to run loose in China Closets
COWARDS THE WORST OF FOOLS!
CONSOLATION

> For all those Englishmen, who will as tenderly be led by the Nose,
> as Asses are. Shakespeare. HEM![1]

The sheer obscurity of this announcement must have attracted the curiosity of many. But it is easy to understand how the weekly circulation of 12,000 claimed by the paper in 1819 could be translated into 12,000 seditious assemblies by the ruling classes. And the paper had a host of imitators: as it put it, in its 'Review of the Past Year' on 7 January 1818:

> The Press was armed in favour of Reform to a degree
> unprecedented. It was the power of a Briareus, who brandished
> a hundred thousand arms, and spoke with more than half a
> million voices. The agents of the corrupt system trembled in
> their dark recesses – the hour of retribution seemed at hand.

This may have been over-optimistic: but undoubtedly Authority was worried. Farm labourers, mill hand, weavers, soldiers – all who had cause to be disaffected – seemed to be reading or listening to someone who could read. And it was *what* they were reading that troubled the ruling classes.

Imitating the Cobbett formula was *The Gorgon* of 1818, a weekly of eight small pages, costing only 1½d. Like Cobbett, it encouraged emigration, pointing out that many people 'love not England for what she *now* is, but . . . a superstitious and traditional veneration for the relics of what they fancy she once has been'. The reader was urged to emigrate, despite the undoubted hardships involved:

> Let him reflect on the evils he has escaped from – the waning
> sun of *Old England* – the Paper Bubble – the Debt and Taxes –
> the myriads of paupers – the fifteen pence and two shillings a
> day for his labour – the soup and salt fish, potatoes and
> almsgiving, charity and Savings Banks: all these he has left
> behind; and, lastly, his ears will no longer be annoyed with
> hearing that '*venerable block*', the British people, roar out 'God
> Save the King' and 'Rule Britannia', to the great edification
> and delight of the Boroughmongers. (7 November, 1818)

The Gorgon advocated practicable reforms, and distrusted abstract theories. Its great aim was universal suffrage, in pursuit of which it attacked all and sundry quite indiscriminately: the royal family (and Cobbett for tolerating it); the Whigs; the Society for the Suppression of Vice; and Orator Hunt, a leading Radical, but described as a 'brazen-faced booby'.

Another writer in the cause was William Hone, an antiquarian bookseller, noted for his religious parodies – parodies for which he was imprisoned following his inability to give bail of £1,000. What gave most offence was his version of the Lord's Prayer:

> Our Lord who art in the Treasury,
> Whatever be thy name,

Thy power will be prolonged,
Thy will be done throughout the empire,
As it is in each session.
Give us our usual sops,
And forgive us our occasional absences on divisions,
As we promise not to forgive them that divide against us.
Turn us not out of our places;
But keep us in the House of Commons, the land of Pensions and
    Plenty;
And deliver us from the People.

Such wit was probably above the heads of the new reading public: but in
1817 Hone started a weekly paper, soon to become *The Reformists' Register
and Weekly Commentary*, consisting of sixteen small pages, price only 2*d*. It
was solidly political, with little light relief. Hone demanded universal
suffrage and annual Parliaments, and, like all working-class journalists,
had no faith whatsoever in any Whig claims to be the reform party. His
writing could be extremely effective, as in his 'Recapitulation' of 15
March 1817:

Borough of Gatton

Proprietors	ONE	Sir Mark Wood, Bart., M.P.
Magistrates	,,	,,
Churchwardens	,,	,,
Overseers of the Poor	,,	,,
Vestrymen	,,	,,
Surveyors of the Highways	,,	,,
Collectors of the Taxes	,,	,,
Candidates at the last Election	TWO	Sir Mark Wood, Bart., M.P. His Son, Mark Wood, Esq., M.P.
Voters at the last Election	ONE	Sir Mark Wood, Bart., M.P.
Representatives returned at the last Election	TWO	Sir Mark Wood, Bart., M.P. His Son, Mark Wood, Esq., M.P.

A more damning indictment of the whole system of borough-mongering
could hardly be imagined – but effected without comment of any kind.
The paper collapsed on 25 October 1817: its author had been in gaol, his
health had been badly affected, and he was in financial difficulties. But
there were others ready to take over.

The Medusa; or, Penny Politician began on 20 February 1818 as an
eight-page booklet, bearing the banner: 'Let's Die like Men, and not be
Sold like Slaves'. It was addressed to 'the public, Alias the "ignorantly-
impatient Multitude" . . . O ye factious, seditious and discontented crew!
will you never believe that you are *happy* . . . ?' As usual, the chief weapon
was sarcasm and the choice of targets wide: political corruption, the
Prince Regent, the Whigs, the Society for the Suppression of Vice, the
law, Sunday schools – in fact, the whole *system*. In its first issue, in a

curious article 'On the public exercise of prostitution', it had advocated 'public stews'. It ran a whole series on 'London parsons in their true character', mentioning (6 March 1819) that 'one vender of piety received only 400 and 80 Pounds for Two HOURS labour in the vineyard!!', and another on 'Law not Justice'. But it reserved its main spleen for political corruption, denouncing

> State leeches . . . useless places, unmerited sinecures, and overpaid offices . . . The Duke of St Albans is still *hereditary grand-falconer, and hereditary Registrar of the Court of Chancery*; and without catching or keeping a hawk, or registering a single gudgeon, entangled in the meshes of the law, he pockets two thousand per annum of the public money, which is wrung from the wants of sickening misery and famished want. The right of his dukeship to seize upon this portion of the public spoil consists in the merit of having had an ancestor who had the honour of being an illegitimate descendent of Charles the Seond, who made his son a duke, in despite of his bastardy, and in despite of the common law, which should have sent his Majesty to the House of Correction, until he gave security to the parish that it should never be burthened with the Royal bantling! The Honourable Henry Addington is still Clerk of the Pells and seizes upon three thousand a year, as his part of the prey; for which the Honourable Clerk is only called upon for the clerkship of signing his quarterly receipt. His claim consists in the merit of having a brother who had been a minister, and is now Lord Sidmouth. Lord Charles George Arden whose claims to public support are more than questionable, is an over-grown porpoise among the loaves and fishes; taking to his single share nearly 38,000 pounds a year of those taxes, which the misery of the people supplies so reluctantly to the profligacy of the state. This is, indeed, a voracious pauper; and he contends for *his right*, his *patent right* as he calls it, with the pertinacity of a sturdy beggar. What a credit to this country, to have an idle Lord devour, for no service, as much as would supply the United States with seven or eight Presidents, each at the salary which is now given to their able Chief Magistrate! (8 May 1819)

The impact of the article was tremendous: place after place, names, amounts, and the significant reference to the United States. Modern historians have stressed the immediate influence of the American Revolution on Radicalism in England: but they have tended to ignore its later influence. The working-class papers did not, and they made the most of the 'contrasts' they could see. Thus, *The Medusa* on 4 September 1819 gave a 'Contrast of the Expenses between a Republican and Monarchical Government'. According to this, America cost only £46,880 a year, the main salaries being those of the President at £5,000 and the

Vice-President at £1,000; but the British system cost £941,850, with the King receiving £120,000 and the Regent £595,000:

> Look at THIS picture and at THAT! What a contrast! . . .
> Look at poor England sinking under her ponderous legal, state and ecclesiastical establishment. Look at her two millions of paupers, her famishing artisans, and her ruined commerce and agriculture. Gracious heaven! are men to be termed *seditious*, because they complain of this contrast? Are they to be termed *incendiaries, anarchists,* and *revolutionists,* because they exclaim to a patient and suffering people, 'There! there is the cause of your privations! Look at the cost of your Kings, your Princes, your Chief Justices, your Lord Chancellors, your Bishops, your Judges, and your Foreign Ministers . . . !

One of the greatest of the Radical journalists was Richard Carlile, who in 1817 fell under the spell of the *Black Dwarf*, borrowed twenty shillings, and invested it in a hundred copies of the paper, often walking thirty miles a day for a profit of eighteen pence. Then he met W. T. Sherwin, an admirer of Tom Paine, who on 5 April 1817 began a sixteen-page weekly, price 2*d*, entitled *The Republican* – a title he was soon to abandon in favour of the less provocative *Sherwin's Weekly Political Register*. Sherwin seems to have been a very timid revolutionary, and he and Carlile came to some sort of agreement, with Sherwin confining himself to printing, leaving the more dangerous task of publishing to Carlile. Carlile promptly republished Hone's parodies, was arrested, and very naturally, could not find bail of £800. He spent eighteen months in gaol – untried, and without redress of any sort. But he was gaining a reputation, and between 1817 and 1818 *Sherwin's Political Register* was submitted to the law officers of the Crown on ten occasions.

The clamour of the Radical journals reached its peak in 1819. Even before Peterloo, the *Medusa* could produce a song hardly likely to gain the sympathy of Authority:

> Britons, rise, the time is come,
> To strike the opposition dumb,
> For though we are oppress'd by some,
> Our wish is to be free:
> Rise, unite, demand Reform,
> Let no tyrant you alarm,
> And if refus'd, then let us arm,
> And fight for liberty!
> (5 June 1819)

When one considers the wide circulation of these papers, one can perhaps sympathise with Authority's concern over the mass meeting of the working classes planned for Manchester, particularly when some of the Radicals, in their well-intentioned zeal to show the country that they could conduct such a meeting with order and sobriety, practised a form of drilling, an exercise not calculated to win the approval of Authority. The subsequent 'massacre' evoked in the Radical press a form of hysteria – and threats of violence. Carlile was well to the fore, for he had actually attended the meeting. But he had allies, all striving to outdo one another in inflammatory appeals. One such was J. Griffin's *Cap of Liberty*, which appeared on 8 September as a sixteen-page weekly, price 2d. Its opening address was typical:

> The Magistrates of Manchester ordered a set of desperadoes to arm themselves and attack a defenceless multitude of men, women and children, peaceably assembled for the recovery of their rights, which had been treacherously lost by those in whom they had confidently reposed them. This certainly is High Treason against the People . . . Mr Carlile . . . declared in his *Political Register* that all hope of reconciliation was at an end, and the People had no other resource but by immediately taking up arms, not for the recovery of their liberties, but in defence of their lives and the lives of their wives and children. How far this appeal to the People may be imprudent it is not for us to determine: but we do not hesitate to declare, that an appeal to the highest authority in the kingdom to defend itself from swords reeking with innocent blood, is not nor cannot be construed into treason.

The Prince Regent came in for special treatment:

> While the Throne thou hast not mounted,
> Stands – but totters to its base;
> And the hordes thou hast not counted
> Give thee yet breathing space!
> While the PEOPLE yet permit thee
> To thy 'vantage nor or never,
> Ere the arm of vengeance hit thee,
> Wake! – arise! – or fall for ever.
> (6 October 1819)

The editor did qualify his hints of violence, as on 17 November 1819 when he announced that he 'although a Republican, does not wish to induce the Reformers to make a Republican form of government their final object, because he believes that the blood which would be shed to obtain it would be more than its equivalent, although when once established it is indubitably the best'. He had, in fact, decided on a more practical approach, and urged his readers not to purchase taxed goods, suggesting alternatives such as a 'Breakfast Powder . . . superior to any coffee which can be purchased at 3s. per pound . . . It is very pleasant to the taste . . . its strength being as nearly as possible in proportion to that of the *excisable* article' (22 December 1819). This particular concoction was named the 'Radical Powder'.

Other papers did not make such concessions. *The Briton*, appearing on 25 September 1819 as an eight-page weekly, price one penny, made its attitude very clear:

> Let us *think*, let us *act* as the brave,
> And *die* for REFORM if need be;
> He's a *blockhead*, a *traitor*, a *slave*,
> Who will not *attempt* to be free.

'Every Briton should be armed', it declared on 23 October. 'Fellow-countrymen, let me again intreat you to learn the use of arms and practise a soldier's discipline.' For good measure, it threw in a savage and remarkably outspoken attack upon the Prince Regent, in the form of a mock advertisement, headed 'Real Bargain':

> To be disposed of, the 'Wild Man of Hanover', and the only motive for getting rid of him is, that his present *keepers* are heartily tired of him. He is a remarkable spendthrift: the thousands he has squandered are incalculable . . . He delights in boasting, cruelty, oppression and blood; and therefore might be placed among the awkward squad of heroic-whiskered Falstaffs, or humane company of Colonel Knox, or be fitly associated with Judge Jefferies, or certain Manchester murderers. The young days of this biped indicated something good. But though he was under the tuition of a very able master, who was as cunning as a Fox, yet his matured age demonstrates that he is fit for nothing . . . He has passed his 50th year; and as his death may be calculated upon, and as he is somewhat corpulent, agriculturists would do well to purchase him for manure.

The aims of *The White Hat*, begun on 16 October 1819 as a sixteen-page weekly, were 'Annual Parliaments and Universal Suffrage'. Again, the general tone was menacing: 'We shall obtain Reform, complete effective Reform, in spite of that borough-mongering oligarchy which has so long lorded it over the purses and persons of the people; or we shall sink into a slavery the most debasing and hopeless that ever nation was cursed withal . . . Neutrality is treason.' According to *The Democratic Recorder and Reformer's Guide* in the same month: 'If ever it was the duty of Britons to resort to the use of arms to recover their freedom and hurl vengeance upon the heads of their tyrants, it is now.'

How dangerous this new type of journalism really was is impossible to estimate. But, understandably enough, Authority was concerned at this spread of Radical papers. As a Secret Committee of the Commons put it, 'they have been circulated with incredible activity and perseverance, in cheap and often gratuitous publications'. The equivalent Committee of the Lords agreed and denounced the 'unremitting activity . . . in circulating to an unprecedented extent, at the lowest prices or gratuitously, publications of the most seditious and inflammatory nature'. Who was behind this free distribution is unknown; Cobbett himself was passionately opposed to the practice. But it was a threat the government could not permit.

At first the government put its faith in an attempt to 'write down' Cobbett. The liveliest of its effusions was *Anti-Cobbett, or, Weekly Patriotic Register*, which appeared on 15 February 1817 as a sixteen-page weekly, price only 1½*d*, with the announcement that the title had been chosen 'not out of any wish to injure that individual, but to counteract his dangerous errors, and criminal violence'. It consisted of essays and extracts from *The Day and New Times*. In particular it made the most of the contradictions between Cobbett's early Tory views and his present Radicalism. Its very first issue quoted Cobbett's opinon in 1794 of what he had then termed the 'reform mania':

> 'If this malady', said he 'is not stopped at once by the help of
> an hempen necklace . . . it never fails to break out into
> Atheism, Robbery, Swindling, Jacobinism, Massacres, Civic
> Feasts, and Insurrections . . . It should be determined, on the
> first insurrection, whether our lives and properties shall be
> secure under the law and constitution of the state, or whether
> they must depend on the mad resolves of illegal meetings.'

It went on to quote, with obvious relish, Cobbett's description of mobs as 'the devil in his worst shape' and of Paine as 'a raggermuffin Deist . . . a blasphemer . . . an infidel Anarchist', before turning its attention to the 'Address to the Journeymen and Labourers (the very hinge of a great plan of Insurrection and Massacre)'. This idea that all the Radical clubs were engaged in some sort of plot loomed large in *Anti-Cobbett's* approach: 'Cobbett will, of course, deny that he had any share in these preparations; but I say he was and is the great, the main instrument in preparing men's minds for it.' In fact, it would certainly seem that the government was convinced that some grand design was in the wind.

Anti-Cobbett usually ended with a verse or a song, as in the issue of 8 March 1817:

> Orator H——T; or The White Feather
> Here's to the *Orator*, boasting bluff,
> And here's to his second, Bill C——bb——tt,
> For both these bold heroes show spirit enough
> When back'd by the boys that can mob it.
>   Orator H——t, Orator H——t,
> Hide the white feather and sham a bold front.

It could always find space for some very sensational stories of atrocities committed during the French Revolution. And from time to time it produced a really serious and positive article, especially on the subject of Reform. On 1 March 1817, for example, it presented an admirable exposition of the traditional theory, commonly associated with Burke, of 'Virtual Representation':

We ARE all truly represented in Parliament – all, I say, men, women, and children – which is much more comprehensible than Cobbett's last new notion of universal suffrage including only men above 21 years of age. He supposes that nobody is represented but those who vote; and they, only by the person for whom they vote. At that rate, a Member for a borough in Cornwall has no concern for the interests of a hundred thousand people in Yorkshire; nay, he cares not for any of the inhabitants of his own borough, except those that actually vote. And this is extremely foolish.

The paper closed with its eighth issue on 5 April 1817, with the somewhat premature statement that 'Cobbett having fled from justice with his ill-gotten gains, and abandoned his deluded followers to their fate, all further exposure of his conduct becomes unnecessary'.

At least, *Anti-Cobbett* had tried to meet the Radical weeklies on their own ground, and at their own price. More expensive was the *White Dwarf*, which appeared on 29 November 1817 as a sixteen-page weekly, price 4*d*. In an address to the 'Labouring classes of Society', it declared (6 December 1817):

We do not expect that every individual among you will derive pleasure from the perusal of this book; but we are certain it will do you no harm, if you will but be candid and impartial enough to read it. Do not say that you are too poor to purchase it, and make that an excuse for not noticing our remarks – we know very well that you contrive to buy other little books . . . Some of our truths may not prove palatable at first . . . Though we cannot promise that it shall prove as violent and blasphemous as some others, we so promise that it shall afford you much more instruction and profit than all the revolutionary trash put together . . . That nothing less than a *revolution* is the aim of these men is too evident to be disputed . . . Hunt, the noisy, and Cobbett, the false.

The paper lasted until April 1818: but it lacked fire. And very early on it was including such items as 'Sketches from real life', 'A Tour through France', and a letter (10 January 1818), with favourable editorial comment, to the effect that 'The Ladies, without a single exception, express their desire to see something for their *entertainment*; declaring that they would feel pleasure in reading your *political* matter if you would but give them a *little in their own way*'. Such concessions to human frailty were scorned by the tougher Radical journalists.

It was increasingly obvious that mere counter-propaganda was ineffective. The Radical agitation continued. Lord Sidmouth, the Home Secretary (and one of the favourite targets of the Radical press) stated that the newspaper press was 'a most malignant and formidable enemy to the Constitution to which it owed its freedom'. Another prominent politician described Cobbett's 'Address to the Journeymen and Labourers of England' as 'one of the most malignant and diabolical publications that ever issued out from the English Press'. He gave the credit for the Derbyshire rising to the press. The Rev. William Butts in 1817 informed the Home Secretary that Cobbett's papers were bought even by paupers and read with avidity. He wrote with some passion about this trade in sedition, with 'poor miserable hawkers, wanting bread, . . . going up and down the country selling 44,000 of the most mischievous publications that were ever put into the hands of man', persuading the ignorant masses that all their misery was caused by taxation, greedy placemen and holders of sinecures, and that their distress could be easily relieved by the government.

The government took sterner action. It began at the top level, with Carlile as its first victim; immediately his report of Peterloo was published, he was arrested. But the government decided to press the more emotionally charged case of blasphemous libel: the re-printing of Paine's *Age of Reason*. Carlile cooperated to the full, and apparently looked forward eagerly to the trial. But he was a poor speaker, and made a very feeble showing; even his warmest admirers had to admit that the Chief Justice had acted with extreme moderation, often under strong provocation, as when Carlile requested that the Bible be read in order to substantiate Paine's arguments. Inevitably, Carlile was found guilty of publishing the work with the intention of bringing the Christian religion into disbelief and contempt; the charge of publishing a seditious libel was never followed up. As Wickwar says, 'one feels bound to regard the prosecution as political, even though the jury found Carlile guilty on religious grounds . . . It was assumed that among poor people radicalism in religion was politically dangerous.' However, the trial had results not anticipated by Authority, despite all the lessons of the past. The circulation of Carlile's paper, now renamed *The Republican*, rose to 15,000, while that of the *Age of Reason* increased even more dramatically, for it had been read into the records as the basis of the case against Carlile, and those records were widely copied by the newspapers. Carlile himself was sentenced to two years' imprisonment and a fine of £1,000 for publishing *The Age of Reason*, one year and £500 for publishing another of Paine's works, *The Principles of Nature*, and security for good behaviour for the term of his natural life, himself in £1,000 and two others in £100 each. He was sent to Dorchester Gaol. His wife continued the business and was promptly under fire: sheriff's officers closed the shop and remained in occupation until Christmas Eve, of all days. It was all in the best traditions of the melodrama, for Mrs Carlile was lying-in during this period. When the officers left, they took with them some 70,000 publications, most of them completely unobjectionable. Legally and morally, the action was dubious, to say the least: a business which had been producing a profit of £50 a week had been ruined. As Carlile put it, in a letter to the Treasury Solicitor:

I am not only imprisoned for three years, but am to a certainty imprisoned as long as the present system of Government continues, as you have not only obtained the infliction of a heavy fine, but at the same time have taken steps to prevent the payment of that fine, with an ultimate intention of keeping me in prison whilst your employers can keep their places.

Such elaborately stage-managed prosecutions were rarely successful; all too often they merely promoted the sale of the publications concerned. But local magistrates took tougher methods. Cobbett himself complained that publicans' licences had been withdrawn if they took in his *Register* and a Shropshire magistrate ordered two men to be flogged for distributing the same paper, 'since when'. he reported, 'I have heard of no others being circulated in this neighbourhood'. This was probably an extreme case. But this local system was considerably extended in 1819, when there seemed a real danger of widespread mob violence, if not actual revolution. The attack was launched not against the actual printers and publishers but against the poor and defenceless hawkers of the Radical weeklies: Carlile was never tried for anything he wrote in *Sherwin's Register* or his own *Republican*, but the small fry who distributed those papers were hit – and hit heavily. As Carlile explained,

> We have pretty good proof that the Attorney-General does not altogether want the authors; he knows that the authors remain authors after committed to prison; but the vendor who has a large family is sure to be ruined and reduced to misery by the prosecution. It is here only that the Attorney-General can act with effect.

Hitherto, prosecutions had been virtually confined to London, but the government had, perhaps somewhat belatedly, become aware of the spread of Radical ideas throughout the country, and of the seventy-five prosecutions of Radical newspapers in 1819 more than half were outside London. Most were aimed at the hawkers and sellers, against whom the whole machinery of the law was brought into play. It was used, according to the indignant Carlile, against

> an old and ailing man, and scarcely able to earn enough in his profession as a shoe-maker to support himself and his wife; he was consequently in the habit of selling political pamphlets to complete the means of living without parochial aid. His defence was that he was a general vender of political pamphlets and did not read them to know what they contained, as his whole time was occupied in doing what little work in his business his strength would admit of.

A cripple in Exeter who had no means of earning a livelihood except by selling periodicals was prosecuted for selling Hone's widely circulated *Catechism*, he was imprisoned until he could find bail, himself in £200 and two securities in £100. Similar prosecutions were going on all over the country. But the threat seemed very real, and Lord Eldon was convinced that something more systematic was needed; Sidmouth agreed, and two of the famous Six Acts of 1819 were directly aimed at the Radical press. They constitute the high-water mark of legislation restricting the freedom of the Press.

The Blasphemous and Seditious Libels Act tightened up the existing laws. It empowered the authorities to search for and seize all copies of a libellous pamphlet after the conviction of the accused, and gave the judge discretionary power to inflict the practically new punishment of banishment for a second offence. Far more important was the Publications Act, or Act to subject certain Publications to the Duties upon Newspapers, and to make other Regulations for restraining the Abuses arising from the Publications of Blasphemous and Seditious Libels. Its purpose was clearly set out in its preamble:

> pamphlets and printed papers containing observations upon
> public events and occurrences, tending to excite hatred and
> contempt of the Government and Constitution of these realms,
> as by law established, and also vilifying our holy religion, have
> lately been published in great numbers and at very small prices:
> and it is expedient that the same should be restrained.

Hitherto only newspapers proper had been subject to the fourpenny stamp duty: it was news, and not views, that were taxed, as Cobbett had discovered. The new Act extended the definition of a newspaper. All pamphlets containing public news *or remarks thereon* on any matter in Church or State, printed for sale and published periodically which did not exceed two sheets or were sold for less than sixpence (exclusive of the fourpenny duty) were to be deemed newspapers. To close a further loophole – and one which had caused trouble in the past – the size of the sheet was fixed. Furthermore, printers and publishers of newspapers as thus defined had to enter into recognizances to the amount of £200 for a provincial newspaper and £300 for one printed in London, Westminster, Edinburgh or Dublin. Finally, persons selling unstamped newspapers were to be fined £20. In the House of Lords, Ellenborough explained the government case:

> It was not against the respectable Press that this Bill was
> directed, but against a pauper Press, which administering to the
> prejudices and the passions of a mob, was converted to the basest
> purposes, which was an utter stranger to truth, and only sent
> forth a continual stream of falsehood and malignity, its
> virulence and its mischief heightening as it proceeded.

The Act exempted from taxation papers 'containing only matters of devotion, piety, or charity'.

The effects of the Act were immediate. The *White Hat* closed on 11

December 1819. Some papers considered resistence, and the *Cap of Liberty* declared on 22 December that:

> Whatever alterations may be necessary in this Publication, to meet the Bills now pending in Parliament relative to the restrictions on the Press, we beg to apprize our Readers that our Publication will be continued as usual; and whatever plans our contemporaries may adopt, this Publication *will not be stamped.* The same plan will be adopted with respect to the *Republican* and *Medusa.*

Nevertheless, the *Cap of Liberty* and *Medusa* had to be combined. Readers received more, but the price was now 6*d.* Carlile's *Republican* and the *Black Dwarf* were also enlarged, but again sold for 6*d.* And the last issue of the *Weekly Political Register* in its cheap form appeared on 6 January 1820, with a tender farewell from Cobbett:

> And now, TWOPENNY TRASH, dear little twopenny Trash, go thy ways! Thou hast acted thy part in this great drama. Ten thousand waggon loads of the volumes that fill the libraries and booksellers' shops have never caused a thousandth part of the thinking nor a millioneth part of the stir that thou hast caused. Thou hast frightened more and greater villains than ever were frightened by the jail and the gibbet. And thou hast created more pleasure and more hope in the breasts of honest men than ever were before created by tongue or pen since England was England. When thy stupid, corrupt, malignant, and cowardly enemies shall be rotten and forgotten, thou wilt live, be loved, admired, and renowned.

> But Cobbett was not to be put off easily. On 29 January 1820 he brought out a new paper, *Cobbett's Evening Post,* duly stamped, costing 7*d* – and small for the price. The whole front page was taken up with advertisements, all publishing notices, and including a specimen of a political carol:

> God rest you merry Gentlemen,
> Let nothing you dismay:
> Remember we were left alive upon last Christmas Day.
> With both our lips at liberty to praise Lord C——h,
> With his practical comfort and joy, and joy,
> With his practical comfort and joy.

The advertisements soon fell off markedly in numbers. And the paper concentrated immediately on slashing denunciations of the new Press regulations and of '"that respectable part of the press", as Lord Castlereagh called it' (3 February 1820). The *Courier* was singled out for special treatment, as in the issue of 2 February 1820, when Cobbett attacked its account of the death of George III:

> How *tender* the heart of the *Courier*; how warm *his* nature; what

noble qualities *he* possessed . . . will be best determined by those who have paid the most strict attention to his huzzaing one of those heroes, the Manchester Yeomanry Cavalry, and who have heard him applaud the chopping down and trampling under foot of numerous unoffending men, women and children. His tender soul melts away in sorrow at the natural decease of a king; but he chuckles and crows at seeing nearly five hundred innocent people chopped about . . . hypocritical court sycophant . . .

Later in the month (24 February) he was still harping on Peterloo, this time with reference to the *New Times*:

Nobody but this man [the editor of the *Courier*] and the Editor of the *New Times* has, that we know, justified the shedding of blood in Lancashire. Nobody else has treated the complaints of the wounded with *ridicule* . . . continually at work to produce a *censorship*; and, in short, to make a breach, never to be healed, between the people and the government.

Cobbett's talents lay in political propaganda rather than in journalism proper. He was well aware of this, and, in a letter addressed 'To Reformers' on 3 February 1820, announced that

The *Register* will be continued weekly. I will never desert nor neglect you. It is on the *Register* I rely for producing *lasting conviction* and *final* success. The *Register* proceeds against the fortress of Corruption by regular and steady approaches: the *Evening Post* acts as a *skirmisher* to keep off the assassin-like assailants, who have hitherto annoyed the main body on its march.

In fact, he produced two versions of his *Register*: a shilling edition on which the duty was paid to obtain free transmission through the post; and a sixpenny edition, about which he remarked (3 February 1820) that 'it may be pleasing to the enemies of "Two-penny Trash" to know, that *four thousand* of each of the *six-penny* Registers have been sold'. The role of the *Evening Post* was thus to reply to the attacks of the other papers, and counterattack in its turn, leaving the *Register* free to carry on its great task without such minor irritations; and the *Post* took up its duties with enthusiasm. But soon Cobbett found another use for his *Evening Post*. On 5 February 1820 he announced his intention to stand for Parliament at Coventry and proposed a public subscription to assist him. His appeal included an account of his whole life and career. He had, he maintained, been sober even when he was a soldier! He had seven children, and, he added, 'I never struck one of them in anger of my life'. And he had a good deal to say about 'cowardly libellers' and the unremitting attacks made upon him by 'the atrocious Daily Press'. The 'Fund for Reform' already amounted to £200, but £2,000 was needed. Every issue published details of the subscriptions apparently pouring in, together with very favourable estimates of Cobbett's prospects. But the subscriptions were usually pitifully small, and Cobbett was defeated. He ascribed his defeat to intimidation and an attempt to murder him.

But the sting had been taken out of Cobbett, as it had from all the Radical weeklies. The new prices precluded the vast majority of 'the people' from buying newspapers. Radical papers continued to be published, but their great days were over – until the struggle for a cheap press was renewed in the 1830s. Nevertheless much had been achieved: the astonishing circulation figures of the Radical weeklies showed that these papers had made politics not only interesting but meaningful to the lower classes. As the *White Hat* put it, on 16 October 1819:

> The great mass of the people of this country, constituting what is reproachfully and contemptuously called 'the lower orders', is now possessed of a very considerable quantity of information, and is become as unlike as possible to the ignorant and beastly mob which gentlemen picture to their imagination, as they sit in their parlours, drinking wine, and reading the *Courier* or *Morning Post*. Thanks to the labour of Cobbett especially, and a host of writers . . . every political subject of importance has been discussed in cheap publications in the most able and ample manner.

The same paper even went so far, in its issue of 13 November 1819, as to maintain that

> The invention of printing itself scarcely did more for the diffusion of knowledge, and the enlightenment of the mind, than has been effected by the cheap presses of this country. Thanks to Cobbett! The commencement of his twopenny register was an era in the annals of knowledge and politics which deserves eternal commemoration.

Not all the Radical writers were as full of Cobbett's praises. But he was undoubtedly the pioneer of a popular press of a new kind, reaching a new class of reader – the common reader – which had suddenly become a threat to the nation's very security.

Already a new threat to the 'respectable Press' was assuming alarming proportions, a threat both to the delicate moral susceptibilities of the upper classes and to their political ease of mind. This was the Sunday newspaper, now flourishing. When in 1822 the Commons ordered the publication of the amount of duty received from newspaper stamps, the Sunday *Observer* was first, contributing £12,773.6s8d to the revenue, followed by *Bell's Weekly Messenger* with £870.13s4d[2] Another attempt had been made in 1820 to suppress Sunday newspapers altogether – an attempt based this time not only on the threat they posed to public morals but also on the fact that too many of them were conducted on 'democratic' lines. According to the *Morning Post* of 27 May

1820, the petition

> set forth that the increasing circulation of Sunday newspapers
> was most injurious to public morals . . . not only for the
> manner in which they employed the printers and publishers on
> the Lord's Day, but from their effect of detaining many other
> persons from attending Divine Service, while morals were
> contaminated by the blasphemy and sedition with which the
> publications were promulgated.

One has to admit that there was some justification in such
criticisms. Most Sunday newspapers began with the noblest of intentions.
According to the opening address of the *Age* on 24 January 1819,

> Morality is the great source of human happiness. Without it,
> there is no dignity in man, no stability in political institutions,
> no confidence . . . Its principles will be held sacred in THE
> AGE . . . The sly insinuation which steals away the purity of the
> female heart; the disgusting scandal hiding itself with
> meretricious decency under the veil of initial letters; the
> purchased paragraph of unmerited praise, or malicious censure,
> shall never find a place in our columns.

Unfortunately, it proved impossible to live up to these high ideals. As
Francis Williams says, 'the Sabbath of the British newspaper reader has
always been bloody and violent'.[3] A very different emphasis soon became
apparent: the main features of the Sunday newspaper of the future were
already being laid down. Typical was *Life in London*, which appeared on
13 January 1822, price sevenpence. It was mainly taken up with boxing
and crime (with particular attention paid to rape), and was often written
in slang. The first issue included, under the heading 'Delicate
Advertisement, or a new species of personal security', an item to the effect
that 'some little time ago an Advertisement appeared in a Morning
Paper . . .:– "Wanted the sum of £100 by a young Lady, just arrived from
the country, for which she will give a consideration of too delicate a
nature to be particularised in a public print".' Some idea of the paper's
literary style and general approach may be gained from its lengthy
account on 7 April 1822 of what it called a 'Turn-up Extraordinary; or, a
Feminine Trial of Skill':

> On the morning of Tuesday last, a great concourse of people
> were attracted toward a spot called the 'Ruins', near St
> George's Fields, to witness the prowess of two Ladies residing
> in Kent-Street, who appeared (attended by two other Ladies as
> seconds) in short jackets, secured at the waist by a
> handkerchief, their hair cropt expressly for the present purpose,
> and *all in prime twig*, determined on a *regular mill*. By what we
> could collect, SAL had been flirting with NAN'S favoured
> Lover . . . The Ladies on coming up to *scratch*, displayed *fine*

science, but were *cautious*. NAN *made play*, but SAL was not *to be had*, and fought rather *shy*. Some manoeuvring ensued when NAN, making a *feint*, SAL attempted to put in a left handed hit, which was well stopped by the former, who placed a blow near the place where Sally took her snuff and which made her *ivories* dance a reel in their box.

The paper also featured a curious series entitled 'The First Corinthian' [the former Prince Regent]:

> He could dance a minuet with a princess with a degree of elegance which every courier envied and every lady admired; and he could *sport a toe* in a horn-pipe at a Ken with 'brown Bess' and 'Sixpenny Sal' with equal éclat. He could *floor* a watchman with all the facility of one of 'the fancy', and he could heal his bruises much more rapidly than any surgeon by the liberal application of the 'oil of palm'; insomuch that the *Charleys* courted his *fists*, and longed for a *flower* at his *hands* . . . There is not a Charley at the West End of the town, who is not ambitious of having his cork *drawn* by *Corinthian* George.

Life in London obviously had aspirations to be a 'society' journal. Like more recent newspapers, it devoted much space to the royal family – of a type all too often on the lines of its 'Royal Anecdote' of 10 March 1822:

> As the Duke of —— passed through the Porter's Hall at ——, he saw a dirty-looking boy standing there. What boy is that? says the Duke. The milk-boy, your Royal Highness. Milk! Milk! from whence? asked the Duke. From the cow, your Royal Highness. Damn your Irish soul, reiterated the Duke to the porter, and walked off.

A few Sunday papers strove to be more serious, but *Life in London* had undoubtedly shown the way along which more and more Sunday papers were to develop, with its emphasis on 'blood and sex' – an emphasis which perhaps culminated in an advertisement which appeared in the aptly named *Paul Pry* of 2 January 1831:

> To Booksellers, Publishers and the Public
> Many have been deterred from taking the CRIM. CON. GAZETTE on account of its title. It is a moral work, and contains not a line to call up a blush on the cheeks of innocence, all the cases being held up to the scorn they may justly merit.

What had undoubtedly helped to assist in this development, and to make the Sunday newspapers increasingly Radical in their tone, was the 'Queen's Affair' of 1820. It has to be admitted that this crisis would have satisfied all the requirements of the most exacting Sunday newspaper of today. For the first time since Henry VIII an English King forced his ministers to do their utmost to get him a divorce, and to deprive Queen Caroline of her royal title. The case involved royalty; it revolved around the eternally fascinating subject of sex (and illicit sex at that); and it became highly political. All the necessary ingredients for muck-raking were there: and the Press as a whole, including (and sometimes led by) that section which liked to think of itself as the 'respectable press', fell on it with gusto.

The leading ministerial (Tory) organ at this time was the *Morning Post*. It first hinted at the approaching crisis on 3 April 1820, when it reported Caroline's announced intention of returning to England and taking up residence in Buckingham Palace – adding, somewhat mysteriously: 'This is a subject which of all others we are most reluctant to discuss; and notwithstanding the above statement, we are not without hope that the Queen will be better advised.' This pious hope was repeated several times, although no explanation was given. Clearly, however, the scandal had become common knowledge, and on 25 May the *Post* complained that

> after a lapse of upwards of three months, we are surprised to find an attempt made to revive the report of the existence of such serious difficulties between his Majesty and his Ministers upon a certain delicate subject . . . With regard to the unfortunate subject on which this rumour was originated, we fear, from the dispositions manifested in certain quarters, that, however great our reluctance, we may hereafter have much to say upon it.

The forecast was accurate enough, if naïve. No true journalist could have resisted the temptations of such a topic, particularly when the political element was already pronounced. A less deserving popular idol than Caroline can scarcely be imagined, but a large section of the population was prepared to regard her as a deeply wronged woman. In much the same way, Wilkes, rake and libertine that he was, had won the support of many of the most sober and God-fearing citizens of the community. The Sunday papers, which reached a poorer section of the community than did the dailies, were quick to build up an image of Caroline as typifying the injustice suffered by millions. The Whig newspapers also saw in her a focus of all anti-ministerial sentiment. The factions were lining up.

The *Morning Post* continued to deplore the whole agitation (27 May 1820): 'We had hoped that so much decorum, at least, would have been observed upon this topic, as to have saved us the painful necessity of entering into any Particulars.' But much as it might wish to play down the scandal, its rivals were soon in full cry, and it felt obliged to warn the Queen to

> turn a deaf ear to your newspaper *advocates*. *Their* object is short and simple – the sale of *Seven Penn'orth*. If the tide

should turn against you, your Majesty would find their friendship to be, like the fawning of the hyena, only to make their bite more deep and deadly. I run no risk in anticipating that, before this article is in print, *thirteen* out of *sixteen* Sunday newspapers (following the example of their prototypes of the Daily press) will, like so many volcanoes, vomit their destructive lava upon the public-houses and barbers' shops of London – all chorussing *professions* in your Majesty's behalf. But, Madam, if reason prevails over passion, you could not deem your cause advanced or honoured by the treacherous partisanship of the systematic eradicators of British loyalty, British morals, and British religion (12 June 1820).

Caroline did not heed the warning, and on her return to England made regular parades through the City, receiving the tumultuous acclamation of the well-organised crowds, to the disgust of the *Morning Post*. Typical of its reports was the issue of 3 July:

> After remaining there for a sufficient time for a mob to collect, she re-entered her carriage, amidst the noisy cheering of a number of chimney-sweeps and other dirty fellows, the very refuse of society, who, being as usual provided with a rope for the purpose, dragged her along all the streets, amidst the most hideous and abhorrent howlings.

The voice of the rabble, the paper insisted, was not the voice of the people.

The Opposition press took a different view – and it was soon to be led by *The Times*. That paper had already displayed some of the chameleon-like characteristics which were to make it unpopular later. Its early attitude to the Radicals had been decidedly hostile, as were its comments on the planned assembly at Peterloo organised by Orator Hunt:

> In speaking of this man and his associates, we are at a loss whether to adopt the language of contempt and ridicule, which would become their personal character and political pretensions, or that of indignation and abhorrence, which is provoked by the mischievous influence which they exercise and the formidable results to which their operation might lead . . . the Hunts, the *Wolseleys*, are nothing without their mob; but by becoming the rallying point of the distressed manufacturers, whose sufferings they exasperate, they exercise the sinister influence of calling some thousand troops round Manchester, of alarming the fears of the local magistrates, and of exciting no small portion of anxiety among the timid all over the country (11 August 1820).

But *The Times* was horrified by the news of the 'massacre' and denounced it in no uncertain terms. Similarly, after some hesitation, it adopted the 'popular' side, and supported the Queen. She was 'but a poor female with nothing but her character to support her through these odious charges' (11 July). And a correspondent wrote approvingly that 'the manly line which *The Times* has pursued with regard to the conspiracy against the life and honour of her Majesty had endeared that Paper to every true and honest-hearted Englishman' (13 July).

With the start of the so-called 'Trial of the Queen' – the introduction in the House of Lords of a retrospective Bill of Pains and Penalties to dissolve the marriage and deprive her of her royal title – the London newspapers ceased to be newspapers at all. They became scandal sheets, devoting page after page, and often the entire issue, to the trial, so that readers could wallow at length in hitherto unplumbed depths of obscenity and scurrility. The *Morning Post* regularly expressed disgust. 'Painful indeed is our duty in having to defile our columns with such uncommonly offensive and disgusting details', it declared on 23 August. On occasion, it even refused to print the more startling items, as on 6 September when it reported that 'the witness hereon proceeded to describe the positions of the Princess and Bergami [her principal lover, according to the Crown], but we cannot pollute our Paper by giving the disgusting description. It was of the most indecent Nature that can possibly be imagined.' But such scruples did not prevent it from printing (in the same issue) such titbits as the following:

> Question Did you observe on any of these occasions the state of the breeches of Bergami?
> Answer Once I saw that Bergami had his breeches loosened from the braces, and the front part half unbuttoned.
> Question On that occasion, did you observe where the Princess's hand was?
> Answer One hand was upon that part . . .

In fact, the *Morning Post* was torn between its reverence for royalty in general and its extreme disapproval of Caroline. Its moral protests may well have been genuine enough, but it was literally driven to devote column after column to the trial – although it put the blame squarely upon its competitors. *The Times* had no such moral qualms, nor did the fact that it was supposedly on the side of the Queen prevent it from plunging happily into the most intimate details of what a German chambermaid had seen when Caroline and her paramour stayed in Carlsruhe:

> What sort of stains were they that you saw? – As much as I have seen, they were white. – Are you married? – Yes. Here the witness became agitated and cried. A glass of water was brought, and some minutes pause took place until she recovered herself. Ask her what the stains appeared to be. – I did not inspect them so narrowly. What I have seen is, they

were white. – Have you ever made the bed of married persons?
– Yes . . . What was the appearance of the marks you saw on
Bergami's bed? – You will pardon me; I have not reflected on
this. – Were they wet or dry? – They were wet.

According to *The Times* (28 August) this particular witness had received
the equivalent of five years' pay to give such evidence.

If the London dailies could devote so much space to the trial, and go
into such rich detail, it is not surprising that the Sunday newspapers,
with their increasing emphasis upon sex and scandal, should have thrown
themselves even more wholeheartedly into the fray. In fact, of course, no
newspaper could ignore such magnificent copy. As the *British Monitor*
explained on 16 July,

> The affair of the Queen is still the only topic of discussion in
> every Journal, daily or weekly, London or provincial . . . The
> whole country seems to have passed under the enchanter's
> wand: questions of real national interest are laid aside or
> forgotten; political differences are suspended, popular
> grievances are overlooked, public measures forsaken or slurred
> over . . . Other topics have had their season; have been, to use
> a vulgar expression, 'a nine days' wonder' – and have been
> forgotten; but the novelty of a House of Parliament sitting in
> judgment upon a Queen of England. . .

At first the *British Monitor*, a Tory paper, favoured a reconciliation to
avoid dragging the royal family through the mud. But as the Queen's
cause was taken up by the Whigs and Radicals the paper adopted an
increasingly tough line. 'La dame Caroline' became 'the Queen of all the
Radicals', who in turn were hailed as 'the gin-drinking reformers of their
country . . . the Chevaliers of the gin bottle'. With sorrow, its editor
declared on 17 September that 'This Paper is read on a day of devotion,
and I have only to regret that I must every Sabbath pollute its columns
with the filthy amours and obscene stories as are told of *la Mere Caroline*
and her paramour BERGAMI'. Nevertheless, he joined heartily in the
general muck-raking, and his issue of 27 August on what the
chambermaid had seen outdid even *The Times* in its scorching detail. At
times the editor displayed a certain wit as in his play on words in an
account on 19 November of a 'Grand Masquerade at Brandy-Burgh
House [i.e. Brandenburg]' attended by 'the ever-upright Bartholomew
Pergami [sic] . . . Her Majesty and Louis Bergami were very much
clapp'd.'

Somewhat late in the crisis appeared one of the most notorious of all
the Sunday newspapers of this period, *John Bull*, with the subtitle *For God,
the King and the People*. Its opening editorial on 17 December 1820 stated
that:

> The shameful licentiousness of a prostituted press, the

infamous tendency of the caricatures which issue forth from every sink of vice and infamy in and near the Metropolis, the inflammatory speeches of knaves and fools, the absurd unmeaning Addresses to the Queen, and the libellous and treasonable answers given to them, are banes to our Constitution, which calls loudly for an antidote.

The attack on the 'prostituted press' is interesting, for it is highly likely that *John Bull* was itself heavily subsidised. As for the 'shameful licentiousness' the new paper denounced, the lead in this field had been taken by the ministerial papers in their campaign against Caroline, and *John Bull* was soon to surpass all their efforts, despite its assurance that 'on the subject of the sickening woman we shall enter into no arguments or discussions'. In fact, the paper concentrated quite blatantly upon that subject, remarking on 28 January 1821 that 'it is said we made a covert attack upon the sobriety of the Queen. This is a mistake: our attack was a very open one!' And this nobody could deny.

From time to time, *John Bull* experimented with verse, as on 21 January on the perennial topic of Caroline:

Oh! deep was the sorrow, and sad was the day
When death took our gracious old Monarch away,
And gave us a Queen, lost to honour and fame,
Whose manners are folly, whose conduct is shame;
Who with aliens and vagabonds long having stroll'd,
Soon caught up their morals, loose, brazen, and bold.

Evidently impressed by the possibilities of this weapon, and somewhat tardily recognising that Caroline was no longer news, the paper proceeded to employ it against a rival, *Independence*, and, having savaged that paper's political views, took up its literary defects. 'We shall', it announced on 28 January, 'be more malicious than usual . . . We let it speak for itself.' And *John Bull* went on to reprint two poems which had appeared in the other paper. The first was entitled 'The Bride of Lausac':

Oh! who is more gay than a bride of Lausac, –
    In her hat is the bustard's feather:
The fur of the hill-fox warms her back,
    And her shoes are of chamois leather.

Hardly more inspiring was 'Isidore – A village Lament':

Where's the young Isidore,
    Rose of the village!
Roams she the barren moor,
    Tills she the tillage?
Her, in her beauty's flower,
    Barbarous Herman,
Spoil'd, in an helpless hour –
    Curse on the German!

John Bull made no comment. There was no need to! But its campaign against Caroline made its name, and by 4 February 1821 it could claim that 'We Sell Seven Thousand Papers; and it is a small computation to suppose than ten persons read each number.'

In fact, the whole crisis had caused a boom in the Press as a whole, and had done much to blunt the effects of the 1819 regulations. The scandal also had interesting repercussions in the legal field. It had made something of a mockery of the 'respectable Press' for the ministerial papers were far more licentious than the Opposition. For this reason, the Tory government was reluctant to take action, as the first victims would have included its own supporters, however disreputable. So the period was one of relative calm and freedom from official prosecution. However, what the government was not prepared to do, certain private citizens were, and in 1820 there appeared the 'Constitutional Association for opposing the Progress of Disloyal and Seditious Principles'. The Association deplored the existing state of affairs, naming as one of the immediate causes 'a licentious Press, which, without excepting even the day of sacred rest, innundates the nation with an unexampled profusion of slanderous, seditious, and blasphemous publications', and it resolved to 'encourage persons of integrity and talent in the literary world to exert their abilities in confronting the sophistries, dissipating the illusions, and exposing the falsehoods which are employed by wicked and designing men to mislead the people'. But it realised from the start that such literary counterattacks would be inadequate, and that tougher measures were needed. Within four months, some 700 subscribed, led by the Duke of Wellington, and having the support of two ministerial papers, the *Courier* and the *New Times*. If it tended to refrain from prosecutions for 'licentiousness' in the moral sense, it was very willing to attack sedition in any shape or form. As Wickwar says, it was out to save the lower classes from the Hunts and Cobbetts and Carliles who were moulding the opinions of the labourer – whose understanding, the Association rather unkindly remarked, 'barely enables him to distinguish betwen a cabbage and a potato'. One of its first victims was John Thelwall, a veteran Radical, editor and publisher of the *Champion*, a Sunday newspaper, price 10*d*, with a sale of only about 600. Then came Thomas Dolby for his *Political Dictionary* in 1821; typical definitions in that *Dictionary* included:

Blasphemy (Ultra-loyal)	Speaking irreverently of corruption in Church or State
Constitution (in Church or State)	Religion without piety, law without reason, representation without constituents, aristocrats without talents, a king without authority, and a people without subsistence

King – from the Saxon word . . .   An abbreviation for *cunning* or crafty, the usual designation of a knave

Press (licentiousness of the)   Fearlessly publishing the truth without fear or reward

There was a minor wave of prosecutions, but the Association was shortlived: it antagonised judges and juries all over the country, and collapsed amid general abuse. The next really serious attack on the liberty of the Press was not to take place until the 1830s.

The Queen's case thus stimulated the press. As the 1820s proceeded, the continuing demand for parliamentary reform and the controversy over Catholic emancipation (among other issues which have given that decade the title of 'the Age of Reform') meant an increasing demand for news. The role of the regular newspaper was still limited: its price was prohibitive to the vast majority. But in London, the industrial Midlands, even in small country towns, cheap subscription rooms sprang up. Public houses, beer shops and coffee-houses all took in generous supplies of newspapers. According to a writer in 1829, 'now no man or no man who can read (and how few are these of those who go to coffee-houses who cannot read), thinks of calling for his cup of coffee without at the same time asking for a newspaper?' But those who could not read (or preferred beer) were also catered for. The *Spectator* of 26 November 1831 reported that 'in most towns of the kingdom, there are public houses, the landlords of which retain readers in their pay, who sit in the place of common resort, and read all the most interesting parts of the newspapers aloud'. Barbers' shops were also a major reading place.

By such means, newspapers were reaching an ever growing public. It has been estimated that every London paper was read by thirty people, and every provincial one by between eight and thirty.[4] Certainly the total circulation increased: in Great Britain as a whole during the period from 1800 to 1830, the annual sale of newspaper stamps virtually doubled, from 16 million to 30 million.[5] The price of the ordinary newspaper and of the Sunday newspaper was 7*d*, and at this price few even among the middle classes could afford them. The answer lay elsewhere. But already the Sunday newspapers were taking the lead: it was calculated in 1829 that the seven London morning papers had an aggregate sale of 28,000, while the Sunday papers had 110,000. From the very start the Sunday newspapers had never been part of the 'respectable Press', and in the early years of the nineteenth century their readers were commonly identified with the 'lower classes'. They were rapidly becoming a significant force, owing their popularity to their judicious blend of scandal, crime and sport, and to the fact that they had become the principal organs of the Radical agitation for reform. But a new and much more dangerous form of Radical journalism was very soon to arise.

5 The growth of a new reading public and the struggle to control it

The idea persists that widespread literacy was an accomplishment of the late nineteenth century, but the reading public in the early years of that century was larger than has often been thought. This new reading public had developed against a background of profound changes, political, social and economic. From 1751 to 1801 the population increased from about seven million to almost nine million, and by 1851 it was fourteen. The most significant increase was in the proportion of the population living in towns, including the new industrial towns – an increase which brought corresponding changes in the geographical distribution of the population and in the class structure as a whole. At the beginning of the century most people were still engaged in farming or cottage crafts, despite the enclosure movement and the growth of factories. But gradually the peasant, the yeoman and the handicraft man were being transformed into the factory-hand: and this process was gathering momentum. The disruption of the old way of life and the concentration of masses of people in cities and towns which were totally incapable of accommodating them produced undoubted physical and moral degradation. English society was shaken as it had not been shaken since the end of the Middle Ages. Admittedly the widening of economic opportunity enabled thousands to climb in the social scale, but on every hand there was a sharpening of class-consciousness, a factor which had been largely lacking in the previous century. To the upper classes civilisation itself depended on preserving the hallowed structure of society, perhaps cautiously modified here and there. The *nouveaux riches* of the middle classes rapidly acquired similar social prejudices, and were to be well content with the Reform Bill of 1832. But to the lower classes – or, rather, to their vocal leaders – what was needed was sweeping and fundamental *change*. Both upper and middle classes were agreed that the supreme threat came from below, and that the growth of the reading habit was to blame.

To say that conditions were against the growth of a working-class reading public would be to put it mildly. In the towns, a fourteen-hour working day was commonplace: those in even the most favoured trades did not get home until 6 or 7 p.m.; not until the sixties was the Saturday half-holiday generally introduced. Another major problem was the absence of light: the window tax was not abolished until 1851, and probably presented an even more formidable obstacle to the people's reading than did the taxes on knowledge; and in most houses tallow-dips or candles were the only sources of illumination apart from the fireplace. So the worker confined his reading to Sundays – hence, of course, the popularity of the Sunday newspapers, although these were far too expensive for the vast majority of the workers. Physical conditions were trying: as Altick puts it, 'How, with a distraught, sickly wife complaining and a brood of ill-fed, squalling children filling the room, and drunken neighbours brawling next door, could a reader, no matter how earnest, concentrate upon a book?' Conditions in rural areas may not have been quite so bad, but again there was little incentive or opportunity for reading. Education was difficult to come by, hours of labour long, and agricultural wages notoriously low.

The changes taking place in society were enough to disrupt a much better system of education than the eighteenth century had possessed, and the first half of the nineteenth century is full of reports showing its utter inadequacy. What educational facilities were available to the poor? There were the charity schools, in great number and even greater variety, often badly organised and highly inefficient. Next in point of time were the Sunday schools, which provided the major outlet for charitable enthusiasm from the middle of the eighteenth century. Webb's guess at the actual attendance in the 1830s was between 800,000 and 900,000 – quite remarkable figures. But the Sunday schools had their own peculiar problems, not the least of which was the natural reluctance of children to spend their only free day in the week at school. Interviewed in 1863, a Gloucester ancient recalled that 'some terrible bad chaps went to school when I first went . . . I know the parents of one or two of them used to walk them to school with 14 lb. weights tied to their legs . . . to keep them from running away'. What is significant in this case is the determination of the parents. Some of the Sunday Schools were incredibly bad, but they were often the only means of education available. There were also the day schools – thousands of them. Most numerous were those of the British and Foreign School Society and of the National Society for Education of the Poor according to the Principles of the Established Church, both enjoying wide philanthropic support. The National Society alone had 230 schools in 1813, attended by some 40,484 scholars; in 1820 it had 1,614 schools, with an attendance of about 200,000; and in 1830, 3,670 schools, with about 346,000 pupils. And there were still other schools, ranging from the tiniest dame school to expensive academies.

The problem was not one of lack of schools. It was rather of their *quality* – and the regularity of attendance. Certainly, in the first half of the nineteenth century, thousands of children never went to school at all, many of those who did attended only sporadically and for very limited periods: at the Borough Road School, the model establishment of the British and Foreign Society, the average attendance was not over thirteen months. Equally, as Webb points out, it seems probable that a far larger proportion of working-class children had at least *some* experience of schools than has been thought, or can be statistically proved. But attendance at a school did not necessarily mean that a child learned very much. Most of the schools for the poor adopted the cheap but iniquitous monitorial system, in which the older pupils took over the teaching, thus imparting all the benefits of their own ignorance to the even more ignorant. All too often the teacher was hopelessly incompetent, and all too often the general attitude was summed up in the remark of a dame school teacher: 'It's little they pay us, and it's little we teaches them.' To make matters worse was the official theory behind popular education. George III's wish that every child should learn to read the Bible struck a most responsive chord. But many still regarded even the teaching of reading as playing with fire. Anything further was madness. As a justice of the peace put it in 1807: 'It is doubtless desirable that the poor should be generally instructed in *reading*, if it were only for the best of purposes – that they may read the Scriptures. As to *writing* and *arithmetic*, it may be apprehended that such a degree of knowledge would produce in them a disrelish for the laborious occupations of life.' Asked an indignant farmer with reference to his labourers and servants:

> What have the schools done for them? . . . What need is there of learning to hold the handles of a plough, or whip a flail upon the threshing-floor? . . . Now, if you lay down a newspaper, and turn your back, your servant takes it up and reads it, and thus neglects his or her work . . . All this is the result of the schools.[1]

In *Nightmare Alley*, Peacock makes his reactionary Mr Flosky lament: 'How can we be cheerful when we are surrounded by a reading public, that is growing too wise for its betters?', while Lord Eldon considered the 'march of intellect' to be 'a tune to which one day or the other a hundred thousand tall fellows with clubs and pikes will march against Whitehall'.

Most influential people of the time, however, supported the teaching of reading. Ignorance made the masses easy targets for demagogues, but if those masses could be herded into classrooms, even if only briefly, they might be immunised against Jacobinism, Radicalism, blasphemy and atheism. All that was needed was to teach the poor to read the Bible. So Lord Brougham maintained that the education of the poor was 'the best security for the morals, the subordination, and the peace of countries', and Southey called for an educated populace 'fed with the milk of sound doctrine'. The whole emphasis was upon religious and moral instruction. Reading was more important than writing, and writing more important than arithmetic, girls should concentrate on sewing.

The system had obvious limitations, but, with all its imperfections, it did teach many to read, however laboriously. An impressive list can be drawn up of self-educated men in this period, men such as James

Lackington, William Chambers and William Hone, all born to poverty and lacking any formal education, but fighting their way to the top. John Freeman estimated at the end of the Napoleonic Wars (without very much in the way of evidence) that two-thirds of the population were literate, while a modern authority concludes that for the period 1832–48 two-thirds to three-quarters of the working classes were. Such figures may appear excessively high, the fact remains that the ruling classes were certainly agreed that more and more of what they were pleased to call 'the industrious classes' could read: *what* they were reading and what they *should* be reading were issues which were to trouble the ruling classes for decades to come, and are still raised today.

The first in the field were the evangelicals, led by the indefatigable Hannah More, with her Cheap Repository Tracts designed quite frankly to drive 'anti-Christian' and 'seditious' literature from the market. The price was low – one halfpenny or a penny. According to Aspinall,

> There had never been anything like it in the history of English books. In the first six weeks (March 3rd to April 18th 1795) 300,000 copies were sold at wholesale; by July of the same year, the number had more than doubled; and by March 1796, the total number sold reached the staggering figure of two million.

Their apparent success encouraged the evangelicals to believe that they had found the right formula. If correct morality and sound religious and political doctrine were presented in wholesomely entertaining tales and verses, humble readers would accept those principles, and the nation would be saved. Very soon others were in the field, and the nineteenth century was to be swamped by a veritable deluge of religious literature, running into millions of copies. As Altick observes, 'it would be futile even to try to estimate how many copies of religious and moral works of all kinds were distributed'. But the effectiveness of this massive campaign was probably less than its promoters supposed. Many of the tracts fell upon very stony ground. And Webb remarks that, 'being paper, an immensely large number of tracts must have gone to light fires or to serve baser but vital domestic purposes which religious writers would understandably not care to mention'. The more robust journalists of the eighteenth century had openly prescribed such uses for their rivals' productions.

It seems clear that Hannah More and her disciples underestimated the intelligence and the independence of the humble worker. Many readers, particularly those who had come under the influence of Radical journalism, realised that they were being talked down to, and Charles Knight was later to blame his competitors for 'using the language of the nursery'. The social message in the tracts was often blatant:

> Beautiful is the order of Society, when each, according to his place – pays willing honour to his superiors – when servants are prompt to obey their masters, and masters deal kindly with

> their servants – when high, low, rich, and poor – when
> landlord and tenant, master and workman, minister and people
> . . . sit down, each satisfied with his own place.

Injunctions to thrift, when there was no money to save; exhortations to work, when there was no work to be had; the insistence on the *duty* to leave one's fate in the hands of an all-wise ruling class, when desperate workers were being mown down or transported – such an approach was hardly suited to a period of intensifying social ferment and dislocation. All too often, the reception given to the eager ladies with their tracts must have been along the lines of the St Albans slum-dweller's 'welcome' to Mrs Pardiggle in *Bleak House*:

> Is my daughter a-washin? Yes, she *is* a-washin. Look at the
> water. Smell it! That's wot we drinks. How do you like it, and
> what do you think of gin, instead! An't my place dirty? Yes, it
> is dirty – it's nat'rally dirty, and its nat'rally onwholesome; and
> we've had five dirty and unwholesome children, as is all dead
> infants, and so much the better for them, and for us besides.
> Have I read the little book wot you left? No, I an't read the
> little book wot you left. There an't nobody here as knows how
> to read it; and if there wos, it wouldn't be suitable to me. It's a
> book fit for a babby, and I'm not a babby.

As a young pickpocket whom Harry Mayhew interviewed at mid-century said, 'Tracts won't fill your belly'. In fact, the enormous circulation of the tracts was among the middle classes, just as it was among those classes that their influence was most pronounced.

Next came the utilitarians, with a somewhat different approach. Like the evangelicals, they had a tremendous belief in the power of education, and of the role of the printing press in it. But they had their own special brand of Truth to disseminate – 'the diffusion of useful knowledge' in the form of good solid facts about mechanics, chemistry, metallurgy and hydraulics. The main organisation was provided by the Society for the Diffusion of Useful Knowledge, formed by Brougham in 1826 to serve the same public for which the Mechanics' Institutes were then being established, skilled working-men. The basic aim was to make their members better workers – 'better' in every sense of the term. But the Institutes were hardly a success in this primary purpose. As Altick puts it,

> However eager he may have been for intellectual improvement,
> the workman was in no condition after a long hard day's work,
> to profit from the instruction the institute offered . . . the sleep
> that overcame him, though not provided for in the
> Broughamites' roseate calculations, was an inescapable fact of
> nature.

The Institutes were soon taken over by the middle classes, between whom and the working classes there was a steadily growing antagonism and mistrust, an antagonism particularly obvious in the clash over the Reform Bill of 1832. In 1827 the Society began to issue a *Library of Useful Knowledge* in fortnightly parts at 6*d* each, the thirty-two closely printed pages being advertised as containing as much as 100 ordinary pages. But it was hopelessly out of touch with its intended audience; quite apart from its price, its idea of suitable reading for the working classes was utterly unrealistic. It expected the common reader to relish a sort of home university course, comprising such topics as Muller's *History of Greek Literature*, Lane's *Manners and Customs of Modern Egyptians*, and Bacon's *Novum Organum*, to mention some of the more exciting features. In fact, the Society was soon being referred to as 'The Society for the Confusion of Useful Knowledge'. Its remoteness from its audience was to be emphasised by the *Westminster Review* of April 1831. As the people whom the Society really intended to reach lived by wages, the doctrine of wages should have been the foundation of all other instruction. Beyond that, readers should have been taught the importance of property and government, the rules of morality, obedience to the law, frugality and kindness. What had the Society done when faced by a wave of rick-burning and machine-breaking in the early 1830s? It had flooded the country with *An Address to the Labourers on the Subject of Destroying Machinery* – a pamphlet which had certainly not found its way into the lower classes, and would probably have been unintelligible to them anyway. It had followed this up with 'two treatises . . . on the Polarisation of Light, and another on the Rigidity of Cordage!'

The essential problem remained. The poor *were* reading. They were reading almanacks – too often of the type described by the *Athenaeum* in 1828 as 'vaporous modifications of palpable imposture, impudent mendacity, vulgar ignorance, and low obscenity'. Equally popular were chapbooks and ballads, usually printed on poor paper, illustrated with a crude woodcut, and selling at anything between a farthing and a shilling. They dealt largely with scandal, executions, natural disasters, and the more gory murders, and were heartily vulgar – and popular: in 1826 the *Last Dying Speech and Confession* of William Corder, who had killed Maria Marten, reputedly sold over one million copies, Even allowing for exaggeration, such a figure gives an impressive clue to the size of the semiliterate public of the time. Finally, there were the cheap periodicals, also immensely popular. Charles Dickens was later to recall how, as a boy, he used to buy the *Terrific Register* – 'making myself unspeakably miserable, and frightening my very wits out of my head, for the small charge of one penny weekly; which, considering that there was an illustration to every number in which there was always a pool of blood, and at least one body, was cheap'. The full title of the publication was *Terrific Register: or, Record of Crimes, Judgments, Providences and Calamities*. It began in 1821 stressing its *moral* purpose:

Sorry we should be to have it supposed that we had no motive superior to the exciting of curiosity, or the enlisting of the passions for mere selfish purposes . . . As meditation is necessarily salutary, we have invited man to scrutinise his fellow in his worst estate, and have accordingly laid before him accounts of barbarities inflicted by savage hordes; cruel punishments with which crime has been visited; barbarous murders; atrocious assassinations and diabolical cruelties; bloody deals and sanguinary conflicts; daring villainies, frauds, plots, conspiracies and rebellions; remarkable robberies, piracies, executions and persecutions for conscience sake . . . well authenticated stories of apparitions and strange and fearful superstitions; disastrous accidents, perilous enterprises, and miraculous escapes by sea and land; awful visitations and singular interpositions; accounts of plague, famine, fire and earthquake; and other special chastisements of Providence.

The *Register* undoubtedly did its best to live up to its promise. Its woodcuts were its great feature. Its first issue depicted the 'Dreadful execution of Damiens for attempting to assassinate Louis XV, King of France'. The woodcut of Damiens tied to a wheel, having his hand burned and his stomach torn by red-hot pincers, left little to the imagination; but it was accompanied by a detailed account of the various tortures and of the screams of the victim. The second issue showed the 'Horrible Murder of a Child', with two women cutting up the body and collecting the streams of blood in a bucket. The illustrations were magnificent. At various times, readers were regaled with the 'Awful Death of Mr Munro', who was depicted in the process of being eaten alive by a tiger; 'Indian barbarity and heroism', a vivid portrayal of torture by fire; and 'Manner of Executing the Russian Pirates on the Volga', which showed four men hanging by hooks through their ribs, and blood running in torrents. According to the accompanying account, such victims might live for four or five days. The climax was perhaps reached with a picture entitled 'The Dead Devoured by the Living', showing an old man in a cave gnawing at a human arm, with heads, legs and other parts all around him. The man had apparently dug up corpses in order to eat them. One can well appreciate the effect these penny horrors would have on an impressionable boy, although the moral purpose behind such effusions is not always easy to detect. Fortunately, not all the cheap periodicals were so horrific: but they too emphasised excitement and romance – an escape from the tedium and squalor of the new industrial towns.

However deplorable from the moral point of view this sensational-ism might be, an even greater threat was contained in the rise of a type of newspaper which offered something more concrete than mere escapism, as the Radical press, largely dormant since 1819, suddenly burst into life again in what has gone down in history as 'the battle of the Unstamped Newspapers'. In November 1830 Carlile began his *Prompter*, a fourteen-page weekly, price 3d, but unstamped. In it he preached the right of revolution under certain circumstances. He was prosecuted, sentenced to two years' imprisonment, and fined £200, with securities in £1,000 for good behaviour. In the event the fine was never paid, the securities never given and Carlile was released unconditionally after eight months in gaol.[2] A familiar figure from the past, Cobbett, also entered the lists with a monthly *Twopenny Trash*, a title calculated to bring back memories of his famous paper of 1816. But other Radical journalists were ready and waiting, men far tougher and more outspoken: and 1831 was to witness a sudden erruption of cheap and unstamped newspapers, all illegal, and all advocating not the moderate reform now being discussed in Parliament, but an extreme – even violent – transformation of the whole political, legal and social structure.

One of the leading lights was Henry Hetherington, a prolific publisher of unstamped newspapers, and a powerful force in the organisation of this revived Radical movement. Early in 1831 he was prosecuted for his *Republican*, price only one penny. He wrote a spirited account of his trial in the first issue (9 July 1831) of what was to become one of the great Radical papers, *The Poor Man's Guardian. A Weekly Newspaper For The People. Established Contrary to 'Law', To Try the Power of 'Might' against 'Right'*. 'Why', he demanded, 'should they attempt to suppress the Poor Man's pamphlet, while they permitted others, published on a larger scale, to remain unmolested? The *Literary Gazette*, *The Athenaeum*, and many other publications were not interfered with.' According to Hetherington, Castlereagh (the villain of the piece with regard to the stamp duty) had not intended his Act to operate against '*separate* and *distinct* pamphlets', but only against 'periodical' publications, and, in particular, Cobbett's *Political Register*, which was published every Saturday. However, his own paper was not a periodical in the strict sense of that term: 'Every paper was a *distinct* and *separate* publication; – they had been published every day in the week, *Sundays* included; – they had been published *four* times a week, *three* times a week, *twice* a week, *once* a week, – but never *two weeks in succession* on the SAME DAY.' The court was not convinced by this ingenious argument. Undeterred, Hetherington pressed on with his *Poor Man's Guardian*, an eight-page weekly, price one penny, and bearing the mottos, 'Liberty of the Press' and 'Knowledge is Power'. Its first editorial was an open declaration of war:

> We are prepared for the fight: it is a mere *legal* one on the part of our persecutors, but a *moral* one on ours: we know that we must suffer, but we are content to do so for the benefit of our fellow-creatures; we have before our eyes the fatal examples of all who have ever advocated the truth; but we shrink not from the worst.

The paper would include not only 'news, intelligence and occurrences' but also 'remarks and observations thereon . . . tending to excite hatred and contempt of the Government and Constitution of the tyranny of this Country, as BY LAW established'.

Hetherington lived up to his word. What might be called 'the Establishment' came under steady fire. And any unusually vicious attack upon his many targets was always assured full publicity. Thus, he reprinted (16 July 1831) Carlile's article in the *Prompter* of 18 June:

> I charge upon the existence of kings and priests, and lords, those useless classes, the common poverty of the labouring classes of mankind. I charge upon them the common warfare and slaughter of mankind. I charge upon their wicked usurpations, their false pretensions, and their general and tyrannical dishonesty, all the social evils that afflict mankind. I make no exception. The royal family in England is as great an evil . . . I cry out to all Europe, and more particularly to my own countrymen, DOWN WITH KINGS, PRIESTS, AND LORDS.

He added,

> We perfectly agree with Mr Carlile on the propriety of abolishing Kings, Priests, and Lords . . . but he does not go far enough – he does not strike at the root of the evil which exists . . . Were there no property, there would be no Kings, Priests, and Lords . . . It is property which has made tyrants, and not tyrants property . . . Down then with property!

The royal family came in for special treatment, as in the issue of 6 August 1831: 'A "King" is *not* a God – he is *not* greater than the meanest of yourselves; – a "King" is a mere MAN; – a "Queen" a mere WOMAN; – and a "Princess" a mere child; – look at them fearlessly, and you will see only Mr and Mrs William Guelph, and their neice [sic] Miss Victoria Alexandrina Guelph!' The following issue reported a petition from the Westminster Union of the Working Classes Parliament requesting it that as

> the princess Victoria (as the Salic Law does not prevail in England) is the heir presumptive to the throne. That, as Queen of England, if she succeeds to the Crown, she will be SUPREME HEAD OF THE WHOLE CHURCH. That your petitioners therefore think there can be no impropriety in praying your Honourable House, *instead of granting HER an increased Pension out of the Pockets of the half-starved working-classes, to address the King*, TO PROVIDE FOR HER *out of the enormous and unmerited wealth of the CHURCH*, by making HER BISHOP OF DERBY, or by appointing HIS SON the Rev. Adolphus Fitzclarence to that See.

The *Guardian* had already dealt with the Church in its first issue: 'She *stinks* – She stinks from *self-corruption* – she BLASPHEMES herself.' But one of the main targets was the middle class as a whole. In its issue of 23 July 1831, it attacked the 'legitimate newspapers' for their welcome to the King of Belgium – and managed to incorporate an assault on the English middle classes:

> We thought that they had had enough of such nonsense as 'Majesty' . . . we hear that carriages and equipages were very plentiful, and, it may be, that the 'joyous processions' were composed of 'Lords', 'Gentlemen', and, perhaps, £10 householders, your 'middlemen' – the idle and useless classes – *the real 'scum of the earth'* – that portion of society which floats on the surface – bloated and unprofitable: such folly suits *them*.

With this sort of social approach, the *Guardian* was naturally extremely hostile to the forthcoming Reform Bill, which it regarded as a betrayal of the people. It denounced *both* parties. But it preferred the Tories, who at least were open and honest in their opposition to the claims of the working classes: 'With our able correspondent do we cry "Down with the Whigs": but we would rather be cursed by the "Tories"; the insidious *serpent* is yet more dangerous than the ferocious *tiger*!' (20 August 1831). Its first issue had made the same point: 'The *Whigs* and *Tories* were two factions opposed to each other in everything but in the destruction of liberty and oppression and plundering of the poor, in doing which they unite together most cordially – the Tories were the violent but honest and avowed enemies of freedom, but the Whigs are the dastardly vipers who sting you in the back.' But well could the *Guardian* say 'DOWN with *both* WHIGS AND TORIES!' Its own programme went much further than the proposals being discussed in Parliament:

> We must have a government unshackled by 'King' or 'Peers' or 'Priests', any other qualifications whatsoever save the free choice of the PEOPLE – in fact we require a government 'annually' (or oftener if necessary) elected by 'Universal Suffrage', 'vote by ballot', and unshackled by any PROPERTY QUALIFICATIONS whatsoever – in other words a *Republic* . . . The Revolution cannot arrive too soon! (20 August 1831).

But in his attacks upon the Reform Bill, Hetherington never forgot the middle classes for very long, and he informed his working class readers that their optimism was utterly unfounded:

> You have been and still are intended to be the common prey: the 'noble' eagles and ecclesiastical vultures have hitherto been feeding upon you; they think you veriest carrion; but nevertheless, have disdained not to fatten upon you; verily, they have satiated themselves; and now, too unwieldy to defend their exclusive spoil, they make way for the *hungry crows*, whose numbers trouble them, to come and also *pick* at you . . . and who are these cormorant crows, but your 'middle men', who have been watching with greedy eyes the 'eagles' of the *state*,

and the vultures of the *church*, devouring you (20 August 1831).

Undoubtedly Hetherington had a talent for invective, and for the telling phrase. And these gifts he did not confine to journalism. He was an active worker for reform and, like Cartwright before him, went round the country addressing meetings and trying to *organise* the movement of protest. His personal efforts were naturally given great publicity in the *Guardian*, as in the report of his visit to Manchester, when it was moved

> That this meeting views with delight and admiration the undaunted manner in which Mr Hetherington advocated the rights of the productive classes of society, in a work entitled *The Poor Man's Guardian*; and pledges itself to support the 'Poor Man's Guardian' – EVEN TO DEATH, as long as it advocates the doctrine of universal liberty.

But any meetings of working-class unions were duly covered. From time to time Hetherington also encouraged the sale of his various other papers. On 13 August 1831 the *Guardian* gave a glowing account of *The Republican*, price one penny, including what it called 'Additional Testimonials in favour of the "Republican"':

> 'The Republican', having a circulation of 20,000 copies, in each page of which republican principles are strenuously advocated – *Blackwood's Magazine*, July 1831.
> With regard to publications such as these which have been read by the hon. member, they could only excite disgust and abhorrence – Extract from the speech of the Attorney-General in the House of Commons, June 28, 1831.

Not surprisingly, Hetherington was soon in trouble. On 6 August 1831 he declared that

> Several of our Readers complain of the great trouble with the hesitation and fear of the TRADE to 'expose for sale' our paper . . . whereby they are compelled to come for it, considerably out of their way, to our shop . . . We have determined upon the expedient of *'lending our paper to read, without deposit*, for an unlimited period, CHARGE One Penny'; we by this means, beyond doubt, evade the 'Act' which only relates to Papers *published for*, or *exposed to* 'SALE': in future, therefore, we shall only 'lend our Paper to read' to the Trade.

Thereafter, the title of the *Guardian* included the statement, 'Lent to Read, without deposit, for an unlimited period, CHARGE ONE PENNY'. The argument was ingenious, to say the least. But Hetherington also mentioned that he had now been prosecuted on four counts. He had replied by letter to the magistrates:

> Henry Hetherington's compliments to Messrs. Hall and Birnie, and informs them that it is not convenient for him to attend at

Bow-Street today, however anxious he may be to hear what possible right they or Mr William Guelph, or anyone else, has to censure his conduct, or call him to account.

As he had not attended his 'trial' himself, he quoted the report in *The Times* – a paper which 'would most certainly give a faithful account of any proceeding intended to suppress the publication of Truth, Honesty, and Justice'. The report took up two pages, with gloating interjections by Hetherington whenever reference was made to the circulation of his papers.

He chose this moment to launch yet another unstamped paper, *The Radical* (a familiar title) on Saturday, 20 August 1831. It was a four-page weekly, 'Lent to read for one year for one Penny'. It asked:

What is a Radical? . . . one who, impatient of enormous taxation imposed by a set of tax-imposers, over whose rapacity he has no control, is determined to procure a remedy for such a foul disease. He is acquainted with the cause: he is aware that it is the present system of government by which the irresponsible, almost self-elected, aristocrats and *Few* contrive to exclude the *Many* from the deputation of Representatives to the Assembly where the taxes are imposed; he is desirous of *eradicating* such a monstrous, unjust, detestable system: he is conscious that a *Whig* or *partial* remedy will prove insufficient for a cure.

Like the *Guardian*, *The Radical* had a very positive policy, and alongside the regular attacks upon the King, the Church and 'The House of Incurables' (the House of Lords) there appeared steady publicity for working-class unions and meetings, with Hetherington urging a general combination of all the various associations. Thus the issue of 28 December 1831 insisted that

The people ought immediately to proceed to help itself. A NATIONAL CONVENTION, *Congress* or *Conference* ought to be formed in London, by delegates of the unrepresented from every principal town, and they ought not to separate till they have declared to the aristocracy, that they, the Delegates of the Nation, were determined to be admitted into the REPRESENTATION, otherwise they form themselves into a NATIONAL ASSEMBLY, and immediately commence a salutary legislation for the excluded multitude . . . The SOVEREIGNTY OF THE PEOPLE might be proclaimed, and the interests of *every man could be represented and attended to*. All this might be peaceably and quietly effected within six months, if the People were active and UNITED . . . No time should be lost. Union should be the motto – AGITATION the method – and the object, a NATIONAL CONVENTION.

Such terms as 'National Convention', 'National Assembly' and 'Sovereignty of the People' smacked too strongly of the French Revolution for Hetherington's assurances of peace and quiet to carry much conviction with the ruling classes.

But Hetherington was not alone in the field, and unstamped newspapers were appearing by the dozen. Comparatively harmless was Owen's *The Crisis; or, The Change from Error and Misery to Truth and Happiness,* which appeared on 14 April 1832. Its main purpose was to promote the cause of Co-operative Societies. It was certainly not a revolutionary paper – and its attitude to politics was at times ambiguous, as on 26 May 1832, when its leading article stated that

> Now when a republican form of government and the subversion and downfall of the established Church are loudly called for by many, as the only measure to effect a beneficial change in the circumstances and moral character of the people of all stations in the world, we lay before them the condition of the people in NEW YORK – the first city of the first republic in the world; a republic which has had all the advantages of the experience of all past ages in its formation, which has no state religion, and which is now uniformly pointed to, as the perfection of human wisdom and the seat of human happiness.

But the article was very different from the usual panegyric. Entitled 'New York. Morals of a Christian City', it presented a vivid picture of the prostitution which flourished there. The number of prostitutes it estimated at 20,000, and the earnings of the trade at eleven million dollars a year.

> Even this enormous estimate [it continued] is less sickening to the moral feelings, than the almost incredible assertion adduced to support his estimate, that each of these miserable martyrs to the vices of a polluted age, frequently from Saturday night to Monday morning, received 15 to 25 men; obtaining as her reward, from 30 to 50 dollars . . . One out of three of the marriageable females of New York at this moment receives the wages of prostitution. One out of every six is an abandoned, promiscuous prostitute.

At this point the author's enthusiasm for statistics rather ran away with him. He calculated that ten million visits were paid to prostitutes every year. The total population was 203,000, of whom 100,000 would be males, of whom again 'adults between 15 and 55, who can be supposed to be regular frequenters of brothels' would number about 60,000. Each of these must therefore pay 160 visits a year, or three a week. Assuming that only half did, in fact, frequent brothels, they must seek the company of a prostitute '*every night of their lives*'. One whole page was devoted to these awesome calculations.

Usually, *The Crisis* was diffuse and ponderous, concentrating upon education, Owen's scheme for 'Equitable Banks of Exchange' (in which workers would exchange surplus produce instead of money), and a complicated and often tedious 'Outline of the Rational System of Society'. It was not a lively paper. Yet there was apparently a demand for such serious and heavy effusions, for according to Robert Owen his paper was an immediate success, and the first issue boasted that 'when we determined to commence our Penny Publication, with the view of attempting to create a new public opinion in every departmnent of society, we did not in the least expect to go to press as we do with a list of actual subscribers for 8,744 copies'. That may have been a modest claim, for, according to the *Cosmopolite* of 28 April 1832, 'Robert Owen has got his Crisis nearly twenty-thousands at starting'.

Far more lively – and politically dangerous – was the *Cosmopolite*, which first appeared on Saturday, 10 March 1832 with the dramatic announcement: 'Our great political master, Paine, has taught us, and we believe it, that *to reason with despots is throwing reason away, and the best of arguments is a vigorous preparation for* RESISTANCE'. Its particular target was the royal family, and on this subject it showed a certain flair. On 19 May 1832 it opened the campaign with a headline 'Prepare! Prepare!! Prepare!!!', followed by an item entitled 'A Series of Caricatures as near the life as possible':

> The LORDS are beaten! . . . The KING'S CLOVEN FOOT! The King has shown the cloven foot. The Patriot King [William IV] is caricatured as the modern Jerry Sneak – as the spoiled child of the royal nursery – as a political cuckold – as the hen-pecked old man – as joining his German frow to cry 'Py a Prougham' – as the modern Lear, driven to madness by his children – as the index or sign-post of Cumber-land's mind – as a political weathercock – as Silly Billy, an idiot from birth – as going the way of the last Sailor King – as the nation's expensive toy, costing half a million a year – and as having all the vices of all the Guelphs. Nothing is remembered of him but his conduct to Mrs Jordan. His brain cannot long bear all this excitement, and we shall soon hear that he has gone mad . . . Crowns, Mitres, Coronets and Whigs for Sale.

It followed up this spirited assault with an even more spirited one, describing the caricature in question:

> One of them represents Billy Guelph as his renowned prototype Jerry Sneak, picking up Adelaide's wearing apparel; in another he is mounted on the back of old Whiskerando of Cumberland, with his naked buttocks – and precious big ones they have given him – exposed to the fury of a good birch broom, in the hands of 'the German Frow'. She is buttoned up in a pair of inexpressibles, commanding him to make no more Peers.

This allusion to the threat of swamping the opposition in the Lords by the creation of more peers was both neat and suggestive. The sale of the caricatures must have risen considerably, and readers would remember the pun.

The Reformer or Schoolmaster Abroad, which appeared on 2 June 1832, price twopence (for sixteen large quarto pages) concentrated on the Tories as the main enemy to reform. It included an item on 'The Pensions and Emoluments of the Duke of Wellington' – estimated at £38,576 per annum, a figure which produced the editorial comment, 'No wonder he does not see the necessity of Reform!' The paper's policy was expounded on 15 June:

> The abolition of tithes; the repeal of the corn laws; a more
> equitable system of taxation; the abolition of the hereditary
> peerage; an equitable reduction of the national debt; . . . a
> reform in the expenditure of the crown; and the abolition of all
> unmerited pensions and sinecures; the doing away with an
> expensive state of religion, and causing society to maintain its
> own ministers; re-modelling the laws, and making the same law
> for the rich and poor; a still more extensive franchise, Etc.

Such aims were radical enough: but the paper did not have the wholehearted support of Hetherington and his friends. It based its appeal on the interests of the middle classes, proclaiming the need for more parliamentary representatives from what it called the 'mercantile class' in order to 'protect commerce from the cruel burthen and shameful neglect which it suffered from both Wigs [*sic*] and Tories'.

There was, however, no doubting the political emphasis of most unstamped newspapers. *The Destructive, and Poor Man's Conservative*, a twopenny weekly which first appeared on 2 February 1833, was primarily concerned with the Church. Its opening issue attacked what it called 'The Disgusting Hypocrisy of the *Saturday Magazine*, the organ of the "religious" tract-mongers'. In this, it reprinted a lengthy item from that magazine – one which perhaps summed up the general attitude of the Church-going classes:

> When you see a rich man who is proud and selfish, perhaps you
> are tempted to think how much better a use you would make of
> wealth if you were as rich as he. *I hope you would*: but the best
> proof that you can give that you would behave well if in
> *another's* place, is by behaving *well in your own. God has appointed
> to each* his own trials, and his own duties; and He will judge
> you, not according to what you think you would have done in
> some different status, but according to what you have done in
> that status to which *He has placed you.*

It was a version of the famous hymn about 'the rich man in his castle, the poor man at his gate': be content with your lot – your rewards will follow in the life to come. But the extract from the *Poor Man's Guardian* which followed took a very different view:

> The miscreant who is capable of writing such stuff as this, could
> be effectually answered, only in one way – and that is by the
> application of the cat-o'-nine-tails to his left shoulder blade, or
> a month's turn at Marshall's factory, under the superintendence
> of the 'billy roller'. One month's strapping, superadded to the
> wholesome change of employment from *tract*-making to cloth-
> making would do more to enlighten his opacity than all the
> *Guardians* we could write in seven years . . . The evidence of
> decrepid limbs – loss of appetite – incessant head-aches, stunted
> growth, and a sore back, occasionally rising in wheals and
> tumours – would soon convince him that many of those evils
> which he now *innocently* believes to be of 'God's appointment'
> are not of so *divine* and *remote* an origin as he supposes.

Another paper, *The Working Men's Friend*, took up the cause of
Ireland. Typically, its first editorial (on 22 December 1832) thanked the
Poor Man's Guardian for its support. The *Guardian* had announced that
'This will be the first time that question, so *vitally* important to both
countries, England as well as Ireland, was ever made the leading topic in
this metropolis of wide and general political discussion'. The new paper
gave a lengthy report of a meeting of the National Repeal Union,
remarking that 'this splendid speech, so rich in eloquence and just
reasoning, has not found its way into the columns of any stamped paper
in England!!!'. In two articles on 9 and 16 March 1833, it condemned out
of hand the Suppression of Disturbances (Ireland) Bill of 1833:

> The bill, the brutal bill, is one of those desperate expedients,
> and the first of a series . . . Will you support such men and
> such measures? Are you not already land-robbed, land-starved,
> and land-butchered, with impunity? Are not all these things
> enough? Must your wives and daughters be ravished too, and
> the streets run red . . . ? By your slaughtered townsmen –
> whose mute reproach God hears from the silent grave – I
> implore you to avert, from England, and from Ireland, the
> hideous bill and its consequences – first, a military despotism to
> support a monopoly – and then a revolution, whose horrors
> casting into shade those of the first French Revolution, will be
> without example in the annals of human calamity.

The *Working Men's Friend* also entered into a field largely ignored by its
rivals, who were perhaps somewhat too political in their approach and
tended to overlook the social problems of the period. On 12 January
1833, under the heading 'Manufacturing Hells', it reported that

> the voluminous evidence taken in the Committee of the House
> of Commons, on the Factories' Labour Regulation Bill, is of a
> nature to make a man almost loathe his species. We could

hardly have believed that such systematic cruelty is practised in this country. We now understand why the labouring people of the manufacturing towns are jealous of the middle classes, and hostile to the Ballot, from a belief that they can only protect themselves from oppression by obtaining, indirectly, a share in the franchise, through the intimidation of the small dealers.

It then proceeded (on 2 February and 2 March 1833) to give considerable publicity to Oastler's famous speech on 'White and Black Slavery contrasted'.

A penny Sunday newspaper which tried to combine working-class politics with a more general appeal – a formula already well established, and still popular today – was *The Man*, which began on 7 July 1833. Its headings included 'Political Unions', 'Accidents, Offences, Etc', 'Police Intelligence', 'Original Poetry' and 'Scraps of Everything' (a very apt title for the odds and ends which followed). Its reports of court cases, giving the actual slang used by witnesses and defendants, were often extremely entertaining. More serious was the section on the 'Spirit of the Contemporary Press'. All the unstamped papers copied freely from one another: but *The Man* did so on a more systematic basis. In this way, any particularly provocative article was assured of the widest publicity: and it was this cooperation which made the cheap press even more dangerous. Despite its more general appeal, *The Man* was primarily a political paper. As usual, it denounced the Whigs, declaring (28 July 1833) that

> the expected collision between the two houses of legislature – the house of haughty, insolent and rapacious titled knaves, and the Whig-serving, dastardly, and inbound house of plunderers – has not yet arrived; therefore the destinies of this great empire will for a time longer, be wielded by the worst portion of the most depraved section of society, the atrocious and nefarious Whigs . . . *vampires*.

More reckless still was its 'Address to Lord Melbourne; On the Weakness and Wickedness of Ignorant Rulers' (8 September 1833):

> I NEVER WILL RECOGNISE either King, Lords, or Commons, *until their authority proceed from the people, and not from usurpation* . . . goaded to desperation by the mad folly, blind intolerance and stupid ignorance of the Tories, and the mendacity, cold-blooded tyranny, and insatiable rapacity of those Arch-taitors – The Whigs; the people, whose interests have been crucified between these two thieves . . . The people are the true source of legitimate power . . . utility should be the basis of all institutions . . . the House of Incurables, the Lords, should be abolished. As for William Guelph, the King. God bless him! he, poor silly creature, is only a ministerial puppet; a mere nonentity, brought forth occasionally to amuse children and old women . . . How are we to obtain our rights? . . .

Adopt the plan now pursuing by the Radicals of the North. Organise yourselves in tens, in hundreds, in thousands; contribute but a trifle of your earnings, however scanty, to a common fund, and PURCHASE ARMS!

This rousing manifesto had, according to the editor, been given to him by an agent of Lord Melbourne – an *agent provocateur*. But, he went on, 'it contains so many truths, is so ably written, and points out the mode of resisting despotic power so clearly, that, *coming as it does from Lord Melbourne* . . . I feel I should be neglecting my duty were I not to give the document entire.' But *The Man* needed little stimulation, and on 11 August indulged in an unusually vicious attack upon the royal family, drawing the King's attention to

the manifold atrocities perpetrated by that sanguinary maniac, his sire; to the disgusting deeds of his late detested brother; and those of his existing relative – Cumberland. Let him blush for the infamy of his royal sisters, and reflect upon the murders, incests, adulteries, fornications, and all the other deadly sins which form the hereditary heir-loom of the deranged family of which he is the appropriate representative.

Something would have to be done about the Radical press. In fact, something was being done. At first, Authority once again sought to 'write Cobbett down'. In the British Museum there is a solitary copy of paper entitled *Cobbett's Genuine Two-Penny Trash. For the month of February, 1831. No. I. Reduced to Three Half-pence for the Benefit of General Distribution to the Labourers of England.* This was genuine enough in that it consisted solely of quotations from Cobbett's *Register* and other writings. But the quotations were cleverly selected from Cobbett's 'early' or 'Tory' period. Thus, the paper maintained, 'the bulk of political reformers is always composed of needy, discontented men, too indolent or impatient to advance themselves by fair and honest means, or too ambitious to remain quiet in obscurity'. Even more embarrassing were Cobbett's earlier views on the working classes:

As for your reading at all, I see no use in it . . . As to a ploughman sitting down to read his book after his labour is done, the idea could never have found its way into the mind of anyone who knew what a ploughman was – take a thousand ploughmen, set them down to their good books after their day's work is done, and in less than ten minutes the whole thousand of them will be asleep – animal amusement is the only amusement they enjoy.

And again,

I have declared as you may find in my 'Porcupine' (that is another work I wrote to convey right notions to the minds of the people), in my *Porcupine* you will find at page 182, I have declared that 'there is no falsehood too great for the *swinish multitude* to swallow – I have called you, I confess, sad names – 'two-legged brutes', 'the silly, noisy, poor sovereign-people of England', 'rough-headed wretches' . . . I am no demagogue – through all the volumes I have put together there will not be found *one single sentiment calculated to obtain favour with the senseless multitude.*

This publication may have made some few readers think twice about what the master had actually said. But with the arrival on the scene of far tougher journalists than Cobbett, stronger measures were required, and the government fell back upon repression. Most of the publishers, if not the authors, of the leading unstamped papers spent at least some time in gaol. The principal target was undoubtedly the *Poor Man's Guardian*, although this favouritism apparently caused some resentment. *The Destructive* on 16 February 1833 reported the gaoling of Watson, the publisher of the *Working Men's Friend*, for selling two numbers of the *Poor Man's Guardian*.

Why [it demanded] was Mr Watson proceeded against for the *Guardian*, more than any other of the unstamped? He sells at least twenty or thirty other publications, all equally obnoxious as the *Guardian* to the Stamp Law; and yet the *Guardian* is the only one selected for persecution! Why is this, Messrs. the Commissioners of Stamps? – Why did you not inform against the *Working Men's Friend*, or the *Cosmopolite*.

The *Cosmopolite* had already had its share of the glory in 1832, when on 28 July it reported, in heavy print, that 'George Pilgrim is incarcerated in the New Prison, Clerkenwell, there to remain Six Months, Bread and Water his only allowance, for selling this our *Cosmopolite* Newspaper for a Penny, without the Blood-stained burning shame of a Four-penny Tax-badge attached to it!' Pilgrim was the publisher of the paper: but he was not prosecuted for the items that appeared in it, but simply for having sold it. And, once again, the main victims were the hawkers and sellers of unstamped newspapers. When not happily occupied in savaging the royal family, the Radical papers bellowed for what they called 'the freedom of the press' – and were full of heart-rending accounts of the arrest of crippled and aged news-vendors, and soliciting subscriptions. According to the *Cosmopolite* of 18 August 1832, 'nearly two hundred individuals have suffered imprisonment for various periods, from one week to six months, in this warfare'. By February 1833 that figure had risen considerably – or so said *The Destructive* (16 February), in one of its customary attacks upon the Whigs:

The most selfish, hollow, rapacious, truckling, cruel, and perfidious faction . . . Need we – to prove their perfidy – point out the FOUR HUNDRED AND FIFTY VICTIMS they have assigned to dungeons, for diffusing cheap knowledge among those who cannot afford to pay a tax of *fourpence* for leave to read a penny-worth of news! . . . As regards the Taxes on Knowledge, the disposition of Ministers is readily seen . . . Lord Brougham tells us in the *Globe*, that its repeal would more than anything else – not excepting even Universal Suffrage – PRECIPITATE A REVOLUTION.

How successful was the repression? On 27 July 1833 the *Working Men's Friend* printed an article on 'Taxes on Newspapers', comparing the United Kingdom (taxed) with the United States (untaxed). According to its statistics, the population of the United Kingdom was 24 million, as against only 15 million. But whereas in the UK there were only 320 newspapers, including 20 daily papers, with a gross circulation of 30 million, in the United States there were 850 newspapers, including 58 dailies, with a circulation of 65 million. As the author put it,

What a marked contrast! The Daily Newspapers circulation of Paris is 100,000; of London, about 36,000; in the former the stamp duty is light, in the latter oppressive. Every large town in America has its Daily Paper – in all Scotland there is not one; in England, only in London (to the number of thirteen); in Ireland, only in Dublin (number seven) . . . The number of newspapers sold annually in England, on the average of 3 years was in

1753	7,411,757
1760	9,464,790
1790	14,035,639
1792	15,005,760
1814	24,000,000
1826	25,000,000.

The circulation of newspapers is not greater now than 5 or 6 years ago, the increase has taken place in the Irish and Scottish journals.

This gloomy picture was based on the stamp returns, and rather surprisingly did not mention the circulation of unstamped papers. On that subject, the *Standard* of 10 September 1833 had a great deal to say. It pointed out that the poor were not taking advantage of the cheap 'innocent and respectable reading' now readily available. But, it went on,

perhaps they have been reading – doubtless they have, and we are enabled, from an authentic source, to give some account of their reading . . . It is a list of the unstamped political publications in defiance of the law, with the late average sale of each:

	Average Circulation
Poor Man's Guardian	16,000

This is printed by Hetherington, an Irish Papist and ex-student of Maynooth

Destructive	8,000

Printed by the same.

It is scarcely necessary to mention the principles of these publications; they are Jacobinical of the latest, bloodiest dye. It will be remembered that Hetherington has preached the use of the dagger as an instrument of revolution. The *Poor Man's Guardian* and *Destructive* circulate in Lancashire

Gauntlet	22,000

The conductor of this is the notorious Carlile – his name is enough

Cosmopolite	5,000

Editor, Detroisier, Principles, Owenite and Republican

Working Men's Friend	7,000

Editor, Watson, Principles, Republican

Crisis	5,000

Conductor, Mr Owen and Morgan, author of the 'wrath of the Bees'. Mr Owen's name precludes the necessity of describing principles.

The Man	7,000

Conductors Lee, the Chairman of Coalbath-field's meeting, and Petrie. Principles, Spencean and Republican

Reformer	5,000

Principles, Republican and Revolutionary. Editor, Lorimer.

These are the principal unstamped publications of London – the reading, with the *Times* and the *Weekly Dispatch*, of the educated democracy of the metropolis. Are men to be turned loose upon such garbage as this? In the country, there are also unstamped newspapers – particularly at Leeds, Bradford, Manchester, etc., all taking their tone from the *Poor Man's Guardian* and the others, which we described as the penny press of London. These are the *primitiae*, the first fruits of the late active exertions in behalf of indiscriminate education.

It is, perhaps, surprising to see *The Times* included in such a list. But the Sunday *Weekly Dispatch* was a very different proposition, with pronounced Radical sympathies, and a very large circulation. What is interesting about the *Standard*'s report – apart from its pithy comments – is the sheer size of the circulation of the unstamped newspapers. That of the papers it listed came to 77,000 a week, and it left out many other papers. It was a hostile witness – and its estimates were conservative. The unstamped papers themselves were claiming even larger sales and influence.

Physical repression had failed. And on 3 September John Mill had written to Brougham condemning

> the illicit publications, in which the doctrines of the right of the labouring people, who say they are the only producers . . . is very generally preached. The alarming nature of this evil you will understand when I inform you that these publications are superseding the Sunday newspapers, and every other channel through which the people might get better information . . . I am sure it is not good policy to give the power of teaching the people exclusively to persons violating the law, and of such desperate circumstances and character that neither the legal nor the moral sanction has sufficient hold on them. The only effectual remedy is to remove the tax which gives them this deplorable power.

The government was not yet prepared to reduce or abolish the taxes on knowledge. It still regarded the growing popular interest in news with suspicion. But it was very willing to tackle the problem from a somewhat different angle. The success of the Radical journalists had shown that workers who laboured sixteen hours a day for two shillings or less could apparently afford a penny or two a week for printed matter. What was needed was cheap but wholesome literature for the masses: not news, and certainly not politics, but general information and, within strict limits, 'entertainment' (but not the sensational fiction already so popular).

There had already been experiments in this field. Hannah More had been one of the pioneers. In 1806 Patrick Colquhoun had advocated a rather different approach: a weekly police gazette 'to excite in the minds of the labouring people a strong sense of moral virtue, loyalty, and love of their country'. Colquhoun proposed to do this by publishing detailed accounts of the juiciest murders, rapes and scandals, justifying his reports on purely moral grounds. He was following a long tradition, and one which was to flourish after him. It was all a matter of definition.

That there *was* a demand for cheap and wholesome literature was perhaps proved by the success of John Limbard's *Mirror of Literature, Amusement and Instruction*, which first appeared on Saturday, 2 November 1822, price 2*d*, and was to last until 1849. The first issue set the general pattern. There was an elaborate woodcut on the front page depicting 'The Tread-Mill at Brixton' (with a two-page report). The rest of the paper was taken up with brief notes on a vast variety of subjects – verse, 'Old Actors', 'Fanatics', 'Nautical Brewing', 'Lying', 'Burning Dead Bodies', 'Law and Lawyers', etc. There was no political emphasis. And this approach was maintained. Always there was an impressive woodcut, illustrating such diverse subjects as 'The Mermaid', 'The Pyramids of

Egypt', 'The Eruption of Mount Vesuvius', 'The Wapati or Giant Elk', 'Laplanders and Rein-Deer'. 'Iron Suspension Bridge over the Tweed', and 'Execution of a Criminal in the Sandwich Islands'. The other items were always brief, and included human interest stories and an occasional, but very short, piece of fiction. But the main emphasis was on general knowledge and 'useful household hints' (including what to do if someone swallowed a clasp-knife). The mixture was harmless enough, and popular. But most of the earlier publications of this type were crude concoctions which did not even approach the ideals of a writer in 1825 who proposed that a paper be set up to address the lower classes 'in a tone of perfect confidence and equality' and encourage them in every liberal and enlightened study; show them 'how differences in rank have arisen in the world, and in what way alone men can rise advantageously from a lower rank to a higher'; and call upon them 'with a voice of authority, to abandon low and brutal vices, and to go on in the grand course of industry, virtuous contentment, and the ambition of knowledge and improvement'

This was the sort of approach which appealed more and more to the upper classes. The guidelines had been laid down, and the basic problems exposed. The social and political mesage of Hannah More had been too blatant; the original approach of the Society for the Diffusion of Useful Knowledge too heavy. What was needed was a judicious blending of the two, leavened by carefully selected and wholesome 'entertainment'. Out of this conviction sprang one of the most spectacular movements in the history of the Press. In 1832 there appeared three cheap – and 'wholesome' – magazines which were to achieve considerable fame: *Chamber's Edinburgh Journal*, on Saturday, 4 February, price 1½d; Charles Knight's *Penny Magazine of the Society for the Diffusion of Useful Knowledge*, on 31 March; and, from the Society for the Promotion of Christian Knowledge, *The Saturday Magazine* on 7 July, price 1d.

The aims of the three were essentially the same. In his opening address, Chambers stated that

> The grand leading principle by which I have been actuated, is to take advantage of the universal appetite for instruction which at present exists; to supply that appetite food of the best kind, and in such form, and at such a price, as must suit the convenience of every man in the British dominions . . . healthful, useful and agreeable mental instruction. I state as my honest conviction, that the people of Great Britain and Ireland have never yet been properly catered for, in the way of presenting knowledge, under its more cheering and captivating aspect, to their immediate observation. The scheme of diffusing knowledge has certainly more than once been attempted on acceptable principles, by associations established under all the advantages of an enormous capital, as well as the influence of a baronial title [Brougham] and the endeavour has

generally been attended with beneficial results. Yet the strongholds of ignorance, though not unassailed, remain still to be carried.

The *Journal* would contain

> original and select papers on Literature and Scientific subjects, including articles on the Formation and Arrangement of Society; short Essays on Trade and Commerce; Observations on Education in its different Branches . . . Sketches on Topography and Statistics, relative to Agriculture, Gardening, Planting, Sheep-farming, the making of Roads and Bridges and Canals; the establishment of Ferries, the best means of Conveyance by Land and Water; Increase of Population; the Use of Machinery to simplify Human Labour and Manufactures, etc. . . . excellent pithy passages from the works of the great British moralists . . . To Artizans, I shall present instructive little paragraphs from the best writers on the various branches of their industry . . . short extracts related to Domestic and Cottage Economy . . . To the ladies and gentlemen of the 'old school', I shall relate innumerable amusing traditionary anecdotes . . . With the ladies of the 'new School' and all my fair young countrywomen in their teens, I hope to be on agreeable terms . . . a nice amusing tale . . . no ordinary trash about Italian castles, and daggers, and ghosts in blue chambers, and similar nonsense, but something really good. I will also inform them of a thousand little receipts and modes of house-wifery, calculated to make them capital wives.

At least Chambers recognised that his potential readers had many and varied interests, and did his best to meet their requirements as he understood them. But, despite all his assurances, the *Journal* made very heavy reading indeed.

The *Penny Magazine* and the *Saturday Magazine* said very much the same, with the latter laying particular stress upon the

> great books . . . very seldom opened by any man nowadays . . . rarely to be met with out of public libraries . . . partly by their occasional perplexity of thought and uncouth manner of speech; and partly also to their size . . . which makes it a work of months, sometimes of years, to get quite through some of them. Nevertheless, they were not without their effect on the world: many of the important truths which they contain, have been preserved and illustrated in later writings, more portable in form and easy of digestion.

One can but admire this *Reader's Digest* approach to the great books of the past – and the felicity of expression. Both the *Penny Magazine* and the *Saturday Magazine* possessed one great advantage over their rival in that they were illustrated, often lavishly so. The *Saturday Magazine* specialised in vivid and spirited woodcuts featuring a 'Juggernaut temple', 'Wild Sport of the East', 'Departure of the Israelites out of Egypt', a 'Gigantic Druidical Idol, as described by Caesar', and 'The Pyramids'. The *Penny Magazine*'s illustrations were not so exciting, and dealt mainly with natural history and the production of sugar, tea, coffee, tobacco and olives. Both stressed the need to combine instruction with wholesome entertainment.

The magazine proved an immediate success. In his preface to the first bound volume of 1832, Charles Knight maintained that circulation in the first month of publication had been 160,000, and was now 200,000. 'It may', he went on, 'be fairly calculated that the number of readers . . . amounts to a million', and this despite the fact that

> in this work there has never been a single sentence that could inflame a vicious appetite; and not a paragraph that could minister to prejudices and superstitions which a few years ago were common. There have been no excitements for the lovers of the marvellous – no tattle or abuse for the gratification of a diseased taste for personality – and, above all no party politics.
> . . . This consideration furnishes the most convincing answer to the few (if any there now remain) who assert that General Education is an evil.

Chambers did not make such formidable claims. On 2 February 1833 he mentioned that 'the sale of the first 12 numbers . . . was confined in a great measure to Scotland; and the quantity then printed (including a portion designed for the supply of future demands) was thirty-one thousand.' It was now distributed in Edinburgh and London, and the circulation was approaching 50,000, despite the fact that

> though sensible moreover, that we might have extended our circulation very much, especially out of Scotland, by the introduction of pictorial embellishments, we have stood steadfast upon letter-press alone, addressing our readers through their understanding, rather than the senses, and thereby making certainly a far less direct appeal to the mass of the public than what is made by the only respectable work which exceeds ours in circulation.

On 1 February 1834 Chambers raised the really significant question: 'It may still be asked – Are these sheets really purchased, and, more than that, are they really read, by the poorer classes?' His answer was a confident affirmative: 'We can answer for our own publication – which we do upon the best evidence – that, though they are purchased also by the middle and upper ranks, they are diffused through the very humblest departments of our society, and not only read, but received into the innermost minds and hearts of those who do us the honour to purchase them.' In fact, their success had encouraged both Chambers and Knight to launch other enterprises. Chambers published a fortnightly *Information for the People*, price 1½*d.*, and a variety of other cheap periodicals. Charles Knight produced a *Penny Cyclopaedia*, issued in weekly parts from 1833, and a whole assortment of other educational offerings. But the essential problem remained: who *was* reading these magazines? As early as 26 January 1833 Chambers had remarked:

> We have heard with regret that, among the more dignified class of our readers – for the *Journal* is read by all classes, as well by those to whom its price is an inconsiderable item of money, as by the multitudinous children of industry to whom its low price barely renders it accessible – a few express themselves dissatisfied with the homeliness of those articles which fall under the description of sketches of society. This kind of society, they say, is not theirs; it is that of our tradesmen.

He followed this up with a homily on tolerance and Christian charity. But later in the same year, the *Standard* (10 September 1833) was to insist that:

> Everybody is aware of the miscellaneous multitude of cheap publications which the last two or three years have called into existence. Some of these have had a very considerable sale; but we have it in evidence that all, without any exception, of an innocent and respectable kind, have been sold, *not* as cheap publications, but in collected numbers, at prices such as the upper and middle classes are accustomed to purchase. We need not hesitate to say, therefore, that those classes which have been the object of eleemosynary education, have not availed themselves of the cheapness of innocent and respectable reading.

Despite growing evidence to the contrary Chambers continued to claim a wide circulation among the poor. On the *Journal's* second anniversary in 1834 he described how 'the shepherd, upon tracts of mountain land, receives his copy, perhaps, from an egg-market man or a travelling huckstry-woman. When perused, he takes it to the extremity of his walk, and places it under a certain stone, where the shepherd of the adjacent farm soon after recovers it.' Even more touching than this rural idyll was the account of how, in a Cambridgeshire village, five boys clubbed together to buy their weekly copy. Three contributed a halfpenny each (which, incidentally, they had been given to put in the missionary box), and the other two walked seven miles to the nearest bookseller. In similar vein was a bookseller's account of the immediate impact of the *Journal* upon the country people:

> Chambers has done what others could not do, even the Tract Societies . . . Not many years ago, I drew £30 annually from trashy ballads, and still more trashy pamphlets, such as *John*

> *Cheap the Chapman, Paddy from Cork*, etc. . . . I no longer keep
> such trash in my shop . . .If you only choose to watch, on
> certain days, the milk-boys returning seated on donkeys or
> donkey-carts, you will discover that almost every urchin among
> them is thumbing *Chambers* in place of a Ballad, and reaping
> the benefit of a partial perusal earlier than either his master or
> mistresses. *Chambers* has done more to wean the people from
> trash, cultivate their minds, and excite their curiosity, than all
> the Tract Societies that ever existed.

Considering that the *Journal* had no illustrations, such comments
suggest a very high standard of literacy among the children of the poor,
but one has always to remember that the educational system in Scotland
was vastly superior to that in England. Chambers returned to this basic
problem in his address in volume IV of 31 January 1835:

> As a single fact illustrative of its extensive reception among the
> working classes, we have been informed that in a single cotton-
> work near Glasgow, no fewer than 84 copies are regularly
> purchased, notwithstanding that in such places a single copy of
> a newspaper or other periodical generally serves a dozen
> readers. But it is not alone among the inferior orders of society
> that the *Journal* is circulated. We have been given to
> understand that it reaches the drawing rooms of the most
> exalted persons in the country, and the libraries of the most
> learned; that, in the large towns, a vast proportion of the
> mercantile and professional persons of every rank and order are
> its regular purchasers; and that, in short, it *pervades the whole
> society*.

The total average circulation was now 55,000. Chambers was
understandably proud of the fact that his *Journal* had won the patronage
of 'the most exalted persons in the land': but this had not been his original
objective. In fact, he was being forced to admit that his magazine did not
reach as far down into the masses as he had at first thought. It was read,
he admitted in 1840, by

> the élite of the labouring community; those who think, conduct
> themselves respectably, and are anxious to improve their
> circumstances by judicious means. But below this worthy order
> of men, our work, except in a few particular cases, does not go
> far. A fatal mistake is committed in the notion that the lower
> classes read . . . Some millions of adults of both sexes, in cities
> as well as in rural districts, are still in this hour in ignorance of
> letters as the people generally were in the middle ages.

There was an unusual note of pessimism here. Also, the facts were not
strictly true. There *was* a working-class reading public, and one growing
steadily in size. But it was not reading the *Journal* – nor, after the initial

response, the *Penny Magazine*. When in 1851 a committee of Parliament inquired into the reading tastes of the poor, one witness stated flatly that he never knew of a poor man taking in the *Penny Magazine*. As for the *Journal*, its sale had been 'almost exclusively confined to the middle classes . . . chiefly among small shopkeepers, not among those dependent upon weekly wages; not certainly among any portion of the working classes earning less than 16s. a week. The 'small shopkeepers' were a far cry from 'the most exalted persons in the land', but the circulation of the *Journal* continued to grow, and by the beginning of 1845 its sale was reported to be approaching 90,000. But its two rivals were in trouble.

Chambers had the advantage that he was a free agent. Despite the heavy emphasis on useful instruction in his *Journal*, he did from time to time try to lighten the mixture with a short story – although his determination to preserve 'moral decency' rather limited his field. As he explained, 'numberless topics and expressions which the conductors of hardly any other periodical work would think objectionable, are avoided by us, and . . . we hardly ever receive a contribution from the most practised writers, which does not require purification before we deem it fit for insertion' (vol. iv, 1835). Both his main rivals were subject to external pressures. Knight's position was particularly unhappy. It had apparently taken some considerable persuasion to get the Society for the Diffusion of Useful Knowledge to support a periodical aimed at the lower classes. Some members considered that a penny magazine was beneath the dignity of the Society. Anything approaching fiction was strictly barred. Even more disastrous was the fact that the leading light of the Society was Brougham, regarded by the Radicals as the arch-traitor, the man who had betrayed the people over the cause of parliamentary reform, and who was responsible for the attack on the freedom of the Press in his persecution of unstamped newspapers. Few indeed were the issues of those papers which did not include an uncomplimentary reference to Brougham – and, in passing, to the *Penny Magazine*. Thus, the *Cosmopolite* of 5 May 1832 contained the item:

> Not worth two-pence a waggon-load. As we were passing
> through Cheapside the other day, one of the flying stationers,
> who appeared to be well supplied with Brougham's *Penny
> Magazine* and the water-closet gazette (*Omnibus*) came up to a
> gentleman walking before us – and pressed him to buy one.
> 'Don't want any of them', was the reply. 'Do buy one, sir –
> only a penny'- – 'Have you any *Guardians, Slaps*, or
> *Cosmopolites?*' inquired the gentleman. – 'No, sir,' replied the
> stationer. – 'Then I won't buy,' he said, 'for I would not give
> you twopence for a waggon-load of those trash'.

By the mid-1840s, the circulation of the *Penny Magazine* had dropped to some 40,000, barely enough to cover costs. In December 1845 Knight took over the paper – which he had hitherto edited 'under the auspices of the Society'. The general aims, he announced, would remain the same, although he intended to offer

> a wider range and a more varied character. IT WILL
> HENCEFORTH be CHIEFLY a MAGAZINE OF
> READING. *Woodcuts* will no longer continue to be the
> prominent feature . . . To the one great object of diffusing *useful
> knowledge* will be added the constant desire to make that
> knowledge *interesting* . . . Important *subjects of information* will
> have their place, in company with *amusing* narrative, real or
> fictitious. Light sketches on *passing manners* may freely range with
> sober essays on *permanent morals*; and the highest obligations of
> *sacred truth* may be enforced in a cheerful spirit.

But there was little real change. It could never be called light reading,
and now it was playing down its main attraction – the woodcuts. The
Penny Magazine died in 1846.

The reasons for its collapse – and the failure of Chambers to appeal
to the working classes – are not difficult to find. They were suggested in
Knight's address on taking over the *Magazine*:

> The literature of the 'Penny Magazine' has invariably
> maintained its ruling character, – that of dealing with general
> subjects in a grave and earnest tone. It has avoided, rather than
> sought, the topic of the day. It has been a safe Miscellany, in
> which all classes might find much information and some
> amusement.

But the *proportion* was wrong, and showed a complete misunderstanding
of the realities of British society. Life was hard and rough, and the vast
majority of the new reading public, often only semi-literate, did not *want*
to be 'instructed'. The politically conscious few turned naturally to the
unstamped Radical newspapers. The rest wanted only to be amused and
entertained. As Charles Dickens put it, 'The English are, so far as I know,
the hardest worked people on whom the sun shines. Be content if in their
wretched intervals of leisure they read for amusement and do no worse.
They are born at the oar, and they live and die at it. Good God, what
would we have of them!' In fact, the worker, whether literate or
semiliterate, demanded entertainment; and he liked that entertainment
rough and raw. Neither Chambers nor Knight had thought seriously in
terms of entertainment, although Knight seems eventually to have
recognised what he was up against, in his final address in the *Penny
Magazine*, when he spoke feelingly of

> those who are carrying out the principle of cheap weekly sheets
> to the disgrace of the system, and who appear to have got
> considerable hold upon the less informed of the working people,
> and especially upon the young . . . There are manufactories in
> London whence hundreds of reams of vile paper and printing
> issue weekly . . . All the garbage that belongs to the history of

crime and misery is raked together, to diffuse a moral Miasma through the land, in the shape of the most vulgar and brutal fiction . . . the cheap booksellers' shops are filled with such things as 'Newgate, a Romance', 'The Black Mantle, or the Murder at the Old Jewry', 'The Spectre of the hall', 'The Love-Child', 'The Feast of Blood', 'The Convict', and twenty others, all of the same exciting character to the young and ignorant.

In fact, the cheap fiction industry was flourishing as never before. Salacious as many of its publications might be to the evangelicals and their allies, they were well adapted to the taste of the reader whose limited education had taught him to read, if little else. At the lowest level, ballads remained part of the local scene, and were to do so for many years to come. 'Popular songs! Three yards for a penny!' was the cry. 'Execution papers' did a roaring trade. Most sported crude woodcuts, often selected without much apparent regard to their aptness. Thus, we are told, 'The Heart that can feel for another' was illustrated by a woodcut of a savage-looking lion; 'The London Oyster-Girl' by a portrait of Sir Walter Raleigh; 'Bright Hours are in store for us yet' by an urn inscribed with the word 'finis'; and 'The Sun that lights the roses' by an engraving of a man thrusting a sword down the throat of a wild boar. At a higher level, there were serial novels by the hundred. In this field, G. W. M. Reynolds was to make himself supreme. On his death in 1899, *The Bookseller* declared that 'Dickens, Thackeray, and Lever had their thousands of readers, but Mr Reynolds's readers were numbered by hundreds of thousands, perhaps by millions'.[3] Reynolds edited the *London Journal*, a very successful if somewhat notorious weekly in 1845, contributing to it a serial, *Mysteries of the Inquisition*. At the same time, he was publishing in weekly numbers his *Mysteries of London*, which eventually reached four volumes. On 7 November 1846 he began his *Reynolds's Magazine of Romance, General Literature, Science and Arts*, price one penny. The title was a fair indication of the contents. Six and a half pages were taken up by a serial, 'Wagner: the Wehr-Wolf. By the Editor'. There followed 'Advice to Young Ladies'; 'Anatomy and Physiology of Ourselves Popularly Considered' – to be continued; 'The greatest Pickpocket in Paris'; 'The Man without a Name'; 'Brewing for the millions'; the 'Provincial Press'; and recipes and anecdotes. But his output was prodigious, and included an apparently unending stream of fiction, under such titles as *The Black Monk, or The Secret of the Grey Tower*; *Almira's Curse, or the Black Tower of Bransdorf*; and, above all, *Varney the Vampire, or the Feast of Blood*. Such tales transported thousands of working men and their families from their own drab and dingy world into a new and exciting world of ghosts, vampires, sinister dungeons, and the like. But every taste was catered for, with such sentimental stories as *Fatherless Fanny* (calculated to wring oceans of tears from their more susceptible readers) and adventure stories on the lines of *The Death Ship, or the Pirate's Bride and the Maniac of the Deep*.

Pearl makes much of the sadism he sees in the 'gaudy descriptions of scourging and torture', the gusto with which floggings, murders and hangings were detailed, and what he terms the 'lush sexuality' with its emphasis on 'the battle of the bulge' (the female bosom).[4] But this is to exaggerate. According to Reynolds, his purpose was very close indeed to that of Knight and Chambers:

> To supply a desideratum which has for some time been acknowledged. The remark on one side has been that certain Cheap Publications contain too much light matter, while on the other side it has been observed that another set of Periodicals are too heavy. To steer the medium course is the object of REYNOLDS'S MAGAZINE.

His emphasis was undoubtedly upon the serials. But, despite its title, *Wagner: the Wehr-Wolf* was remarkably restrained. The illustrations might at times include 'Instruments of Torture', but they were not shown in use; the second issue of the *Magazine* depicted 'A Guillotine Scene in France', but the knife had not fallen; the third, 'The bloodstained Altar', and nothing more. One wonders what the *Terrific Register* would have made of such wonderful material! Most of the illustrations were in fact portraits of eminent persons. And there was also a pronounced educational strand, with 'Popular Papers on Science', 'The Moral Elevation of the People', and so on.

The problem of finding the 'medium course' remained. Reynolds laid more stress on 'entertainment'. Chambers and Knight pressed on with their programmes – programmes which, though well-meant, were totally unrealistic. With the growth of industrialisation and urbanisation, the masses needed recreation as never before. They wanted to *escape*. And so, with the exception of a small aristocracy of labour (whose members would intellectually probably have put most of the upper classes to shame) the new reading public rejected the *Penny Magazine* and *Chambers's Journal*, and turned instead to more exciting periodicals. At the same time the success of the unstamped papers had indicated that a fair proportion of the working classes was reaching the stage of political consciousness. But both Chambers and Knight deliberately excluded politics. To many of the Radical leaders, this avoidance had a sinister connotation. The *Poor Man's Guardian* defined the 'useful knowledge' as 'namby-pamby stuff published expressly to stultify the minds of the working people and make them spiritless and unresisting victims of plunder and oppression'. And there was some truth in the charge.

In their main objective, both Knight and Chambers failed. Nevertheless, both were landmarks in the development of popular journalism, bringing wholesome reading to many who had not hitherto been able to afford it. And their amazing initial success produced something of a boom in the field of cheap periodicals, with the appearance of such new offerings (some of which the two pioneers would not have approved of) as the *Half-Penny Magazine*, the *Christian's Penny*

Magazine, London Penny Journal, Girl's and Boy's Penny Magazine, and, on the lighter side, the *Penny Comic Magazine, Penny Story Teller,* and *Penny Novelist.* For better or worse, the reading habit was spreading as never before.

6 The age of *The Times*

In the background, one London newspaper had been rising steadily to a position of dominance: *The Times*. It is all too easy to write the history of the press around this paper and so overlook such even more significant developments as the growth of the reading public and of a 'popular' press. But in any such history, *The Times* must necessarily play a leading part. Its rise symbolised the growing independence of the Press from government and party control – indeed, from any control whatsoever.

The Times possessed one immediate advantage over its rivals: technical superiority. From its foundation it had been closely interested in improved printing methods: it was in fact established to promote a new 'Logographic' press. Now, in this decisive period, it was always technically ahead. The first successful adaptation of steam power to the printing press – by Frederick Koenig – was rightly described by *The Times* as an invention second only in importance to that of Gutenburg himself. In 1813 John Walter paid £1,100 each for two double machines, and £250 each for two steam engines. The first issue so produced appeared on 29 November 1814. It was a remarkable advance: from 250 sheets the hourly rate was raised to 1,100. By 1827 the rate had risen to 4,000, printed on both sides. So *The Times* was ready to cope with its forthcoming tremendous growth, for hitherto any real expansion had been limited by the printing rate. However, its growth depended upon other factors also. There was obviously little point in printing off thousands of sheets if few people were prepared to buy them; advertisers in particular required not only a large circulation but one worth appealing to, from the business point of view. That sort of public would first have to be convinced that the newspaper in question represented *their* interests, socially and politically. All these interrelated factors were obvious in the rise of *The Times*.

Advertisements were the great feature. To take a random example, in the issue of 5 August 1819 the whole of the front page was taken up with advertisements, 149 in all, often in tiny print; there were thirty-eight, mainly to do with publishing, on page 2; and the whole of page 4, the last page, was devoted to twenty-four publishing notices, and eighty-five miscellaneous trade announcements, with the emphasis on 'Situations Vacant'. By the 1830s, the numbers had increased markedly, and *The*

Times was now regularly producing Supplements in the form of 'double' or eight-page issues, often packed with advertisements. The issue of Saturday 3 July 1830 consisted of eight pages: and it contained no less than 600 advertisements! It is not surprising to be told that *The Times* paid in 1829 £16,332 in advertisement duty (at 3s6d an advertisement). The *Morning Herald* paid £7,325; *Morning Advertiser* £5,560; *Morning Chronicle* £3,714; and *Morning Post* £5,854.[1]

But advertisements alone would not sell a newspaper, and *The Times* was already winning a formidable reputation for its news and opinions. There were early pre-rumbles of 'The Thunderer', and as early as 1823 Hazlitt in the *Edinburgh Review* could remark that, '*The Times* is, we suppose, entitled to the character it gives itself, of being the "leading journal of Europe", and is perhaps the greatest engine of temporary opinion in the world. Still it is not to our taste... It might be imagined to be composed as well as printed with a steam engine.' The editor of *The Times*, Thomas Barnes, seems to have agreed with the criticism, for he wrote to a correspondent who had submitted some articles that they were

> good as far as they went, but they wanted a little devil in them
> . . . Newspaper writing is a thing *sui generis*; it is in literature
> what brandy is in beverages. John Bull, whose understanding is
> rather sluggish – I speak of the majority of readers – requires a
> strong stimulus. He consumes his beef and cannot digest it
> without a dram; he dozes composedly over his prejudices which
> his conceit calls opinions; and you must fire ten-pounders at his
> densely compacted intellect before you can make it comprehend
> your meaning or care one farthing for your efforts.

As an honest estimate of the capacities of newspaper readers, not only for his own time but for all time to come, this statement could scarcely be improved on. But already Barnes's motives – and consistency – were being questioned. Over the decision of *The Times* to support Caroline, Crabb Robinson wrote, on 13 October 1820:

> *The Times* has pledged itself by one uniform course of
> justification of the queen to go on to the end. I have no doubt
> Walter really thinks he is doing right, and I believe he may be
> – but he is not aware perhaps how much he is influenced in the
> line he is pursuing by finding that since the trial the sale of the
> paper has risen from seven to more than fifteen thousand!!!

Similar charges were to be made regularly. According to Hazlitt (admittedly a hostile witness), writing in *The Edinburgh Review*, May 1823, the paper

> takes up no falling cause; fights no uphill battle; advocates no
> great principle; holds out a helping hand to no oppressed or
> obscure individual. It is 'ever strong upon the stronger side' . . .
> It is valiant, swaggering, insolent, with 100,000 readers at its

heels; but the instant the rascal rout turns round with the 'whiff and whim' of some fell circumstance, *The Times*, not constant *Times*, turns with them.

In support, the *Morning Chronicle* derived considerable amusement from printing in parallel columns, what *The Times* had said the day before, and what it had said earlier. Barnes had a ready reply to such taunts: the important thing was not what had been said *then*, but 'whether what we say *now* is true and just'.

Behind these exchanges lies one of the most important – and difficult – of all the problems which face historians of the newspaper press. Do newspapers guide and mould public opinion – or do they merely reflect it? The problem was brought up by Lord Grey, who had a very poor opinion of Barnes, and who deeply resented the attacks so regularly made on him in *The Times*. Newspapers, he said, could be divided into two categories: those which sought to lead public opinion, and those which took their tone from it. In the second class, *The Times* was pre-eminent, for it was conducted without the least regard to principles of any kind, but solely with the view of extending its sale. One of Queen Adelaide's ladies in waiting once remarked, according to Brougham (another of *The Times*'s targets), that the paper would change if ten copies less were sold. There was undoubtedly some truth in these accusations. *The Times* did modify its political opinions when it found that its circulation was being adversely affected. But this did not necessarily mean that it was, in the words of the *Quarterly Review* of January 1831, 'the most profligate of the London newspapers, and the most impudently inconsistent in everything except malice and mischief'. Le Marchant put the case more fairly when he said that Barnes was remarkable 'for the quickness with which he caught the earliest sign of public opinion'. But that public opinion was not that of the masses but of the new aristocracy of wealth, steadily gaining economic power but poorly represented in Parliament and increasingly politically-minded, although *The Times* had deplored Peterloo, and had taken the 'popular' side over the Queen's affair. More venturesomely it supported Catholic Emancipation against the ultra-Protestant *Morning Post* and its allies, the *Morning Journal*, *Standard*, *St. James's Chronicle* and *John Bull*. It was soon to adopt the crucial cause of parliamentary reform, and again it chose the 'right' side – so that Barnes could announce triumphantly in March 1832 that:

> It has been asserted again and again that our sale has decreased in consequence of the part we have taken in that great measure, and thence was inferred the indifference and indisposition of the people to Reform. We want no better criteria of the feelings of the people. Our sale for the year 1830 was 3,409,986. For the last year (1831) it was 4,326,025, so that the increase has been nearly 1,000,000 . . . Such is the indifference to Reform! . . . . We observe that the great Conservative paper, the *Morning Post*, sells about 2,000 a day.

In all this, *The Times* reflected accurately the growing liberalism of the period. Politically, it had achieved its objectives in 1832, further than which it did not wish to go. It urged its readers to be content with the extension of the vote into the middle classes, and its readers needed little urging. For the poor, it had sympathy, as demonstrated in its opposition to the new poor law. But it had a hearty distrust of 'democracy'. Because it represented so perfectly the views of the middle classes – now regarded as the enemy by the working class leaders – it brought down on itself far more abuse than did such papers as the *Morning Post*, the organ of the traditional ruling classes. Cobbett in particular reserved some of his choicest epithets for it: 'that cunning old trout', 'that ranting, trimming old *Times*', 'that brazen old slut', and 'the bloody old *Times*'. To do *The Times* justice, it was similarly denounced by the Tory press, and it was soon to become the bane of the Whig government as well.

The government continued to offer inducements in the way of exclusive information and official advertisements. But in 1834 *The Times* proudly announced that it had declined accepting such advices because its own information service was earlier and more reliable. As to official advertisements, it soon became obvious that government departments had to place their notices in those newspapers which had the largest and most significant readership. No longer did it pay newspapers to be subsidised. In effect, the leading newspapers were largely beyond control, and Wellington ruefully admitted that 'we have no power over them'. Bad newspapers were still ready to sell themselves, but they were not worth buying. No newspaper with any reputation would accept direct money from the government. Of course, most continued to have dealings with important politicians: but they had to avoid any open and avowed connection with them.

Politicians did not accept this situation easily. The Tories were particularly concerned during the campaign for Reform. In 1829 Croker had suggested that a cabinet minister instead of the Parliamentary Secretary of the Treasury should be made responsible for 'instructing' friendly newspapers. His suggestion revealed the new stature of the Press – and also forecast, with some acuteness, the future importance of 'propaganda':

> the times are gone by when statesmen might safely despise the journals, or only treat them as inferior engines which might be left to themselves, or be committed to the guidance of persons wholly unacquainted with the views of the ministry. . . . The day is not far distant when you will (not *see*, or *hear*) but know that there is someone in the Cabinet entrusted with what will be thought one of the most important duties of the State, the regulation of public opinion.

The Tory worries became even more serious in 1831, with the collapse of the *Morning Journal* and the defection of the *Courier*, a paper which had been more closely connected with the various Tory ministries since 1807 than any other. They could still rely on the *Morning Post*. They had also two evening papers, the *Standard* and the *Star*, the latter having a sale of only 150 in 1830. There was some talk of setting up a new morning paper on the same scale as *The Times*, but the project was abandoned, for as Lord Lowther explained, 'it is no easy matter to establish a morning paper on the same scale as *The Times* and the *Herald*. The first cost would be from £30,000 to £40,000'. The Tories were driven back on the *Morning Post*. That paper was once again demonstrating its extraordinary resiliency. Its whole career had been one of ups and downs. It was now on the way up again, and its leading article of 1 July 1830 boasted that the sale had increased by upward of a thousand a day since the previous year. Politically, it appealed to the aristocratic and landed interest. But it had won a reputation for snobbery, and a writer in *Fraser's Magazine* in 1836 was to call it, 'the pet of the petticoats, the darling of the boudoir, the oracle of the drawing-room, and the safe recorder of ballroom beauties and drawing-room presentation'. There was an element of truth in the charges. Unfortunately, from the point of view of the Tories, Byrne, who controlled the paper, preferred this form of prostitution to the political variety, and Lord Lowther reported in May 1831 that

> We can make nothing of the *Morning Post*. Old Byrne has a sale for his fashionable news, and *we* had authority to assist him with reporters and a Parisian correspondence, but he would neither delay his press nor give room for such intelligence. I conclude he knows his own trade better than we do, and that he would not risk the readers of his fashionable news for the prospect of making his paper a more decided political one.

Once again, in fact, a newspaper was demonstrating its independence, and despite the lure of political assistance the *Post* preferred to go its own way. But it took an increasing interest in politics after 1832, when it seriously feared a revolution. And its political approach became lively in 1835, when Disraeli began writing for it. In a leading article (24 August) on the general theme that the 'reformed' House of Commons was no more representative of the people than the House of Lords, Disraeli wrote, with particular reference to the Whigs:

> And of whom is this knot of rebels formed? First and foremost, of course, of the Popish rebels [i.e. those who had voted for Catholic Emancipation]. The other society is led by Mr HUME and his Utilitarian, and rather *Brutalitarian* allies . . . They altogether form a company utterly contemptible in point of number, intelligence and influence in the country . . . The vast majority of these men . . . are illiterate persons. HUME, for instance, can neither speak or write English; his calligraphy reminds one of a chandler's shop, and his letters resemble a butterman's bill . . . All the petty plunderers, would-be Commissioners, and other small toadeaters, for the sake of a

possible dinner and probable job, laud them with great praise. But the ignorance of WARBURTON rather staggers even these parasites . . . WAKLEY is a lighter order of mind . . . He would make an admirable cad, or a first-rate conductor of an omnibus.

In another article, he described the Attorney-General as 'this bowing, fawning, jobbing progeny of haggis and cockaleekie'. According to Disraeli, his contributions were responsible for the growing circulation of the *Morning Post*. Barnes obviously appreciated their appeal, and commissioned Disraeli to write 'The Letters of Runnymede' – though warning him against his 'most surprising disdain for the law of libel'.

The *Morning Post* was probably the chief rival of *The Times*, referring to its 'shameless mendacity and effrontery' and 'its utter disregard to truth and honesty'. Edward Sterling, the original 'Thunderer', was singled out for special treatment: he was 'the cockney leader-writer . . . It would be idle to attempt to reason with a person at once so uninformed and so presumptuous.' But such pleasantries were by no means confined to the two papers. According to another, 'We think it was Sheridan who said, "Let your satire be as keen and as polished as your sword"'; but the *Times* knows no other weapons than a club or a butcher's cleaver; its language is such as only might be expected from the gentlemen of Billingsgate and the gentlemen of St. Giles's.'[2]

And Daniel O'Connell (who had suffered much at the hands of *The Times* in its reporting of his speeches in Parliament) demanded of the House in 1835:

> Was he not to speak of that vile journal which had falsely, foully, and wickedly calumniated him every day, and on every subject – a journal which exhibited the foulest instance of political tergiversation that had ever disgraced the press of England – a journal whose talent had served only to enhance the price of its prostitution . . . ?

At the same time, the *Morning Chronicle* could describe the *Morning Post* as 'that slop-pail of corruption'; *The Times* called the *Chronicle* 'that squirt of filthy water'; and the *Morning Journal* regarded the editors of the *Post* and the *Courier* as 'contemptible scribblers . . . who scarcely would be ranked by Linnaeus in the class of Mammalia'. Honours were about even.

The Times may have enjoyed its occasional rough-and-tumble in the gutter. Otherwise, it continued upon its majestic way. Its earlier uncertainties were forgotten: more and more, it was coming to look upon itself as an authority in its own right. It had strongly supported the cause of parliamentary reform: 'Thunder for Reform' – 'The Bill, the whole Bill, and nothing but the Bill'. But very soon it fell out with the Whigs, particularly over the new poor law, which it regarded as an injustice to the poor. Barnes was apparently convinced that the Whigs had lost their enthusiasm for moderate reform. But the split was more general. On 25

June 1834, with characteristic violence, *The Times* lashed out at Palmerston, the Foreign Secretary: 'What an offensive union is that of a dull understanding and an unfeeling heart! Add to this, the self-satisfied airs of a flippant dandy, and you have the most nauseous specimen of humanity – a sort of compound which justifies Swift in the disgusting exhibition of the Yahoos.' Next, it started on Brougham, and Lord Durham wrote: 'What a terrific and bloody attack *The Times* is making on Brougham. Can he survive it, politically or morally? I could not, I know, if I felt myself open to such damning imputations'.

Something would have to be done about *The Times*. As early as 1831 a Colonel Fairman had fervently declared that 'that filthy concern, *The Times*, which spares neither age nor sex, public bodies nor private individuals, which at a less degenerate age would have been burnt by the common hangman, ought to be forthwith checked in its flagitious course of unparelled infamy'. In September 1834 a writer in *Blackwood's Magazine* had argued that an established press was as important as an Established Church for the preservation of the rights of property and the maintenance of order against the efforts of a 'democratic' press to destroy both. In time of war, he went on, the government never hesitated to spend fifteen millions on both the army and the navy; but

> a hundreth part of that sum, judiciously applied, would buy up the whole Press of London, and turn the great majority of the national talent into the defence of order and justice . . . The time, we are persuaded, is not too far distant when a leader in this defensive spiritual militia will rank as high in public estimation, and unquestionably be equal in public importance to a first-rate debater in either House of Parliament, or a victorious commander of our land or sea forces.

The Times was certainly convinced that moves were afoot to destroy the independence of the Press. On 22 December 1834, after the fall of the Whig ministry – a fall to which *The Times* had contributed handsomely – it declared that

> The management of the press was one of the aims of the late Government, and if the attempt had been carried to success, it would have ended in a rotten representation of public opinion, similar to the rotten representation of the people before Parliamentary Reform. There were Gatton and Sarum newspapers – nomination journals . . . A committee regularly organised, an inquisition and secret tribunal, used to hold daily sittings in a Government office, and contrive things for the reward of the servile and the damage of the intractable.

How true this accusation was is not known. But certainly Brougham was not alone in his opinion of *The Times*. Had not Lord Lyndhurst said in 1834: 'Why, Barnes is the most powerful man in the country'? And, according to the *Saturday Review* – admittedly set up to attack the paper in question – 'No apology is necessary for assuming that this country is ruled by *The Times*. We all know it. It is high time we began to realise the magnificent spectacle afforded by British freedom – thirty millions of *cives Romani* governed by a newspaper' (3 November 1835). Brougham himself seems to have believed that the best way to injure *The Times* was to reduce its circulation, by supporting the Radical agitation for the repeal of the so-called 'taxes on knowledge'.

Some progress had already been made in that campaign, mainly to the advantage of *The Times*. All restrictions on the size of newspapers had been removed in 1825, in which same year the stamp duty on supplements containing only advertisements had been lowered to twopence. In 1833 the advertisement duty was reduced from 3s6d to 1s6d (and it had been calculated by Bulwar in 1832 that an advertisement of twenty lines in a London morning newspaper would, if published every day for a year, cost £202 16s – whereas in New York it would have cost only £6 18s8d. There remained the major problem of the stamp tax itself. Undoubtedly the Radicals – and some Whigs – were sincere in their campaign. But one is forced to the conclusion that the reduction in 1836 of the stamp tax from 4d to 1d was not so much motivated by the Whig belief in the diffusion of knowledge, or the Radical conviction that the unrestricted circulation of the printed word would usher in the millenium, as by sheer political expediency: the determination to 'stop *The Times*'. In fact, just as the abandoning of the licensing system in 1695 had been achieved on purely practical and party grounds, and with no enunciation of great principles, so the 1836 Act was primarily political. It was certainly not wanted by the main newspaper proprietors themselves. They had passed on the whole duty of 4d to the public: but they never paid that 4d. They received a discount of 20 per cent intended to cover 'wastage', but the wastage was seldom more than 5 per cent, so that most of the discount represented a sort of hidden bonus for the proprietors. Had they now reduced their price by 3d, they would actually lose a halfpenny on the deal. In fact, they made their new price 5d, instead of the 4d generally expected.

Brougham seems to have been convinced that his policy had succeeded; and the newspaper returns of 1837 did in fact suggest that *The Times* was losing ground, with a circulation of 11,000 against the *Morning Chronicle*'s 9,000. But thereafter *The Times* swept to a position of quite extraordinary dominance. By Barnes's death in 1841 it was selling more than twice as many as the *Chronicle, Herald* and *Morning Post* combined, and by 1850 four times as many. There had never been anything quite like *The Times* before. Britain was becoming the greatest industrial and trading country in the world: and *The Times* spoke for the industrial and mercantile classes. Perhaps never before or since has a newspaper so faithfully reflected the dominant interests of an era. As Lord Clarendon expressed it in 1848:

I don't care a straw what any other newspaper thinks or says.

They are all regarded on the Continent as representing persons or cliques, but *The Times* is considered to be the exponent of what English public opinion is or will be, and as it is thought that whatever public opinion determines with us, the Government ultimately does, an extraordinary and universal importance attaches to the views of *The Times*.

The material basis of *The Times*'s success was provided by the supplements. Three or four times a week the paper produced a supplement, which the 1836 Act taxed at one halfpenny. But this tax was not passed on to the public. *The Times* calculated that so long as the number of advertisements balanced the cost of printing, paper and taxation, it would pay to present the supplement free. Competitors were more or less correct in their opinion that, as the advertising rates then were, the supplements were in themselves uneconomic. But they *did* pay in circulation, if not in advertising profit. The other newspaper proprietors sought instead to reduce their price. In June 1846 the *Daily News* dropped its price from 5d to 2½d and managed to increase its circulation from 4,000 to over 20,000 – though it was mocked by *The Times* as the 'twopenny halfpenny paper'. In fact, its price was too low, and it was soon in financial difficulties. In 1847 the *Morning Chronicle* reduced its price to 4d, but still fell behind, returning to 5d in 1848. *The Times* sailed on regardless: its circulation in February 1848 was 30,000, and it made no effort to increase that circulation – which, according to Mowbray Morris, the manager appointed by John Walter II, could have been doubled in two years. Nor did *The Times* attempt to increase its advertising. In fact, after 1850, the paper stayed aloof from such mundane matters. As John Walter III saw it, the paper could not be improved.

In terms of prestige it was the only paper. Its circulation – and, more important, the *quality* of its circulation – made its support vital to politicians. In 1839, it had backed another winner, when it supported the Anti-Corn Law League. Under J. T. Delane, the editor after 1841, its influence in high circles grew, statesmen, for reasons of their own, supplied it with highly confidential information, and so contributed to its reputation for omniscience. The sheer power of *The Times* was admirably displayed in 1851, when the paper attacked Louis Napoleon, much to the irritation of that sovereign. But his ambassador was obliged to report to him:

Someone has told you, Prince, that the hostility of *The Times* and the *Morning Chronicle* was provoked by pecuniary subsidies. Nothing could be more false than such an assertion and believe me, on such an important subject I would not make a statement without being absolutely certain. It is possible that third-class papers like the *Sun*, *Standard*, etc. etc. might be purchased. But the enterprise of *The Times* and *Morning Chronicle* are backed by too big capital, their political management is in too many hands, for it to be possible to buy them for any price whatsoever . . .

The prosperity of *The Times* is founded on its very large number of readers, who give it more advertisements than to any other newspaper. Moreover, it is an axiom among the founders of this paper that to retain a great number of readers one must anticipate public opinion, keep it alive, animate it, but never break a lance against it and give way every time it declares itself in any direction and even when it changes its attitude to change with it . . .

Although less than in France, political men in England are sufficiently anxious about newspaper criticism to have tried often to buy an organ so widely circulated as *The Times*: but they have always failed. Sometimes by personal influence, positions, and other baits, men have succeeded in influencing its policy, but with money, never . . .

I know very well that some newspaper editors, among others even the editor of the *Morning Post*, complain continually that *The Times* is venal; but venal in the sense that it has no political convictions, thinks only of shop, is not influenced either by the country's interests or the desire to impose its own opinions, but merely by what it considers profitable to its own business; yes, doubtless! But venal in the sense that its policy can be influenced with money, that is absolutely false.

As a summing up of the general attitude of *The Times*, this report could hardly be bettered. Louis Napoleon seems to have considered bribery. He then turned to threats, and tried to frighten the English government into some sort of action to restrain *The Times*. The whole matter came up in Parliament, where Lord Derby brought up the old problem of the independence of the press – and its responsibilities:

If, as in these days, the press aspires to exercise the influence of statesmen, the press should remember that they are not free from the corresponding responsibility of statesmen, and that it is incumbent on them, as a sacred duty, to maintain that tone of moderation and respect even in expressing frankly their opinions on foreign affairs which would be required of every man who pretends to guide public opinion.

In reply, *The Times* simply published a clear and defiant statement of its right to criticise heads of state, ministers and politicians without any qualifications whatsoever.

In fact, a new power had entered politics – and a potentially dangerous one. As Croker wrote to Brougham on 21 July 1854, 'There has grown up, and is still growing, an influence over the conduct of ministers so imperious that the Speaker, instead of demanding from the Sovereign freedom of speech had much better ask it from *The Times*'.

'Our most secret decisions are made public . . . somehow or other this evil should be corrected', complained Aberdeen in February 1854, and Lord John Russell wrote to the Queen that 'the degree of information possessed by *The Times* with regard to the most secret affairs of State is mortifying, humiliating and incomprehensible'. It was recognised by friend and foe alike that *The Times* could make and unmake governments. It had revealed that power in the Crimean War, when the paper probably reached its zenith. Its enemies charged it with having largely caused that war. During the course of the war, it had destroyed a ministry, forced the removal of a Commander-in-Chief, and aroused public opinion to the need for a thorough overhaul not only of the army medical services but of the army as a whole. The reports of its war correspondent, W. H. Russell, particularly with regard to Florence Nightingale, had brought war home to the people more vividly than ever before. Indeed, the information published in *The Times* was so detailed that a British official complained that 'our spies give us all manner of reports, while the enemy never spends a farthing for information. He gets it all for 5d. from a London newspaper'.

The Times had attained an extraordinary – and frightening – eminence. As Francis Williams has so aptly explained,

This eminence did not leave its controllers unscathed: they were no more immune than modern press lords from the corrupting influence of their own sense of power. Egomania is an occupational hazard to successful newspapermen. They did not escape it. They came to regard *The Times* as so much superior to all other human institutions as to be above criticism even when it was wrong; subject to none of the common obligations to justify itself by facts.

When Mowbray Morris was called before a committee of the House of Commons to substantiate insinuations published by *The Times* that all the Irish Members were in receipt of bribes, he acted very much like the editor of a modern tabloid called before the Press Council. The press – or at any rate *The Times* – had, he indicated, the right to do whatever it chose and was required to explain to no one. He was asked if he extended his idea of the privilege of the press to facts as well as to opinions. He replied briefly, 'To everything whatever'. To the question whether he was willing to offer any explanation or justification of the charges brought against the Irish Members, he answered shortly, 'I am not'. After which, as the *Manchester Guardian*, then a bi-weekly, but a vigorous one, commented, 'The gentleman bowed, retired, and went home to dinner, convinced no doubt that the Czar of Russia, the Member for Bucks [Disraeli] and *The Times* newspaper can defy the whole of mankind'.

The power of *The Times* may perhaps have been exaggerated by contemporaries: but they were remarkably unanimous as to the danger. Lord John Russell, on his resignation, commented that, 'for me who have had my full feast of office, it does not much matter, but if England is ever to be England again, this vile tyranny of *The Times* must be cut off'.

Once again, something would have to be done about *The Times*, and something more drastic than Queen Victoria's solution that 'the Editor, the Proprietor and the Writers of such execrable publications' should be ostracized from the circles of 'higher society'. But what could be done? *The Times* had won its supremacy largely because of the business ability of its proprietors and the genius of such editors as Barnes and Delane. It had won its position in fair competition. It had shown considerable enterprise in making use of the most up-to-date services, with forwarding agents at Alexandria and Malta, and permanent agents in Marseilles and Boulogne. The overland mail under Delane cost £10,000 a year. On the domestic front, *The Times* might be a supporter of the established order, and suspicious of all forms of radicalism. Yet, at the same time, it was acutely aware of the 'Condition of England' question and of the various social and economic evils: and it urged humanitarian reforms. It had mounted a major campaign against the new poor law of the Whigs; it even showed sympathy for Chartist agitators transported for their protests; and it ran many columns from special correspondents concerning the ill-treatment and flogging of pauper girls in work-houses. And even in its most majestic period, it could rarely be called dull or stuffy. Its issue of 2 January 1841 contained a Homeric crime report from Mansion House:

> Matilda Stratford, a woman of great strength of body, was brought before the Lord Mayor, charged with having beaten a man, and also with having, upon being taken into custody, whopped some policemen, and broken several panes of glass.
>
> The prisoner, who was said to have fought several men at different times, swaggered up to the bar as if she feared no man, and displayed an awful clenched fist. The complainant said that, without receiving the slightest provocation, the virago attacked him. 'Mind your eye, old fellow', said she, and in an instant gave him a straightforward pelt between the eyes. She then tore his coat and shirt, and when the policemen were called to his assistance she turned upon them and fastened upon them like a tiger. The policemen said that the woman had been frequently charged with having assaulted men, women, and children. When she was tipsy, she did not care how many were opposed to her.
>
> The Lord Mayor – Why, Matilda, this is a very bad account that I hear of you.
>
> Prisoner – It is, indeed, my Lord.
>
> The Lord Mayor – What can you say for yourself?
>
> Prisoner – I'm blest if I remember anything about it.

> The Lord Mayor – What! you were so much intoxicated
> that you forget what happened?
> Prisoner – Just so, please your Lordship. Wasn't I
> precious lumpy! But it is all the fault of the
> new year.
> The Lord Mayor – Well, you shall begin the new year
> at the treadmill.

And *The Times* could seldom resist the temptation to descend from its lofty pedestal to join in the rough-and-tumble of the newspaper wars of the period. Macaulay it called 'Mr Babbletongue . . . hardly fit to fill up one of the vacancies that have occurred by the lamentable death of Her Majesty's two favourite monkeys'. Its review of Brougham's *The Oration of Demosthenes upon the Crown. Translated into English, with Notes* was possibly the longest ever given to a book in any newspaper, being spread over half-a-dozen issues. According to *The Times* 'there is not one single page in the two hundred and sixteen pages, in which there are not, on an average, three or four blunders, which would be unpardonable even in a stripling of fourteen . . . foul, wallowing, boisterous and un-English.'

The other daily papers were outshone by *The Times*, but they remained important. The *Morning Chronicle*, with a circulation in 1850 of only 3,000, had considerable political influence. The *Morning Post* was still a force in the country, mainly because of the excellence of its reports of the debates in Parliament. Unfortunately, it had a gift for supporting the losing side. It had opposed parliamentary reform in 1832, declaring that 'no Minister will ever be able to manage a democratic House of Commons'; later, the last battle for Protection was fought in its columns. It saw itself always as the champion of Protestantism, especially in Ireland. And it deeply distrusted the trade union movement. Nevertheless, its conservatism did not stop it supporting Ashley's factory legislation. And it displayed a fiercely independent attitude in 1852, when the Derby government sought to transform it into an avowed Tory newspaper. Algernon Borthwick, the editor's son, to whom overtures had been made, declared that 'I would not defend your Malmesbury, Derbys, Walpoles, etc. at any price, as a mere hired organ bound to praise their stupidities as well as their well-doings. It is our independence and our late attacks upon several members of Government that have made them feel our value'. His father would not entertain the idea of publishing ministerial handouts without the right to rewrite them. 'We cannot', he said, 'on such terms, or indeed on any other, sacrifice that independence of party, and that strong adherence to principle which constitutes the character and the chief value of a newspaper.' Like *The Times*, but perhaps for a different reason, it was adamant on the necessity of independence. In this way *The Times* influenced the other major newspapers. In much the same way they were forced to try to compete in the technical field. Great emphasis was placed on foreign news, and the rivalry was fierce to get the latest information, as a report in the *Hampshire*

Advertiser of the reporters awaiting the arrival of the packet-boats shows:

> A few persons who, if it be a winter night, would scarcely be
> recognisable, disguised as they appear to be in greatcoats,
> comforters, and every kind of waterproof covering for the head,
> feet, and body. These persons are the outport Newspaper
> agents. They make for the head of the quay, and each jumps
> into a small yacht, which instantly darts from the shore . . .
> Cold, dark and cheerless as it may be, the excitement on board
> the yachts is very great in calculating which will reach the
> steamer first, and at no regatta is there more nautical science
> displayed . . . While making for the shore, sometimes in the
> most tempestuous weather, perhaps the rain peppering down,
> and the wind blowing great guns, or thunder and lightning
> over head, the foreign journals are hastily examined by means
> of a lantern, similar to that used by Policemen, the most
> important items of foreign News which they contain are
> immediately detected, and the form in which they must be
> transmitted to London arranged in the mind. The agents are
> landed as near as possible to the electric telegraph office,
> sometimes on the shoulders of their boatmen through the surf
> or mud. They arrive at the telegraph office, and to write down
> their messages is the work of a few minutes only . . . Before a
> foreign mail packet comes alongside the Southampton dock
> wall hundreds of persons in London, eighty miles distant, are
> reading from the public journals with breathless interest the
> news she has brought . . . The news has affected the public
> funds, and induced numbers to risk the acquisition and loss of
> whole fortunes.

But perhaps even more significant developments were taking place
in other fields. *The Times* was undoubtedly the greatest newspaper of
them all, and it has become customary to think of it as the characteristic
paper of the period. But it must always be remembered that the most
widely read papers were the Sunday papers – and that if we are to
examine the actual culture of the period, we must start with this basic
fact. Whereas by the end of the 1840s it has been estimated that the total
circulation of the London daily newspapers was 60,000, the Sunday papers –
the *Dispatch, Chronicle, Lloyd's Weekly, News of the World*, and their rivals –
was 270,000.[4] At the same time, there had been a renewed growth of periodicals combining sensational and romantic fiction with recipes, household
hints, and advice to correspondents – mostly at a more 'popular' level
than the 'popular education' journals of the previous decade, and
learning from their mistakes. If we are to understand the emotional and
intellectual temper of more than a very modest number of the British
public, the works of Reynolds and *Eliza Cook's Journal* are more
important than *The Times*.

To turn from the newspapers proper to periodicals and magazines is to confront a mass of material so wide in its appeal and so overwhelming in its sheer quantity as to defy description, let alone classification. At the bottom of the pile, from the point of view of respectability, were such journals as *Paul Pry*, the *Town* and the *Age*. All professed a moral purpose. The declared aim of *Paul Pry* in 1856 was to 'strip society of its baseness and hollow cant' – which it proposed to do by studying the 'Gay Women of London . . . their history, habits and haunts . . . the mode of life, income, supporters and connexions of the Children of Night . . . together with sketches of brothels and brothel-keepers, pimps, fancy men, bullies and decoys, interspersed with recondite anecdotes of love, seduction and prostitution'.[5] All advertised pornographic books. The *Town* offered a particularly fine selection, despite some doubts as to who had written what:

> *Tales of Twilight: or, Entre Chien et Loup*; containing the adventures and intrigues of a company of ladies prior to their marriage, as related by themselves; showing the deceits practised upon men, by the artful, the prudent, the modest, and demure. By Madame la Comtesse de Choiseul-meuse, authoress of *Julia, or I've saved my Rose, Amelia St. Far or the Fatal Error, Eugenia, or where is the woman who wouldn't?* etc. etc. Translated from the French, and illustrated with eight fine engravings coloured.
> *Julia: or I have saved my Rose:* Being the Amorous History of a Young Lady of ardent imagination; who, amidst the voluptuous temptations to gratify the sensual passions, succeeds in preserving her Maidenhead from destruction. By Madame H——, and authoress of *Amelia St. Far, or the Fatal Error, Tales of Twilight*, etc. etc. A new edition, containing eight fine Plates. Price 10s.6d. *Onanism Unveiled, or the Private Pleasures and Practices of the Youth of both Sexes*, in all their branches, showing its insidious progress and prevalence among schools, particularly female, pointing out the fatality that invariably attends its victims; developing the symptoms, the cause of the disease, the means of cure, as regards simple gonorrhoea, etc. Translated from the last edition in French of the celebrated M. Tissot, and illustrated with a fine engraving presenting the awful consequences of this revolting habit. 3s.6d.
> *Sainfroid and Eulalia*; or the intrigues and amours of Sainfroid, a Jesuit, and Eulalia, a Nun, developing the gradual and imperceptible progress of Seduction of a highly educated Young Lady, who became, by the foulest sophistry and treachery, the victim of debauchery and libertinism. Translated from the French and illustrated with beautiful plates. Price 5s.6d.[6]

All specialised in epigrams and poems of an extremely dubious type. By and large, they survived only as scandal and blackmailing sheets – and all were periodically charged with libel.

At a somewhat higher moral – if not always literary – level were popular periodicals to feed the interests of a public just above the level of literacy. And here the problem of classification becomes immense. The dividing line between what might be called a newspaper and a periodical emphasising sensational fiction was often very nebulous indeed, as the encyclopaedic title of *Bell's Penny Dispatch, Sporting and Police Gazette, and Newspaper of Romance* would suggest. The exact number of newspapers and periodicals will probably never be known, despite the heroic efforts of that pioneer in newspaper handlists, *The Times Tercentenary Handlist of English and Welsh Newspapers, Magazines and Reviews* (1920), and the later work of H. G. Pollard and W. Graham in *The Cambridge Bibliography of English Literature* (1941). According to Charles Knight, the number of weekly periodicals (not newspapers) issued in London on a Saturday in 1846 was about seventy-three.[7] They comprised two literary papers, twelve economic and social journals, fourteen penny and halfpenny magazines, three tracts, five musicals, and thirty-seven weekly sheets forming separate books. Of these, the weekly sale of the most important amounted to almost 400,000 copies. The *London Journal* stated that 227 *monthly* periodical works were sent out on the last day of July 1846 to every corner of the kingdom. In addition, there were thirty-eight quarterlies.

As Dodds remarks, merely to list some of the titles at random is instructive. His list includes: *The Almanac of the Month: a Review of Everything and Everybody*; *The Annals of Philosophical Discovery and Monthly Reporter of the Progress of Practical Science*; *The Builder*; *The Cricketer's Companion*; *The Electrical Magazine*; *The Friend of the African*; *The Gas Gazette*; *The Teetotal Times*; *Journal of the Working Classes*; *The Family Journal of Useful Knowledge* . . . And there were scores of others, catering for every conceivable taste. At the top stood the well-established quarterlies, well edited, well written, and ranging over every field of culture. The greatest was probably *The Edinburgh Review or Critical Journal*, begun in 1802, and associated with such eminent names as Sydney Smith, Macaulay and Brougham. Then came the *Quarterly Review* of 1809, with its own galaxy of stars – William Gifford, Coleridge, Sir Walter Scott – followed by *The Westminster Review* of 1824, with John Stuart Mill and George Eliot. Their high quality limited their circulation, as did their price: few people could afford to spend six shillings on a single magazine. In their heyday, both the *Edinburgh Review* and the *Quarterly* had sold some 13,000 copies; by 1841, the first was down to 7,000, while the *Quarterly* claimed 8,500. The reason for their decline – a decline in circulation, but certainly not in influence – was the increasing competition from weekly reviews and from new monthly magazines, many of excellent quality, but somewhat lighter in tone, and cheaper. Among the weeklies might be mentioned *The Athenaeum* (1828) and *Notes and Queries* (1849); the monthlies included *Fraser's Magazine*, established in 1830, with Carlyle, Charles Kingsley, Ainsworth and Thackeray among its contributors; *Bentley's Miscellany* (1837–68), with Dickens and Ainsworth; *Tait's Edinburgh Monthly Magazine* (1834–61), with De

Quincey, Leigh Hunt, J. S. Mill, Cobden and Bright; and *The Edinburgh Monthly Magazine*, better known as *Blackwood's*, which began its long career in 1817. Most cost 2s6d a month. They were intended for the drawing-rooms and libraries of the well-to-do.

As might be expected, religious magazines were exceedingly numerous. As many were heavily subsidised, they flourished accordingly. In 1854 they included *The Record* (Anglican, 1818), *The Patriot* (Nonconformist, 1832), *The Watchman* (Wesleyan, 1835), *The Tablet* (Roman Catholic, 1840), *The Nonconformist* (1841), *The Jewish Chronicle* (1841), *The English Churchman* (1843), and many others. Even the Mormons had their periodical, *The Latter-Day Saints' Millennial Star*, established in 1840, and with a circulation of 22,000 in 1851. As was also to be expected in this age of increasing technological advance, the number of technical journals increased rapidly. Few interests were not catered for: there were *The Lancet*, *The Mechanic's Magazine*, *The Repertory of Patent Inventions, and other Discoveries in Arts, Manufactures and Agriculture*. The sheer variety is amazing. Obviously, many had a restricted circulation: they were either expensive, or highly specialised in their appeal. But what were the great majority of the people reading? There were still working-class papers urging radical reform, and Chartism naturally produced its newspapers. But these were mainly in the Midlands and North, and centred round Feargus O'Connor's *Northern Star and Leeds General Advertiser*. Otherwise there would seem to have been a distinct lull in radical journalism, and the 1840s were the period of the 'family magazine', made up of pious reflections, practical household hints, and informative articles, with a leavening of fiction and poetry. The basic philosophy behind many of the family magazines was once again that of teaching the poor to be happy with their lot. They must accept without question the condition into which they had been born. To be poor was not a crime (although the practical attitudes towards the poor might often suggest so): it was an estate marked out by divine providence. As Wilberforce expressed it,

> The more lowly path of the poor has been allotted to them by the hand of God . . . it is their part faithfully to discharge its duties and contentedly to bear its inconveniences . . . if their superiors enjoy more abundant comforts, they are also exposed to many temptations from which the inferior classes are happily exempted.

Rewards would, hopefully, follow in the life hereafter. The emphasis was on *work*, with thrift, sobriety and piety the principal virtues, at least for the 'industrious classes'. It is easy to be cynical about this approach, which was very much in line with the interests of the prevailing class society. But there is no doubting the complete sincerity of men like Wilberforce, and the very success of the family magazines suggests that such sentiments were generally shared.

The Family Economist: a Penny Monthly Magazine, begun in 1848, perhaps summed up the general approach. It was to be devoted 'to the Moral, Physical and Domestic Improvement of the Industrious Classes', and its frontispiece portrayed a contented industrious family surrounded by such slogans as 'Education is Second Nature', and 'Labour rids us of Three Great Evils, Irksomeness, Vice and Poverty'. Another very popular paper of this type was *The Family Herald* of 1843, with the subtitle, 'Useful Information and Amusement for the Million'. Its sixteen large quarto pages cost only one penny weekly. The contents of its first issue set the pattern for years to come. There were two stories, a 'Weekly Calendar', 'Natural History No. I', 'Industry and the various modes of rewarding it', 'Family Matters', 'Letters from Aunt Peggy to her Niece', some good advice on the respective duties of wife and husband, verse, riddles, puzzles, and 'Random Readings'. The mixture was apparently successful, and in 1844 the paper was boasting that it was 'extensively circulated . . . it is extremely gratifying to us to learn that the volume is likely to be placed on the shelves of both the rich and the poor' (4 May 1844). Its motto was still 'Interesting to all – Offensive to none'. In 1849 appeared *Eliza Cook's Journal*, price 1½d – a remarkable success, having a circulation of between 50,000 and 60,000 within a few years; its homespun verse apparently provided the sort of inspiration many of the public wanted, and behind it was the typical approach of the period:

> Many an enlightened intellect, many a sensitive spirit, is bound to a wheel of grinding poverty, bitterly restricted in sympathies and hopes, yet wearing the mien and manner of elevated content . . . and a strong lesson it is, when we see a mind and soul of Nature's finest workmanship take the scanty pittance doled out to them by Fortune, and bravely, humanely, and cheerfully 'make the best of it' . . . Let us . . . emulate the example of a Divine Teacher, and 'make the best of it'.

The audience lapped it up. According to *Reynolds's Magazine* of 13 February 1847, 'Miss Eliza Cook is, *par excellence*, our national poetess. The sweet simplicity – touching pathos – and natural truthfulness of her compositions appeal to every heart.' Apart from her own effusions, the first issue of the *Journal* included a story entitled 'Three Hyacinths from Heaven' and 'Lessons for Little Ones', by Peter Parley, who candidly admitted that 'everyone knows that Peter Parley likes to blend the useful with the instructive; that when he writes a story it is always with a moral aim; that when he writes a book he always has in view to make his little readers *better* as well as wiser'.

The same note was struck again and again, although not always, fortunately, with the somewhat sickening sentimentality of *Eliza Cook's Journal*. In 1850 John Cassell launched *The Working Man's Friend and Family Instructor* as a penny weekly, with the announcement that 'This sort of journal is wanted at the fireside of the Working Man, to improve his evening after a day of toil. Our object has been that of instruction rather than of mere amusement.' But the lesson of the past had been learned – few readers wanted instruction pure and not-so-simple – and the *Working Man's Friend* included stories as well as its heavier material. Another magazine which succeeded better than most in combining edification and amusement was *Howitt's Journal*, begun in January 1847. It rapidly won a reputation in the field of cheap but well written periodicals, and at its height had a circulation of 25,000. It took a keen interest in cooperative movements and the efforts of the working classes to improve themselves by education, but it never allowed such interests to become an obsession, and carefully diluted its serious content with woodcuts and light entertainment.

Perhaps the best-known of all these periodicals was Dickens's *Household Words*. Its first issue, on Saturday 30 March 1850, price twopence, declared that

> in the Bosoms of the young and old, of the well-to-do and of the poor, we would tenderly cherish that light of Fancy, which is inherent in the human breast . . . To show to all, that in all familiar things, even in those which are repellent on the surface, there is Romance enough, if we would find it out.

The moral aim remained, but the touch was lighter. It was a family magazine aimed at all ages and both sexes; the stories were often heart-rending, but humour was never lost sight of; nor was the social purpose behind the publication, and features about such problems as the water supply, cruelty to animals, life in the mills and conditions in the workhouses appeared regularly.

The great difficulty, as always, was the blending of instruction and entertainment into an attractive whole. Many potential readers were antagonised by the blatant didactic approach of many of the 'family' magazines. And many on the fringe of literacy wanted not so much to keep up with the world as to escape from it. They wanted adventure and excitement – something *different*. Even Dickens was too heavy for them. They turned to the indefatigable Reynolds, and to Lloyd, whose *Penny Sunday Times, and People's Police Gazette*, begun in 1840, was to be the parent of a whole host of weekly papers. At first his emphasis was on news, but he soon branched out. In September 1841 he produced a *Companion to the Penny Sunday Times*, which purchasers of that paper received free. The *Companion* consisted solely of fiction – a serial, 'The Miller's Maid', and such stories as 'Blanch: or, The Fearful Mystery of the Doomed House', 'The Saucy Hell-cat and the Indiaman, by a Bluejacket', and 'Ansalmo the Accursed, or the Skeleton Hand'. All were illustrated; but, although the gore was plentiful enough, the emphasis was mainly upon what might be called good clean fun.

Even more important developments were to come. Many printers had made use of woodcuts to illustrate stories and general items, but none of the major newspapers seems to have realised the force and impact of this approach. In 1842, one Herbert Ingram decided to start a journal which would be totally dependent on illustrations – an idea without precedent at the time. The first issue of his *Illustrated London News* was delayed so that it could cover the Queen's fancy dress ball at Buckingham Palace. At the last minute came news of a great fire in Hamburg. Ingram sent to the British Museum for a print of Hamburg, from which his artists rapidly prepared the required illustrations, adding flames, smoke, and crowds of sightseers. To readers brought up on the tiny eye-crippling text of Victorian newspapers, the *News* was a revelation. The first issue was a sell-out of 26,000 copies. In ten years, the circulation reached 150,000, and it continued to grow, hitting a new record in 1863 when its special issue marking the wedding of the Prince of Wales sold no less than 310,000. In fact, the paper quickly became part of the social fabric: the country might listen to *The Thunderer*, but it looked at the *Illustrated London News*.[8]

A new era in journalism had dawned – helped, of course, by technical advances. Paddle-steamers and railways were making travel vastly easier and faster than ever before. News came in from distant parts of the world in times that appeared unbelievable. The first issue of the *Illustrated London News* included reports from New York brought across the Atlantic by Brunel's 'Great Western' in twelve and a half days. The second issue started with an account of the overland mail route from India – reduced to sixty days in 1836, and then to as little as thirty days and ten hours in 1841. Spurred on by Ingram's obvious success, Lloyd launched his own *Lloyd's Illustrated London Newspaper* on Sunday, 27 November 1842, price twopence. By 11 December he claimed that 'this cheap Journal has already reached a circulation of 100,000, consequently giving it an advantage over any other of the present day. The country circulation is 35,000, which we send by Saturday's post, and upwards of 65,000 are sold in London on Sunday.' But Lloyd was tireless. His *Illustrated London Newspaper* of 27 November 1842 announced the forthcoming appearance of a 'New Work – Sixteen Large Quarto Pages for One Penny!!! *Lloyd's Penny Atlas and Weekly Register of Novel Entertainment*', with the emphasis on what he called three continuous romances. This announcement was repeated on 11 December, together with an illuminating list of Lloyd's other ventures:

> *Lloyd's Penny Weekly Miscellany*, each Number containing Sixteen Large Quarto Pages of closely-printed original matter, consisting of Tales, Romances, Etc. of sterling merit, by celebrated Authors, and may justly be called The Wonder of the Age.
>
> The Largest, The Cheapest and The Best Family Paper is *Lloyd's Penny Sunday Times and Police Gazette*. – This Cheap Colossus of the press is allowed to be the most useful, amusing, and instructive Journal in existence, and enjoys a circulation unprecedented in the annals of literature. In its columns are to be found something to please every taste, and nothing that can offend the most fastidious is ever admitted .

> . . . The Weekly Sale of this Extraordinary Paper is *Ninety-Five Thousand!* . . .
>
> > *Lloyd's Companion to the Penny Sunday Times*; which, next to its predecessor, is universally admitted to be the best paper published as it contains more original Tales, Romances, Etc. Etc. . . . than all the cheap periodicals of the day combined.

Lloyd was obviously proud of his productions, and, despite his stress on fiction and illustrations, never lost sight of his avowed moral purpose. The first issue of his *Penny Atlas* emphasised this:

> True morality – sound reasoning – and exalted sentiments may be more easily, more effectively, and more pleasantly conveyed to the mind through the medium of works of fiction than by any other means . . . We have ever found, in our intercourse with our readers, that those fictions in which the innocent – although environed by snares, and nearly brought to destruction by the wicked and designing, ultimately triumphed, and proved the goodness of right over might, were welcomed and read with delight. Can there be a more convincing proof of the ennobling power of Romance, if it be directed in the proper channel? . . . Hence we punish and confound the vicious – hence we defend, applaud, and bring off victorious, the innocent, dealing a poetical, and in our innermost hearts believe, a practical justice upon evil doers.

Lloyd seems to have got away with his exciting and gruesome woodcuts and his stories of vampires and hunchbacks, cannibalism and murder – probably banned from respectable houses, but still immensely popular. His many rivals were not so fortunate. *The Weekly Dispatch* had its own correspondents overseas and claimed a circulation of 60,000 as early as 1843, but it tended to emphasise 'police news'; according to *The Illustrated London News*, 'it is essentially the organ of the crime districts of England, and its circulation will always be proportional to the existing amount of depravity in the land. It keeps its venom well set in the teeth of society.' Singled out for special attention was the *London Journal*, which had a circulation of 100,000 when it achieved the distinction of a mention in the Select Committee on Public Libraries in 1849. There was no open indecency, but witnesses were inclined to think that such penny publications had 'perhaps a worse tendency than books positively indecent or immoral'[9], the argument being that the latter were at least open in their evil designs, and were also too expensive for the poor to buy. To superior intellects the popular periodicals may well have presented a somewhat frightening indication of what the popular mind fed upon; the same problem remains today. But it is difficult to agree with the *Spectator*, a quality journal, that

> If posterity judge of the present age by its newspapers, they will form a rare opinion of it . . . Among the news, the rascalities of

life occupy a most disproportionate space. The steady unobtrusive exercise of the domestic virtues . . . is the commonplace of life, and affords no salient points to the news-caterers. But the adventures of Lord Huntingtower and the swindling leeches who clung to him . . . the will-forgeries, poisonings, adulteries, stabbing of sheep by clergymen, etc. – these fill up the news-columns as attractively as their dramatized versions do the minor theatres. The rottenness of life is sought out by the newsmongers as the rottenness of cheese is by the epicure.

The newspapers and periodicals so far mentioned merely touch the surface of the fantastically assorted reading matter offered to the public. One might mention *Punch*, which began its long career on Saturday, 17 July 1841. Its humour was then surprisingly broad, it was full of frightful puns, and it had a pronounced social and humanitarian policy. The Duke of Wellington's statement that in 1841 England was 'the only country in which the poor man, if only sober and industrious, was quite certain of acquiring a competency', *Punch* branded as 'a heartless insult thrown in the idle teeth of famishing thousands'. In its Christmas issue of 1841, it published Hood's 'Song of the Shirt'; and it regularly denounced harsh sentences for juveniles, flogging in schools and in the army, and the treatment of destitution as a crime. Religious publications remained enormously popular – and one reason for the unpopularity in respectable households of *The Weekly Dispatch* was its anti-Church bias, but there was room in 1840 for a periodical whose sole policy that was: *The Parochial Expositor: Or, Anti-Church and Rate-Payers' Gazette*. This consisted of savage attacks on 'parish plunder', 'parish jobbery' and the 'misapplication of charity funds'. It was also libellous in that it printed the names of those accused of cruelty and swindling, and it is hardly surprising that its second issue, 1 October 1840, was headed 'Diabolical Threats to Intimidate and Assassinate the Author'. Very different was the *Colonial Intelligencer; or, the Aborigine's Friend* of 1847, the organ of a typical Victorian institution, the Aborigine's Protection Society, and devoted to the evils of imperialism. 'The history of discovery and colonisation', it declared, 'is a history of crime, fraud, and blood-guiltiness.' Rather wider in its appeal was a new penny Sunday paper in 1851, *Everybody. A Weekly Budget of Everything*. Finally, in the true tradition of the *Terrific Register* was another Sunday newspaper, *Death Warrant*, launched on 20 January 1840, price three-halfpence, which proposed to offer a

Reprinted Record of Facts – compiled from authentic sources, of the most dreadful Battles by Sea and Land; Horrible and Mysterious Murders and Suicides, Plagues, Pestilences, Famines, Earthquakes, Storms, Shipwrecks, Conflagrations, Death-Beds, and every other appalling Calamity incidental to the Life of Man . . . exceeding in intensity and agonizing interest, any work ever published; showing how Man is dazzled and betrayed by the Vanities of the World, and that the real occurrences of this life far surpass, in an Extraordinary degree, any Events which can possibly be depicted in the pages of Fiction and Romance.

True to type, it went on,

The Death Warrant will achieve for the People a Grand Moral Lesson, it will inevitably strike Terror into the Hearts and Minds of Thousands, and bring back to their Memories the too often forgotten but solemn admonition, 'In the Midst of Life we are in Death'.

That moral message was reinforced by a cheering woodcut in heavy black of a skeleton, with, above it, the words, 'A Check to Pride and Vanity', and below, 'My Turn Today, Tomorrow Your's also'.

Who read these orgies of sensationalism and their more sober 'family' competitors? Fortunately, a contemporary record is available, in a series of articles sponsored by Henry Mayhew in 1849–50 on 'Labour and the Poor', for the *Morning Chronicle*. His sixth letter reported on the reading habits of Manchester operatives: 'every London publisher knows that Manchester furnishes no unimportant part of the literary market of England. I was very desirous of ascertaining, therefore, the species of works most in demand amongst the labouring and poorer clases.' He applied to Abel Heywood, the most enterprising bookseller in the area. According to Mayhew, 'that species of novel, adorned with woodcuts, and published in penny weekly numbers, claims the foremost place. The contents of these productions are, generally speaking, utterly beneath criticism.' The average sale of what he rather unkindly calls 'weekly instalments of trash . . . literary garbage' (mainly published by Lloyd) was 6,000.

Of the penny weekly journals [he went on], some of them, such as *Barker's People*, political and democratic, but the greatest number social and instructive, the Lancashire sale is:

Barker's People	22,000
Reynold's Miscellany	3,700
Illustrated Family Journal	700
London Journal	9,000
Family Herald	8,000
Home Circle	1,000
Penny Sunday Times	1,000
Lancashire Beacon	3,000
Plain Speaker	200
Potter's Examiner	1,500
Penny Punch	360
The Reasoner	150
Chat	200

Of these publications, the *Lancashire Beacon* and the *Reasoner* are avowedly infidel . . .

Of the better class of weekly publications, generally selling at three halfpence, Mr Heywood makes the following returns:

Domestic Journal	600
Eliza Cook's Journal	1,250
Chamber's Journal	900
Chamber's Information	
For the People	1,200
Hogg's Instructor	60
People's Journal	460.

The sale of *Punch* is 1,200. The *Family Friend* sells 1,500 monthly at 2d; The *Family Economist* 5,000 monthly, at one penny . . .

In answer to enquiries as to whether he could apportion particular classes of books to particular classes of readers, Mr Heywood replied that the comic or quasi-comic tales, and humorous publications, were principally bought by shopmen and clerks; that the school of the monstrous novels, and the more rabid democratic papers, supplied the literary thirst of the mass of the operatives, and that the better weekly publications were taken by the superior classes of the work-people. The women were terribly fond of mixed love and raw-head-and-bloody-bones stories.

Clearly there had been a tremendous expansion in sheer *output*. Technical advances were important. The Fourdrinier paper machine and the Cowper and Applegarth cylinder press created something of a revolution in printing. With manual labour, no matter how efficient, impressions of 50,000 to 80,000 could not be put out, but in 1835 a foreign visitor watched with amazement twenty steam presses turning out the *Penny Magazine*, each at 1,000 sheets an hour. There remained the problem of distribution – a development assisted by the spread of the railway and the reform of the Post Office. This problem inspired *Household Words* in its first issue (30 March 1850) to produce an article on 'Valentine's Day at the Post Office':

It blew, rained, hailed, snowed newspapers. A fountain of newspapers played in at the window. Waterspouts of newspapers broke from enormous sacks, and engulphed the men inside. A prodigious main of newspapers, at the Newspaper River Head, seemed to be turned on, threatening destruction to the miserable Post Office. The Post Office was so full already, that the window foamed at the mouth with newspapers. Newspapers flew out like froth . . . All the boys in London seemed to have gone mad, and to be besieging the Post Office with newspapers . . .

But what chaos within! Men up to their knees in

newspapers on great platforms; men gardening among newspapers with rakes; men digging and delving among newspapers as if a new description of rock had been blasted into these fragments; men going up and down a gigantic trap – an ascending and descending-room worked by a steam-engine – still taking them nothing but newspapers! All the history of the time, all the chronicled births and deaths and marriages, all the crimes, all the accidents, all the vanities, all the changes, all the realities, of all the civilised earth, heaped up, parcelled out, carried about, knocked down, cut, shuffled, dealt, played, gathered up again, and passed from hand to hand in an apparently interminable and hopeless confusion, but really in a system of admirable order, certainty, and simplicity, pursued six nights every week, all through the rolling year!

In a later article (1 June 1850) Dickens produced figures to support his vivid account. In 1848, as many as 64,476,708 stamps had been issued to the 150 London and 238 provincial newspapers; 7,497,064 to the 97 Scottish papers; and 7,028,956 to the 117 Irish. He pointed out that in 1809, only 29½ million stamps had been issued, dropping to 24 million in 1821. Obviously, there had been an impressive expansion of the press, particularly of the cheap 'popular' press. Such an expansion – and the circulations claimed by the 'popular' periodicals – would suggest a parallel growth in general literacy. But the few figures available hardly support such an assumption. In 1843, 33 per cent of the men, and 49 per cent of the women marrying in England and Wales are said to have signed the marriage register with a cross.[10] By 1853 the figures were still 31 and 45 per cent respectively. Admittedly, the ability to sign a register is not an accurate indication of an ability to read, and we must remember that this was a period in which reading was more commonly taught than writing. The general picture of children's education – particularly in the lower classes – is hardly attractive, but at the adult level there was a great deal of activity. In 1842 the Rev. R. S. Bayley opened the first 'People's College' at Sheffield, and by 1846 more than a thousand operatives had passed through it. It was run by a committee of working-men, and taught, among other subjects, Latin, French, German, education and logic. Another college was established in Nottingham in 1846. The village of Edwinstowe had its own Artisan's Library and Mutual Instruction Society, which held classes five evenings a week, free to all villagers, teaching reading, writing, arithmetic, music and drawing – a more practical and realistic programme. In Nottingham again, the working-men established a number of 'Operative Libraries', situated in public houses. In March 1845 Samuel Smiles, whose book *Self-Help* was to become the Bible of all working-men who aspired to improve their conditions, delivered an address in Leeds on 'The education of the working classes', showing, by citing the lives of famous men, that adverse conditions cannot repress the human intellect and character, if it be determined to rise; that Man can triumph over circumstances and subject them to his will; and that knowledge is no exclusive inheritance of the rich and leisured classes, but may be attained by all. Tied in with this whole movement were the Mechanics' Institutes. In 1850 there were 700 of them, with more than 107,000 members and libraries of nearly 700,000 books. But the mechanics who planned them were progressively crowded out as more and more of the lower middle classes took them over, much to the resentment of the more intelligent operatives.

The vast mass of the people were not touched by these efforts of the more enterprising. The real answer lay in establishing a reasonable system of elementary education. But here again the problems were enormous. In 1843 the government, stimulated by Ashley, brought in its Factory Bill to reduce the working hours of children. Included were provisions for the compulsory education of factory children: classes were to be set up under the main control of the Church of England. And then the storm broke. The Catholics naturally objected, but so too did the more politically conscious Nonconformists. The ensuing controversy was hardly encouraging. It resulted in the abandonment of the educational clauses and the holding-over of the Bill itself. Nevertheless, more and more people could obviously read, and certainly far more than the educational figures would suggest. But the growth of the reading public was a slow process, and hardly comparable to the quite remarkable expansion of the printing trade generally. It would seem that, with the abolition of most of the 'taxes on knowledge' and the technical advances of the period, reading matter in general was becoming far cheaper, and that the great expansion was largely absorbed by the already literate sections of the community. This meant primarily the middle and lower-middle classes, which were themselves rapidly expanding in a changing society and economy. To them must be added a growing number of working-class readers. Inadequate as their educational opportunities might be, many had learned to read however painfully. And in the encouragement of this type of reader, the efforts of Reynolds and Lloyd must not be overlooked: they did much to stimulate the reading habit, although, according to their many critics, both contemporary and modern, with disastrous results.

7 The provincial Press, 1701–1854

Towards the end of the eighteenth century, according to the oft-quoted London *New Monthly* (vol. 48, p. 137):

> there was scarcely a single provincial journalist who would have hazarded an original article on public affairs. Their comments were confined to the events of their own towns and districts so sparingly administered, with such obvious distrust of their own ability, and with such cautious timidity, that they were absolutely of no account. The London papers, a pot of paste and a pair of scissors supplied all the materials for the miscellaneous articles, and the local intelligence was detailed in the most meagre formularies. The provincial journalist of that day was in fact not much above a mechanic – a mere printer – and intellect had as little as possible to do with it.

These were harsh words – and there was some truth in them. Nevertheless, the provincial press had made significant advances since its very uncertain and tentative beginning. It was now a firmly established part of local life, sometimes controlling large circulations and extensive spheres of influence. It had reached the stage when its more enterprising printers were prepared to throw off their former dependence upon the London newspapers, and take an active and individual part in both local and national politics.

With the lapse of the former restrictions on the printing trade generally in 1695, competition in London became intensive, and it was not long before trained printers left the capital to seek their fortunes elsewhere. The excitement of the times, the proliferation of London newspapers (with the consequent multiplication of confusing, if not flatly contradictory reports), and the cost of a subscription to a London newspaper, all presented an opportunity for an enterprising country printer to provide, in one cheap weekly newspaper, the most important items contained in the various London newspapers – and of the written newsletters. Admittedly, there were risks involved: the size of the local reading public was an unknown quantity. The first printer to take the risk would seem to be Francis Burges, who in 1701 began the *Norwich Post*. In 1702 there was probably a paper in Bristol – and in or about the year

1704 one in Exeter. Thereafter, the number steadily increased – although the provincial newspapers shared the difficulties of their London colleagues regarding the various Stamp Acts and the periods of what was called a 'dearth of news', and casualties were heavy. By the end of 1760 there were only thirty-five papers in existence, out of the 130-odd which had been started in fifty-five towns. Such a total may not seem impressive, but in this period papers had been established which were to survive into the present century, such as the *Bath Journal*, *Bath Advertiser*, *Chester Courant*, *Coventry Mercury*, *Derby Mercury*, *Gloucester Journal*, *Ipswich Journal*, *Leeds Intelligencer*, *Leicester Journal*, *Sussex Weekly Advertiser*, *Newcastle Courant*, *Northampton Mercury*, *Norwich Mercury*, *Reading Mercury*, *Salisbury Journal*, *Stamford Mercury*, and *Worcester Journal*.

It had been a time of experiment. Today the possession of a local newspaper is regarded as one of the most accurate indices of a town's importance, but this was not so in the early eighteenth century, when much depended on the presence of a printer able and willing to take the risks involved. Such towns as Norwich and Bristol stood in a class of their own as regards population and importance; others had their own attractions – they were market towns, county capitals or sea ports. Up to 1760 Bristol had seen nine local newspapers; Manchester eight; Norwich, Exeter and Newcastle seven each; Nottingham five; and Bath, Derby and York four each. But Cirencester had a newspaper in 1718, a year before York; the tiny St Ives in Huntingdonshire witnessed no less than three attempts to found a newspaper before 1720; and Maidstone had one in 1725. At the other end of the scale, Birmingham, with a population of some 15,000 in 1700, had no paper at all until 1732, and no successful one till 1741; Coventry had to wait until 1741, Doncaster, Halifax and Sheffield until the 1750s. Perhaps the most surprising case of all was Liverpool, which, after an abortive attempt in 1710, had no newspaper until 1756. However, by 1760 the general trend was clear: not only were newspapers being produced in a growing number of towns, but they were being produced more and more in the Midlands and north, the areas which were already showing signs of that development which was later to be dignified with the title 'Industrial Revolution'.

The provincial newspaper was essentially a weekly: its whole claim to support lay in the completeness and impartiality of its 'collection' of news from London papers. It made no claim to originality, and certainly not to giving local news. Instead, it boasted of the number of London newspapers it used. The *Protestant Mercury* of Exeter thus asserted on 7 October 1715 that its contents were 'impartially collected, as Occasion offers, from the *Evening Post*, *Gazette*, *Votes*, *Flying Post*, *Weekly Pacquet*, *Dormer's Letter*, *Postscipt* [sic] *to the Post-Man*, Etc. So that no other can claim to have a better Collection'. The printer accepted no responsibility. As the *Northampton Mercury* so disarmingly explained on 13 March 1721, 'we hope our candid Readers will not condemn our *Mercury* for the many Falsities that have of late been inserted therein, as we took them all out of the London Printed Papers, and those too the most creditable'.

The provincial newspaper was to retain this character throughout most of the eighteenth century. If anything, the list of sources became even more extensive, so that in 1745 the *Cambridge Journal*, a relatively minor paper, could declare that its collection of news was taken from the

> *Amsterdam, Utrecht, Hague, Leyden, Brussels, Paris*, and *London Gazettes*; the *Paris Ala-Main*; *London, General* and *St. James's Evening Posts*; *London Courant*; *Daily Advertiser*; *Daily Post*; *Daily Gazetteer*; *Universal Spectator*; *Old England Journal*; Dublin and Edinburgh News-papers; and *Wye's, Fox's* and other Written Letters, besides Private Intelligence.

In effect, the local newspaper was local only in the sense that it was printed locally. Local news was kept to a minimum. For one thing, with very few exceptions the country towns of this period were little more than rather sprawling villages, in which any exciting titbit would be spread by gossip long before a newspaper could put it into print, while local insularity ensured that whatever was news to one small community would be of no interest whatsoever to others. And it could be dangerous. As the *Northampton Mercury* put it (23 January, 1721), 'publick Reflections may bring an Odium upon the Paper, the Business of which is to amuse rather than reform'. So the country papers steered well clear of such controversial issues as enclosures, the game laws, the laws of settlement, and the administration of justice.

Nevertheless, significant developments had taken place. With the physical enlargement of the newspaper which was the unintended result of the Stamp Act of 1712, the country printers in general found themselves with twelve small pages to fill. Nearly all now included a section on 'Remarks on Trade', comprising lists of goods imported and exported at the London Customs Office or, more often, the 'Bear Key'. Most also gave lists of bankrupts and the prices of stocks – and threw in, for good measure, the 'London Bill of Mortality', with all its weird and wonderful causes of deaths in the capital. As the tempo of economic life began to quicken, and despite the reduction to four pages following the 1725 Stamp Act, such papers as the *York Courant, Leeds Mercury*, and the various Manchester papers continued this economic emphasis, giving lists of the imports and exports not only in London but in Hull nd Liverpool. Similarly, the Bristol newspapers began to give considerable coverage to their own seaport, with the *Bristol Oracle* announcing on 21 July 1744 that

> for the Future, an exact Account of every Ship enter'd outwards, the Place where bound, the Master's Name, and as soon as it can be known, the time of its intended arrival, will be publish'd (Weekly), for the better Information of all Persons who may have Occasion to correspond with their Friends beyond the Seas . . . And as a further Encouragement to all Pursers and Masters of Ships to give proper Notice to the

Public, for the better Carrying on so useful a Project, he
likewise promises to insert all News gratis.

By the early 1750s the newspapers of Bristol and Newcastle were virtually
trade papers, with their main emphasis on local shipping and commerce.
With the publication in 1756 of *Williamson's Liverpool Advertiser*, the
provincial trade paper may be said to have been born. So detailed were its
extracts from Lloyd's List, the course of exchange, tables of wind and
weather, the winds at Deal, local shipping news – and, of course,
advertisements – that it had little space for ordinary news. The accuracy
of its shipping reports received an unexpected testimonial during the
Seven Years War, when on 2 March 1759 it published a letter signed by
some forty local merchants: 'The Publishing a List of the Ships that enter
Outwards and sail from the Port every Week, we have too much Reason
to apprehend, has been a very bad Consequence this War: We therefore
desire that for the Future, you will omit it from your Paper.' It would
seem that the French privateers were keen students of the reports.

Most country papers filled up their additional space with what was
called 'Instruction and Entertainment', the variety of which makes
description almost impossible: it varied from moral and didactic essays
and verse to lengthy histories of England, from extracts from such
London society papers as the *World, Rambler* and *Covent Garden Journal* to
the highly ambitious series on 'The Geography and Natural History of
the World', published in 1739 by both the *Newcastle Journal* and the
Lancashire Journal. This particular project was rather too ambitious, and
both printers were forced to admit that 'we find every Taste does not so
much relish the Natural History of the World'.[1] No paper approached the
record of the *Cambridge Journal* which, from 1749 to 1753, gave its readers
a weekly instalment of a novel, working its way through more than a
dozen (although, according to a frequently quoted story, the printer of
the *Leicester Journal* was once so short of material that he was reduced to
reprinting chapters from the Old Testament each week, getting halfway
through Exodus before the foreign mails provided him with rather more
up-to-date news).[2]

The evolution of the provincial newspaper from a primitive
news-sheet to the proud purveyor of 'intelligence, instruction and
entertainment' had been accomplished without much difficulty. Any
possible objections were silenced by editorial assurances that no material
news would be excluded in favour of more general fare. But the evolution
of the political paper was a very different proposition. Admittedly, a few
stout individuals threw themselves into the fray from the very beginning.
Henry Cross-grove, printer of one of the earliest Norwich newspapers,
won considerable notoriety for his political activities, and even had the
temerity to plunge into the field of local politics. He was, needless to say,
frequently in trouble with the authorities. Philip Bishop of Exeter was
prosecuted in 1716 for having reprinted a ballad entitled 'Nero the
Second' – in which the parallel to George I was too obvious. His

punishment, according to an obviously unsympathetic rival printer reporting in the *Protestant Mercury*, was to have been 'to stand in the Pillory three several Times, and to have his Ears (if not his Hands also) cut off and nail'd to the same; To be whipp'd at the Cart's Tail three several Market Days round this City; And to be imprison'd during life; A Sentence indeed too mild for his inexorable Villany'. Perhaps fortunately for him, Bishop had died in gaol during the lengthy legal proceedings. But, quite apart from the risk of such penalties, most country printers had an even more powerful reason for keeping out of politics – the financial one. The adoption of a firm party line would inevitably estrange potential customers and might even encourage a rival to set up a newspaper in the opposite interest. In general, the country newspaper's aim was to be the county newspaper, read by Whig and Tory alike. The *Derby Mercury* candidly announced on 21 February 1734 that, 'as it is undoubtedly my Interest to be equally willing and faithful in serving all Parties, so I hope all who read my News Paper may be convinced that I am so far from being such a Bigot as to act contrary to that Interest'. This studied neutrality was probably the ideal of most printers. But local competition often forced their hand, and there were always the politically-minded individuals, such as the Farley family of Exeter and Bristol, and the printers of the *York Courant* and the *Newcastle Courant*. As early as 1724, a government agent reported that

> the country printers in general copy from the rankest papers in London; and thus the poison is transmitted from one hand to another through all his majesty's dominions. How far this may tend to the corrupting the minds of his majesty's subjects, and how detrimental it may prove to the state, your lordship is a competent judge.[3]

This assessment was perhaps exaggerated in view of the general timidity of the provincial printers, but it was to become increasingly accurate, with the *York Courant* regularly reprinting *The Craftsman*'s political essay – an example followed by the *Newcastle Courant* and *Farley's Bristol Newspaper*. Edward Farley, of *Farley's Exeter Journal*, preferred the more inflammatory *Mist*'s. And, if modern historians have tended to assume that the political influence of the provincial press was negligible, that view was certainly not shared by Authority in the early eighteenth century. The government's main problem was lack of information, and the early prosecutions were local and spasmodic. But from 1726 a Mr Bell of the Post Office had the duty of purchasing copies of all the newspapers printed in England, Scotland and Ireland for the perusal of the Treasury Solicitor, who then reported to the Secretaries of State 'when the King or Government are traduc'd or slandered'.[4] This systematisation produced immediate results in the prosecution for high treason of Edward Farley in 1728 for reporting Mist's notorious 'Persian Letter', and the prosecution in 1731 of John White of the *Newcastle Courant* and Samuel Farley of Bristol for reprinting the 'Hague Letter' from *The Craftsman* (see above,

p. 44). But the problem continued. As always, the Opposition papers had the advantage: they were so much more *exciting*. After 1742 the *London Evening Post* became the favourite source, and there were few country newspapers indeed which did not find room for its waspish verses and satires.

Another problem was the reporting of parliamentary debates. Every provincial newspaper included extracts from the written news-letters, and these extracts regularly gave details of the debates. They were often extremely brief, but they were remarkably well informed, containing information which no London newspaper dared to print. Thus, on 5 December 1717, the Nottingham *Weekly Courant* gave its readers an account of one of the most daring speeches of the session, when the Jacobite leader 'Mr Shipp[en] reflecting upon his Majesty's Speech, and saying that he neither understood our Language nor Constitution, which differs from a German Province . . . [was] order'd to withdraw to the Tower'. In these extracts, the country papers possessed their one great advantage over the London papers. It was an advantage which had its dangers, and from time to time the House took action. In 1718 and 1719 all the Exeter printers were summoned to the bar of the House and taken into custody; in 1728 Robert Raikes, of the *Gloucester Journal*, suffered a similar fate; later, it was the turn of the York printers. All pleaded guilty, and were discharged upon payment of their fees (which were by no means light). But the extracts from the news-letters continued until the 1760s, when London papers appeared which were prepared to report parliamentary debates.

One of the most formidable problems facing the country printers was that of distribution. In the very early days customers in town had their papers delivered to their door, while those from outside were expected to pick up their copies on market day. But the printers soon realised that they must address themselves more and more to potential readers in the surrounding countryside – thinly scattered, perhaps, but providing the natural public for a local newspaper if it could be supplied cheaply and punctually. So developed the new profession of newsman, whose job it was to deliver the newspaper together with the various other wares sold by the printer and bookseller. As the circulation grew, agents had to be appointed in the various local towns and villages – agents who organised their own delivery systems. In this way was evolved the distribution system which was to remain in operation until well into the next century. The routes followed by the newsmen radiated out from the printing office like some great spider's web, with each agent in turn the centre of a smaller web. The distances covered by the newsmen were often surprisingly great: a newsman of the *Manchester Magazine* did a round trip of one hundred miles; one Peter Pass carried the *Manchester Mercury* to Bolton, Wigan, Preston and Kendal, a distance of some eighty miles, and returned within two days to begin his travels for the *Liverpool Advertiser*. So familiar a sight did these newsmen become that the printers rarely thought it necessary to describe their routes. By 1760 it would seem that the smaller papers employed half-a-dozen, but the *Reading Mercury* in 1743 claimed fifteen, the *York Courant* had at least twelve, and the *Newcastle Journal* fourteen. Similarly, the number of agents increased considerably, and in 1743 the *Reading Mercury* named thirty-six and the *York Courant* forty-three. But no means of distribution was ignored: according to the *Cambridge Chronicle* in 1762, it was

> dispatch'd Northwards every Friday Evening by the Caxton Post, as far as York, Newcastle and Carlisle; into the Counties of Cambridge, Bedford, Hertford, Essex, Huntingdon, Lincoln, Nottingham, Leicester, Rutland, Northampton, and the Isle of Ely by the Newsmen; to London the next Morning by the Coach and Fly; Eastwards by the Yarmouth Carrier to Suffolk, and to several Parts of Norfolk, etc. by other Conveyances (27 November, 1762).

By such means, the country newspapers were distributed through surprisingly extensive areas. It was no idle boast when the *Reading Mercury* in 1743 declared that it was 'distributed throughout Berkshire, Buckinghamshire, Oxfordshire, Wiltshire, Hampshire, Surrey, Sussex, and part of Kent and Middlesex'. In the north, the spheres of influence were even wider.

Circulation also grew steadily, from 100 or 200 in the very early years to between 200 and 400 in the late 1720s, and to much higher figures thenceforth. In its first issue, dated 14 July 1739, the *Newcastle Journal* stated flatly that 'we now sell nearly two thousand of these Papers weekly'. In 1775 the *Manchester Magazine* claimed a sale of 1,200. By 1773, the newly established *York Chronicle* could claim between 1,900 and 2,500. And all three faced local competition. It is clear that even by 1760 the greater provincial newspapers could have a circulation of 2,000, although many had far less.

'The profits of a newspaper', declared the *Reading Mercury* on 10 July 1797, 'arise only from Advertisements.' That had certainly not been the case earlier in the century, when advertisements had been little more than incidental items. For many years, according to the *Liverpool Chronicle* (6 May 1757) 'it was thought mean and disreputable among tradesmen of wealth and credit to advertise the sales of their commodities in a publick Newspaper'. And as long as circulation and distribution remained limited, there was little point in advertising, when everybody knew everybody else's business. As late as 19 January 1742, the *Manchester Mercury* pointed out that

> as it is a Happiness peculiar to the Trading Part of the Kingdom, that such Articles as are to be sold or lett at a reasonable Rate hereabouts seldom want Advertising, the Printer . . . is oblig'd to have more News than others in his Paper, which must certainly be more entertaining to almost all Persons than Advertisements of such a House, Farm, etc. to be lett at 30, 40, or more Miles Distance.

Nevertheless, as economic life developed, so too did the number of advertisements increase. By 1740 the four-page *Newcastle Journal* regularly devoted at least one and a half pages to advertisements, and by 1753 not only pages 3 and 4, but frequently page 2 as well, with trade announcements occasionally even encroaching on the front page. The *York Courant* similarly gave three-quarters of its space to advertisements, as did the *Ipswich Journal*. Such papers were becoming 'Advertisers', containing some 2,000 'paid' advertisements a year together with numerous publishing notices and quack advertisements in which the printers themselves were concerned and which, presumably, did not bring in any cash. Most provincial newspapers had only 1,000, and some far less.

The actual income from this source is difficult to estimate. No printing office records have survived – if, indeed, any were kept. What have survived are various copies of papers in which prices have been written in against the advertisements, whether paid, and the number of times to be inserted. Unfortunately, in only two cases are such copies numerous and detailed enough to provide anything like accurate information. In the twenty-six weeks of the *Liverpool Chronicle* between 6 May and 28 October 1757 there were 795 advertisements of varying length, of which 761 were paid for. The final income, after deducting the advertisement duty, would have amounted to only £49.2s. In the fifty-eight issues of the *Reading Mercury* between 25 January 1762 and 7 March 1763 there were 1,481 advertisements, with the final profit £125.6s[5]; even the giant *Newcastle Journal* with its total of some 3,000 advertisements would receive only about £4 a week. And it is clear from some of the plaintive comments written against advertisements that bad debts were a permanent problem.

Income from sales was similarly small. The average country paper of the 1750s had a circulation of about 1,000 a week, which would bring in roughly £8 gross. Out of this had to come the stamp tax, payments to newsmen, newsprint, the cost of London papers and newsletters, wages, rent and various other expenses. It would seem unlikely that, adding the income from sales and advertisements together, the average printer would clear as much as £5 a week. Some undoubtedly cleared far less. But in the eighteenth-century, and well into the nineteenth, no country printer relied solely on a newspaper for his livelihood. He was first and foremost a general printer. He sold the innumerable forms demanded by Authority even in those days of *laissez-faire*. Some idea of their scope may be obtained by the list advertised in the *Oxford Gazette and Reading Mercury* of 10 February 1745:

> The following Blanks, viz. Parish Certificates, Warrants for
> Removal of poor People, Warrants for Overseers of the Poor,
> Warrants for Collectors of the Land Tax, Warrants for
> Assessors of the Land Tax, Receipts for the Land Tax,
> Warrants to appoint Surveyors of the Highways, Warrants for
> Collectors of the Window Tax, Affidavits for burying in woollen,

> Copies of Writs for the King's Bench, ditto for the Common
> Pleas, Subpoena's for the Assizes, Warrants to search for stolen
> goods, Tickets and Biscuit-Papers for Funerals.

Many country printers produced broadsheets on local trials. Some went even further: Collins of Salisbury, Newbery of Reading, and Goadby of Yeovil and Sherborne managed successfully to break into the exclusive ring which then controlled the London book trade, achieving national reputations. Most sold patent medicines, filling their advertisement columns with lengthy and often nauseating accounts of the 'diseases' their offerings would supposedly cure. Others again conducted what would now be called employment agencies; Andrew Hooke of Bristol kept a coffee-house; William Chase of Norwich and Robert Williamson of Liverpool were auctioneers. Some sold wall-paper, old rope, charcoal, Old Jamaica Rum and pocket watches. The list is endless. Clearly, the country printers were men of considerable initiative and enterprise, and the newspaper was only one, and that not the most profitable, of their activities.

Nevertheless, profits could be made. In 1724 or thereabouts John White offered his niece £50 a year 'to resign the materials and all she was worth in stock' for the management of the *York Mercury*. In 1769 a half-share in the *Ipswich Journal* was bought for an annuity of £20 – a surprisingly small sum for so important a paper, but there were family interests involved. Also in 1769, Joseph Pote, one-time printer of the *Eton Journal* and a very well known bookseller and publisher, assigned his business to his son on payment of £600, plus £450 for the stock, £200 a year, and £50 for rent, board and lodging. (The stock in question consisted of a vast quantity of knives and forks, buttons, combs, rings and similar oddments.) The case was obviously exceptional, but it does show how profitable a country business could become. In 1774 Francis Newbery, of Reading fame, sold his share in the *Sherborne and Yeovil Mercury* (a minor paper) for £200. Equally, a series of solicitor's letters show that between 1771 and 1789 a quarter-share in the *Salisbury Journal* reached the remarkably high figure of £1,300. And when Robert Raikas II retired from the management of the great *Gloucester Journal* in 1802, he seems to have received an annuity of £500, the value of the whole business being estimated at £1,500 a year.

In such ways, behind the protective screen provided by the multifarious activities of the printers, the provincial newspaper had been able to develop. By the end of the century it had become a firmly established part of local life. Moreover, with the increasing competition, the tendency was for the areas of distribution to contract. The earlier efforts to produce not merely the county paper but the paper of several counties had drained the resources of the printers, and in such papers, local news could play no vital part. But increasingly the printers were forced to abandon such ambitious projects and concentrate instead on the more practicable aim of publishing the local newspaper, a paper in which local news items might assume an important role. The country paper still relied heavily on the London press for its news; its views it continued to take from those papers, usually stressing its complete impartiality (although it was surprising what could be achieved by a judicious selection of sources); and most tried to avoid local controversies. But the way was opening for a true local newspaper voicing local views. With the rise of Radicalism and the outbreak of the French Revolution, issues were appearing which people could feel deeply about. During the uproar over Wilkes, a politician was to ask: 'How is it possible that the farmers and weavers of Yorkshire and Cumberland should know, or taken an interest in the Middlesex Election?'[6] The answer was clear: this new political awareness and knowledge was in great measure due to the press, and in particular the provincial press. Admittedly, the views the provincial newspapers expressed were those of the London newspapers. But this ignoring of purely local issues and the concentration upon politics had its advantages. For the first time, a political agitation on almost a national scale had become a possibility – and the provincial press must rank high among those centralising forces, whether political, economic or social, which were making national unity. The provincial press was reaching the stage when its bolder and more enterprising members might react to the changing conditions, and advance beyond the type of newspaper so scathingly described by the *New Monthly*.

One might have expected the first reaction to take place in what was becoming the industrial north, with the growing economic and social problems of the so-called Industrial Revolution. But much still depended upon the individual. Rather surprisingly, rural Cambridge was to be the home of one of the pioneers in the transformation of the provincial newspapers, in the person of Benjamin Flower, a Dissenter who had travelled in Europe and witnessed some of the earlier scenes of the French Revolution. The local paper was the pro-Tory *Cambridge Chronicle* of Francis Hodson, a typical eighteenth-century country printer. He would have much preferred to print a paper which would be read by Whig and Tory alike, but the French Revolution forced his hand, and he came out strongly in favour of the war and of Pitt's repressive measures – and the domination of local elections by Tory grandees. He had little sympathy for parliamentary reform.[7] In 1793 Flower launched his *Cambridge Intelligencer*, emphasising the need for 'an independent and impartial Newspaper' and supporting the cause of reform. From the outset he sought to instruct public opinion and offer solutions for the problems of the day. To such ends he developed the use of the editorial article: the war he denounced as unjustified, unchristian, and liable to ruin the country; at the same time, he plunged into local politics, continually attacking the patronage and corruption in both borough and county elections. He represented something new in provincial journalism: he had outgrown the 'scissors and paste' tradition, and had thrown off the former dependence upon the London newspapers. He had little support in conservative Cambridge, but he acquired a national reputation among reformers, and was favoured with advetisements from the Sheffield Constitutional Society, the London Society for Constitutional Information, and the London Corresponding Society. He claimed a weekly circulation of 2,700 in 1797 (most of it from outside Cambridge). But his outspokenness finally led him into a libel action in 1799. He was found guilty, fined £100, and sentenced to six months in Newgate. In 1803 he gave up the unequal struggle. Until the repeal of the corn laws became a vital issue, Cambridge was hardly likely to be a suitable base for organised protest. It is, perhaps, surprising that he should have been allowed to pursue his very radical policy for ten years. Other pioneers in the field were not so fortunate.

To some extent, his enterprise had been anticipated by Joseph Gales, of the *Sheffield Register* (1787–94). With the outbreak of the French Revolution Gales quickly forgot his professed impartiality and began printing extracts from the various Radical leaders praising the Revolution and urging a similar, if less violent, reformation in England. The extracts he supplemented with original leading articles. He was a powerful writer, closely associated with the Sheffield Constitutional Society, to whose meetings he gave the fullest publicity. By May 1794 he claimed a circulation of over 2,000 a week, but this very success brought disaster: he was indicted for conspiracy, and fled to France. But others were in the field. In Manchester the Radicals were driven by the refusal of the existing local papers to publish their case into producing in 1792 a newspaper of their own, the *Manchester Herald*. It lasted only a year before Authority stepped in, and the printers fled. In Sheffield the radical *Sheffield Iris* succeeded the *Register*, but its editor was imprisoned twice for libel in 1795 and 1796, and, understandably, lost much of his reforming zeal.

These early provincial radical papers were ahead of their time. Outside London there was little real discontent, and political consciousness was only in its embryonic stage. But 1815 brought not only peace but also economic depression, and a sudden flare-up of Radical journalism, particularly in the north, where the London unstamped papers enjoyed an extensive distribution, with Manchester well to the fore. According to *The Times* of 11 August 1819 (just before Peterloo):

> The shop of Wroe, the printer of the *Manchester Observer* in that part of Market-Street which has been called 'Sedition Corner', is perpetually beset with poor misled creatures, whose appetite for seditious ribaldry, created at first by distress, is whetted by every species of stimulating novelty. *Medusas, Gorgons, Black Dwarfs*, and all the monstrous progeny begotten by disaffection upon ignorance, are heaped on the table or in the windows, with hideous profusion, and the money which should be expended in buying bread for their families is often squandered on the purchase of such pestilent publications.

At the same time, most provincial centres were producing their own

Radical newspapers. The *Manchester Observer*, begun in 1818, achieved national fame and notoriety, claiming a sale of 4,000 just after Peterloo – the highest circulation of any provincial newspaper of the time. But Boston had its penny *True Briton* in 1819, Birmingham its *Birmingham Inspector* and its *Edmond's Weekly Register* (price 3*d*), Coventry its *Lewis's Coventry Recorder* (price 4*d*). There was also the *Dudley Patriot*, costing only twopence, and bearing the motto 'God armeth the Patriot'. Most were largely made up of extracts from the London Radical papers.

The government was well aware of the dangers involved in this flooding of the country by subversive newspapers. Of the seventy-five prosecutions of Radical papers in 1819, more than half were outside London – mostly aimed at the hawkers and sellers. One of the major victims was James Wroe, who, after Peterloo, brought out an anonymous account of that affair in weekly parts, some of which sold over 12,000 copies. The account was admittedly savage, as were the reprisals: an apprentice who had sold a copy received four months' imprisonment; the wife of one of Wroe's journeymen received six months for a similar offence, her seventeen-year-old daughter being fined £5; Wroe's ten-year-old son was fined sixpence; Wroe himself was found guilty on eight charges, imprisoned for twelve months, and fined £100 (his sentence was apparently only for publishing two issues of *Sherwin's Register*, and the other seven charges remained). The expenses involved meant ruin for Wroe, and Manchester was to be without a working-class newspaper until 1829, when the *Manchester and Salford Advertiser* appeared.

In fact, the early working-class provincial newspapers rapidly faded away. Their place was taken by Radical papers of a very different type, run by middle-class reformers, tough, ambitious, eager for parliamentary reform – but with scant sympathy for the demands of the extremists. The old-style country papers remained, but a new spirit was in the air (although even as late as 1819 the *Exchange Herald* of Manchester could make the remarkable assertion, coming as it did from the largest of the unrepresented towns, that the people were 'better and fully, and more freely represented at the present moment, than they ever were at any former time'. The new middle-class reformers of Manchester were soon to make clear the absurdity of such statements; indeed, Manchester gained national notoriety, with its awful slum conditions, the vast growth of the cotton industry, and the increasing cleavage between capitalists and workers. Leeds had similar problems, as did most towns in the Midlands and north. The basic problem was the collapse of the whole system of local government – a system totally incapable of coping with the quite unprecedented problems presented by the rapid growth of huge towns where only rather sprawling villages had existed before.

A typical middle-class paper of this period was the *Leeds Mercury*, which was to win a national reputation. In 1801 Edward Baines had purchased the copyright, the goodwill of the associated printing business and the printing materials for £1,552, of which £1,000 was lent by eleven backers, all but one dissenters and reformers. His aim was to transform the *Mercury* into a paper of opinion, and from the start he included leading articles, at first tentative, but becoming increasingly outspoken. When he took over, the circulation was only about 700 or 800 a week; by 1806 it approached 2,000; and by 1833 it was about 5,500, the largest of any provincial newspaper. Throughout his life Baines took a prominent part in charitable causes: he felt deeply for the distressed operatives – but had no sympathy for the Luddite machine-breakers. Above all, he urged parliamentary reform as the only way to achieve more enlightened policies. But he disliked both the objectives and the temper of the rival movements for universal suffrage and annual parliaments: he wanted calm, *moderate* reform. From 1820 on his son, Edward Baines II, was increasingly in charge. Like his father, his social aim was to heal the class cleavage between masters and men. He was well content with the Reform Bill, contending that it could open the way to many reforms beneficial both to the working and the middle classes. But the operatives wanted *immediate* reforms. It seems doubtful if many were passionately concerned over that rather abstract ideal, the vote. What they wanted was the ten-hour day. The Baineses believed that this agitation went too far. As Read puts it, 'they (the operatives) wanted an eleven-hour limit for children under fourteen. Working-class families depended upon the wages of children, and the *Mercury* contended that it would be false benevolence to reduce too drastically the hours (and therefore the wages) of those children. Moreover, reduced hours meant reduced output and higher prices.' In fact, the Baineses combined a genuine sympathy for the poor with an extremely hard-headed business approach. Surprisingly enough, the ten-hour agitation had virtually started in the pages of the *Mercury*, when it published on 16 October 1830 Richard Oastler's famous letter on 'Slavery in Yorkshire' – admittedly with an editorial note deploring the 'undue warmth and violence' of Oastler's language. Oastler's attitude was hardly calculated to promote that union of masters and men which the *Mercury* urged: he portrayed the masters as tyrants to be hated. He was soon dropped. But the paper was rapidly losing whatever reputation it ever had among the working-men: its very practical and rational approach to the ten-hour question saw to that – as did its obvious lack of sympathy for the anti-poor law agitators, whom it described as 'the most violent, perverse, and wrong-headed men that could be collected together in England'. Equally, it has to be remembered that the paper was a supporter of the Municipal Corporations Act, and a steady advocate of expenditure on public parks, improved street lighting, paving and sewering, and higher standards of building, although strongly opposed to any form of central control.

The Manchester equivalent to the *Leeds Mercury* was the *Manchester Guardian*, established in 1821. It was at first radical in tone, but soon came to be regarded as the champion of the commercial interests of the town. By the middle of 1822 it was selling about 1,000 a week; but 3,000 was passed by the end of 1825, and 4,000 was reached by 1834, while the number of advertisements rose impressively until by 1840 it was the most successful provincial newspaper in this field. It appealed to the *laissez-faire* principles of the cotton manufacturers. In every strike, it came out on the side of the employers; it opposed the restriction of hours of labour of children in factories; it welcomed the new poor law. At the same time it campaigned for local improvements and was a strong advocate of education, declaring that 'were the ravings of Stephens, O'Connor, Richardson, Oastler, Etc. addressed to instructed audiences, they would be innocuous'. One wonders what form the 'instruction' it supported might take. In Sheffield, the middle-class reformers had as their organ the *Sheffield Independent*, unusual only in the way it related all problems to the corn laws. Were they repealed, trade would so expand that the demand for labour would exceed the supply, and working-class conditions would have to be improved.

The predominance of the 'Big Three' middle-class papers was not achieved easily. Other middle-class papers appeared advocating principles reminiscent of the earlier Radical Movement. One such was the *Manchester Times*, begun in 1828 under the editorship of Archibald Prentice. A tremendous enthusiast for the Reform Bill, he blamed the aristocracy, pensions and sinecures for the heavy taxation. At the end of 1829, he reproduced Cruickshank's drawing entitled 'The Greatest Unhappiness Principle', commenting that under the existing system, ninety-nine industrious operatives had to work at subsistence level to keep one aristocrat in luxury:

> Who that looks upon the little bloated monster, – the
> representative of corn-monopolies and tax eaters, – crammed
> till he is reduced to the most helpless imbecility, and the poor
> starving wretches of the same family who have scarcely strength
> enough to hold out their hands in supplication for a portion of
> that abundance which is wasted on him, can fail to recognise
> an illustration of the 'Greatest unhappiness principle'?

Such a passage might well have been written by Cobbett, and one can understand why the Manchester manufacturers preferred the approach of the *Guardian*. But Prentice failed also to appeal to the working classes. Though critical of the poor law, he did not support the noisy agitation. Over the ten-hour question, he took up a middle position, refusing to believe that masters deliberately made slaves of factory children, but at the same time appreciating the humanitarian motives which inspired that particular agitation. But his great interest was the Anti-Corn Law League, and in his zeal for that movement, he neglected such features as local gossip and news which helped to sell newspapers, and to increase their influence. 'I was often told', he wrote in his memoirs, 'that it would be more to my interest if I made the *Manchester Times* more of a newspaper. It mattered not. If journalism was not to effect public good, it was not employment for me.' Provincial journalism had obviously moved far.

Much more radical, at least in its early years, was the *Manchester and Salford Advertiser*, begun in 1829, and the most successful working-class paper in the north before the foundation of the *Northern Star*. It had no hopes of the Reformed Parliament, denounced both political parties, and called on the people to take the initiative and start movements which the Parliament would be unable to ignore. By 1837 its circulation was over 3,800, which put it ahead of the *Manchester Times*: but then it lost much of its radical enthusiasm, and appealed more and more to the middle class, a class already well supplied.

The situation was much the same in Leeds. Again, the 'typical' middle-class paper, the *Leeds Mercury*, was challenged by a middle-class paper which wanted to go much further – the *Leeds Times*, begun in 1833, whose editor from 1839 to 1842 was Samuel Smiles. The paper regarded 1832 as inadequate, and demanded further and more radical reform of Parliament. It emphasised the need for union between the middle and working classes; it was very much against the poor law – and it ardently supported the repeal of the corn laws. It was trying to attract working-class support. But, according to Read, 'like the *Manchester Times*, though to a lesser extent, the *Leeds Times* suffered from being too advanced for many middle-class manufacturers and yet too middle-class for many of the working classes'. The paper's circulation in 1837 was about 3,500 a week; but this fell to about 1850 by early 1839. There was also the *Leeds Patriot*, from 1828 onwards a working-class paper and an ardent supporter of the ten-hour movement. Its enthusiasm for the cause proved its undoing: in 1832 it criticised the way a local merchant treated his work-people, and the merchant replied by claiming damages. The case was settled out of court, but the costs were too heavy and the paper collapsed.

But there was other competition to face, this time from conservative Tory papers. The old-established *Leeds Intelligencer* was one of the first such papers to use the new techniques. Its motto from 1829 onwards was 'The Altar, the Throne and the Cottage', and it sought to unite the old landed society and the operatives of the new industrial society against the selfishness of the middle-class manufacturers. In 1841 it denounced what it called the 'millocracy of wealth', and the *Leeds Mercury* replied: 'Mr Holland speaks of the mill-owners as the grand cause of the sufferings of the working classes. A more flagrant absurdity was never put on paper. The mill-owners to a great extent *offer* labour and wages, but they compel no man to accept them'. The *Intelligencer* heartily supported the ten-hour movement, and it condemned the poor law as 'a monstrosity in legislation calculated to disgust as well as astonish'. This attempt to woo the workers was not highly successful, and the workers generally were not impressed by the idea of an alliance with the aristocracy. Nevertheless, the paper enjoyed a certain success: its circulation rose to 3,000 after 1836, and over 4,000 in 1841. Its Manchester counterpart was the *Courier*, which again displayed the Tory paternalistic spirit. It was founded with the explicit intention of fighting the middle-class reform papers, but did not really expect many working-class readers. Again, it achieved some considerable success: there was obviously local support for its campaign that 1832 had gone too far.

One can hardly say that the industrial towns were starved of news and views, particularly if one remembers that London newspapers continued to flood the country. According to an advertisement of 'The Manchester Coffee and Newspaper Room' of John Docherty, a Radical reformer and trade union leader, in 1833:

> This Establishment affords advantages never before offered to the Manchester Public, combining Economy, Health, Temperance, and Instruction, in having a wholesome and exhilarating beverage at a small expense, instead of the noxious and intoxicating stuff usually supplied at the Ale-house and Dram-shop, together with the privilege of perusing the most able and popular publications of the day, whether political, literary, or scientific, in a comfortable and genteel apartment, in the evening brilliantly lit by gas. COFFEE – 'As a Medicine, strong Coffee is a powerful stimulant and cordial; and, in paroxysms of the Asthma, is one of the best remedies' – *British Cyclopaedia.* 'Coffee has been the favourite beverage of many distinguished men. Napoleon and Frederick the Great drank it freely; Voltaire liked it very strong, and Leibnitz drank it also during the whole day. In France, this beverage is in universal respect. In fact, throughout the continent of Europe, it is generally drank' – *British Cyclopaedia.*

The daily papers taken in were the *Morning Chronicle, Morning Herald,* and *The Times;* the evening papers, the *True Sun, Standard, Courier;* the tri-weekly *Evening Mail* and *Scotsman;* weekly papers, *The Court Journal, Cobbett's Register, Manchester and Salford Advertiser, Manchester Times, Manchester Courier, Manchester Chronicle, Manchester Guardian, Glasgow Liberator, Liverpool Mercury, Leeds Mercury, Dublin Weekly Register, Belfast Northern Whig, Atlas, Spectator, The Age, Examiner, Bell's Life, Lancet, Weekly True Sun, Weekly Dispatch, Athenaeum, Destructive, Mechanics' Magazine, National Standard, Poor Man's Guardian, Gauntlet, Chambers' Edinburgh Journal, Thief, Dublin Chronicle,* and 'most of the penny publications'; the monthlies were *Blackwood's Magazine, New Monthly Magazine, Metropolitan Magazine, Tait's Magazine;* and quarterlies, the *Westminster Review* and *Edinburgh Review.* And the terms were reasonable: 'Reading 1 d. Cup of Coffee (sugar and cream included) 2d. Bason [*sic*] do.do. 3d. Pot do.do. 5d. Cup of Tea do.do. 2½d. Pot of Tea do. 6d. Bread and Butter 1 d. Roll and Butter 2d. Toast and Butter 3d. Eggs, One Penny each'.[8] Certainly, all literary and political tastes were catered for. But the appeal was aimed squarely at a middle-class audience, despite the inclusion of such papers as the *Poor Man's Guardian* and 'most of the penny publications'. The establishment could have attracted few indeed even of the elite of the skilled workmen.

The ordinary workers could not afford coffee-houses, and they probably preferred the 'noxious and intoxicating stuff usually supplied at the Ale-house and Dram-Shop'. There, they would probably find an adequate supply of the unstamped papers. A London newspaper, *The Standard*, produced on 10 September 1833 a list of 'unstamped publications in defiance of the law', giving the *Poor Man's Guardian* a circulation of 16,000 and the *Destructive* 8,000, adding that both circulated in Lancashire. It continued, 'in the country, there are also unstamped newspapers – particularly at Leeds, Bradford, Manchester, etc., all taking their tone from the *Poor Man's Guardian* and others'.

The reduction of the stamp duty in 1836 was hailed by the middle classes as a great stride towards the freedom of the press: but it virtually killed the unstamped papers, both London and local. It reduced the difference in price between the stamped and the unstamped newspapers, making it less profitable to continue the latter, particularly at the risk of prosecution. 'The reduction upon stamps has made the rich man's paper cheaper, and the poor man's paper dearer', said the *Northern Star* in 1838. The triumph of the middle classes and their newspapers seemed to be complete: but the greatest threat to that predominance – and, indeed, to the Establishment as a whole – was to come. While the middle classes were basking in the sunshine of their victories, the working classes were looking to Chartism and to the *Northern Star*, which first appeared in Leeds on 18 November 1837. Feargus O'Connor was in complete control of the paper, and from the start made it fairly obvious that he intended to use it as a vehicle to advance his personal career. At first, the *Northern Star* was a general working-class paper, giving much space to the poor law, trade unions, and O'Connor's dream of a huge alliance between English operatives and Irish peasants. His own role in all three issues was assiduously publicised, with his many public speeches reprinted in full, together with his lengthy editorials. The paper was an immediate success, despite its price ($4\frac{1}{2}d$). By February 1838 it was selling over 10,000 a week – more than the twice-weekly *Manchester Guardian* or the weekly *Leeds Mercury*. This spectacular growth, as an editorial pointed out, proved that hitherto no single organ had satisfactorily voiced the grievances and aspirations of the working classes.

O'Connor did not immediately support the Charter, sponsored as it was by the London Working Men's Association, a moderate body not at all to his liking. Only when the popularity of the Six Points became apparent did he take up the cause. Thereafter he – and the *Northern Star* – dominated it. No other leader had at his command so powerful an organ of personal publicity. Other Chartist papers, such as the *Northern Liberator*, *The Charter*, and the *Southern Star* had their influence. But the *Northern Star* became accepted as the national organ of the movement. Correspondents were appointed in every town or village where the slightest indication of Chartist activity existed, and the paper claimed in 1841 that its reporting costs were £500 a year. In its columns isolated incidents and small meetings gained significance as part of a greater whole, and working-men throughout the country could see themselves as part of a great movement.

In 1839 the paper achieved its full glory. It consisted of eight pages, with six columns to the page. In appearance, it was curiously out-of-date, and its advertisements were strikingly reminiscent of eighteenth-century newspapers. Thus, its issue of Saturday 5 January 1839 included a description of a runaway apprentice, publishing notices, and quack medicines – 'Atkinsons's Infant Preservative', 'The celebrated Rose Liniment', 'Mrs Young's Female Pills', 'Restorative Pills . . . certain and effectual remedy for every stage and symptom of the Venereal Disease', and 'A Certain Disease cured within one week . . . so simple and plain, that parties of either sex may cure themselves without even the knowledge of a bedfellow'. But the emphasis was purely political – focused on O'Connor, with the paper devoting considerable space to such occasions as 'Soirée given to Feargus O'Connor, Esq., by the numerous party of his friends and admirers in Edinburgh' and the 'Tour of Feargus O'Connor . . . At this stage . . . Mr Fergus O'Connor entered the meeting, and was hailed with several rounds of the most deafening cheers, followed by waving of hats and clapping of hands for several minutes' (16 February 1839). But the *Northern Star* was always willing to give credit where it was due. It referred very respectfully to such papers as the *Northern Liberator* and the *Western Vindicator*, and on 13 April 1839 published the prospectus 'For the Establishment of a Newspaper in the Midland Counties, in the Interest of the Working Classes. The NOTTINGHAM CHRONICLE *and Midland Liberator* . . . in 6000 Shares at Five Shillings each, no person to have more than 20 shares, excepting the Proprietor.' The aims of this paper were:

> The Reform of the Reform Act – Universal Suffrage, Vote by Ballot, Etc. – in fact, a restoration of the Old English Constitution, which in effect says, 'no man shall be taxed who is not represented'. An entire revision of the present system of taxation, which robs the poor man of two-thirds of his earnings, and cheats the shopkeeper of half his profits. An equal admission to the law – justice to the poor, as well as to the rich. Cheap and honest Government. A fair Day's Wages for a fair Day's Work. The annihilation of all Church rates. The total abolition of the Corn Laws.

It also gave publicity to such enterprises as 'Blanchard's Old Established Newspaper, Periodical, Pamphlet-Office and News Room' in Hull, run by a man who obviously appreciated the fact that many working-men could not afford to spend a penny a day to read newspapers. The advertisement (23 February 1839) ran:

> The News Room . . . is still open every day from Eight in the Morning till Ten at Night, on extraordinary low terms, viz: One Penny per Day, Fourpence per Week, one shilling per Month, or two shillings and six-pence per Quarter. London and

Provincial Daily and Weekly Newspapers, Magazines,
Pamphlets, Etc. taken in great variety and in all shades of
politics.

> *News Lent to read*
> *(first day of publishing, 1d. per hour, and 1d. for two hours every*
> *succeeding day).'*

Then followed the significant announcement:

> *Important to the Working Classes*
> *Fellow Townsmen,* – Believing that a great struggle is about to be
> made between the Aristocracy and the Democracy in the
> coming Spring, both in Parliament and out of Parliament, and
> having long witnessed with regret the want of facility to the
> Working Men of Hull to discuss soberly and read quietly all
> sides of the political questions which now agitate this great
> oppressed country, I offer Free Admission to all Operatives
> every succeeding Monday Evening from Six o'Clock to Ten in
> my News Room.
> *Mark! Free of all Expenses.*

By such means, the *Northern Star* sought to bring home the message
of Chartism to all and sundry. Its leading articles – and the speeches of
O'Connor – could hardly be called violent. They were popular, with
jokes and plenty of rhetoric. Only occasionally did a more sinister note
appear, as in the advertisement on 'Street Warfare' in the issue of 1 June
1839:

> Now publishing, a Series of Weekly Letters, price 1d. each, on
> Street Tactics . . . To prove the errors of some recently
> published military instructions, the probable battles of
> Birmingham, Glasgow, and the English cotton and wollen
> districts are sketched with a careful consideration for all
> possible occurences. The author having a practical knowledge of
> the use of arms, and anxiously sympathising with the Chartist
> Struggle.

Again, on 17 August 1839 it reprinted what it called 'a nervous and well-
written article' from the *Western Vindicator*, entitled 'The Coming
Struggle':

> People – The time for *talking* is past; the time for *action* is come,
> and it is now the duty of every man, woman and child to
> reflect, in secret, upon the power possessed by the people to
> carry out the principles of Democratic Government; the time
> has come for deeply reflecting on the power possessed by the
> masses to carry out the recommendations of the Convention;
> the time has come when, by a bold and energetic display on
> the part of the people, the power of the aristocracy may be
> destroyed for ever.

The *Northern Star* flourished. On 2 February 1839 it claimed that 'the number we sold last week was 17,640; This Week we have now (Thursday night) orders for 27,000'. Such claims it was able to substantiate by publishing on 1 June the 'Official Return of Stamps 1st January to 31 March 1839 . . . Yorkshire Newspapers – Weekly Averages', together with a gloating editorial commentary. The purchase of stamps was a most unreliable way of arriving at a paper's actual circulation, but it was usually the only method available. According to these particular returns, the *Northern Star* completely dominated the field, with 32,692; its closest rival was the *Leeds Mercury*, with 9,692; only two papers, the *Leeds Intelligencer* and the *York Courant*, topped the 3,000 mark; the rest lagged far behind, with no less than nine below 1,000. A similar account on 17 August 1839 gave the *Northern Star* a weekly average of 42,077. Its growth was extraordinary, as was that of Chartism itself. Naturally, both met intense opposition. The *Leeds Mercury* denounced the movement from the start, describing the demand for universal suffrage as 'downright absurdity'. Education might, one day, make universal suffrage possible, and the working classes should concentrate on education. In language strongly reminiscent of Charles Knight it declared that

> The true objects to which the attention of the Working Class should be directed, and the only means by which they can ever attain either political influence or personal happiness, are these – Education, Religion, Virtue, Industry, Sobriety, Frugality. These are *Six Points* of a thousand times more importance than the Six of the People's Charter. These would make them *deserve* the suffrage.

The demand for annual parliaments, it went on, was misconceived, and it emphasised that Members of Parliament were not delegates, and that to pay them was a 'most transparent scheme of a *pack of demagogues to pension themselves on the Public*'.

Prentice of the *Manchester Times* also distrusted Chartism, describing its leaders as 'noisy braggarts whose only object is to put money into their purses', and who were trying to do too much. In 1839 he outlined *his* programme: free trade (and especially the repeal of the corn laws); triennial parliaments, with one-third of the Members to be elected annually; secret ballot; a redistribution of seats; and a suffrage based on an education test. The *Sheffield Independent* was in general agreement. The corn laws had caused people to take up 'newly fangled chimeras'. And it supported the idea of an education test: 'The candidates for the Suffrage shall first be required to read a few sentences, or half page of an ordinary book; and then of himself to write a few sentences, or half a page of an ordinary book; and then of himself to write a few sentences about what he has read'. Such a system would encourage education and would bring about universal suffrage when the people were ready for it.

Nothing could stop the *Northern Star*, apparently. It sold unprecedented numbers in the first half of 1839, when the National Petition was being prepared and the National Convention (with its overtones of the French Revolution) was sitting. Its maximum sale at this time was probably over 50,000 a week. That figure was not maintained for long, but the paper was still remarkably successful. Its circulation revealed not only the extent of working-class enthusiasm but also the fact that widespread illiteracy need not necessarily be an obstacle to a working-class newspaper. The success of the *Northern Star* fluctuated as the success of the Chartist Movement fluctuated. The key year was probably 1842, when, according to Arthur Bryant,

> Britain came nearer to revolution than at any time in her history save in the Peasants' Revolt of 1381. Compared with it, the General Strike of 1926 was a milk-and-water affair. At a time when the only poor relief was organised on a parochial basis designed for the village, a prolonged industrial slump brought wholesale wage reductions and mass unemployment, and with them famine, to the entire manufacturing districts of the North, Midlands and Clyde. By August, the workers were starving and desperate, and open insurrection broke out in South Lancashire, Staffordshire, and the West Riding'.[9]

It was this economic discontent which the Chartists sought to exploit and turn into a general strike for the Charter – and certainly the disturbances were by no means entirely Chartist fomented. Chartism failed – largely because the Chartist leaders were never clear as to their ultimate purpose: they split very early into a moderate wing stressing peaceful agitation and a far more radical wing urging direct action. They called their general strike – the 'Sacred Month' – at a time when industries were closing down and when workers were begging for employment. More significant, the new and ever-growing class of superior artisans, involved in the great development of factories and railways, tended to woo respectability: they looked to trade unionism to secure their rights, and threw their social weight behind the middle classes. And the English middle classes, unlike the French, were at one with the aristocracy in defence of the established order; moreover, the aristocracy included active philanthropists and humanitarians. But the disturbance of 1842 – and the terrible Irish famine which followed four years later – did much to arouse, however belatedly, the conscience of the upper and middle classes to the realisation of the need for some amelioration of the conditions of the working classes. The great days of the *Northern Star* were over: its circulation fell to about 9,000 a week in 1843, and 7,000 in 1844. Of course the radical papers continued to agitate, but the old fire had gone. The future lay with the middle-class papers and their cause, the repeal of the corn laws.

The significant fact is that the provincial newspapers had now completely abandoned any pretence to neutrality, and were devoting more and more space to politics, both national and local. According to the *Champion*, a London Sunday newspaper, even as early as 1836 (2 October),

> with the exception of two or three newspapers, almost exclusively devoted to commercial matters, each of the provincial journals now sustains a political character. Of the 175 newspapers published out of London (excluding those published in Wales) 100 are of Liberal politics, and 75 advocate the principles of the Tory party. There are 60 journals which have an average circulation of 1000 and upwards per week – namely, 37 Liberal journals, and 23 Tory journals. The aggregate circulation of the 37 Liberal papers is 72,193 per week, which gives an average weekly circulation of 1951 to each; the aggregate circulation of the 23 Tory papers is 31,606 per week, or 1374 per paper.

The main newspaper wars were naturally taking place in the industrial areas. But radical papers were liable to crop up in quite unexpected places. Brighton had its *Brighton Patriot and Lewes Free Press*, an evening paper, as early as 24 February 1835. Its initial aims were well within the tradition: parliamentary reform and the vote by ballot; disestablishment of the Established Church; abolition of the corn laws; abolition of sinecures and pensions; opposition to a standing army in time of peace, and so on. Its emphasis was primarily political, but it did regard itself as a local newspaper. Inevitably, the paper embraced the Chartist cause, but its approach was moderate, and it favoured moral force as against direct action. On 2 April 1839 a letter from 'Gracchus' on 'The Approaching Revolution' was reassuring: 'Let not the reader be alarmed. There is nothing terrible in a revolution unless it is attended by carnage and violence, and this in England will be wholly unnecessary if the people are true to themselves.'

Perhaps the *Patriot* was most happily employed when attacking its local rivals, particularly regarding their circulation claims. One may well be surprised to learn that, as early as 1833, Brighton had three local papers. The *Patriot* lost no time in questioning the claims of its competitors, and in so doing performed a most useful service. Most newspapers of this period based their circulation figures on their newspaper stamp returns, and those returns have largely been accepted by later historians (admittedly in the absence of any other evidence). The *Brighton Patriot* demolished such claims. On 25 August 1835, in an article entitled 'A Challenge', it produced an 'Extract from a Return made by the House of Commons showing the number of Stamps issued to each of the Provincial Newspapers in the year ending 1st April 1833'. The returns for the Brighton papers were: *Brighton Guardian* 44,000, *Brighton Gazette* 41,000, *Brighton Herald* 26,000. According to the *Patriot*, 'The above LIE has been kept standing in the columns of the Brighton GUARDIAN for about two years and shows to what paltry subterfuges the conductors of that journal resort in order to impose on the public'. In fact, it went on, the government, after due examination of the problem, had stated that 'SUCH RETURNS MUST ALWAYS BE INCOMPLETE AND FALLACIOUS'. As the *Patriot* explained,

> If, indeed, the Proprietors of papers were compelled to purchase their stamped paper at the Stamp Office – if the name of every paper was stamped upon the sheet before it was taken to the Office – if this were practised, then indeed the number circulated by each journalist might be accurately known. But at present it is utterly impossible to ascertain any thing relative to the circulation of papers.[10] Some persons purchase a portion only of their stamps at the Stamp Office, and the rest of the London wholesale stationers. Others, again, purchase the whole of their stamps at various stationers – a portion at one house, and a portion at another – and change their stationers perhaps half a dozen times a year. Sometimes a great number of stamps are purchased for a particular newspaper, but as soon as they reach the newspaper or stationer's office, they are sold to others – perhaps to a dozen different country proprietors.

In agricultural Cambridge the newspaper wars took a different turn, with the ultra-Tory *Cambridge Chronicle* increasingly challenged by more liberal rivals. The *Chronicle* was a staunch advocate of the Anglican Establishment in England as well as Protestant ascendancy in Ireland. It opposed Catholic emancipation and the reform of local corporations and Parliament; and it favoured the retention of the corn laws. On the other side, the *Cambridge Independent Press* in the 1820s led the attack on the Cambridge Corporation and also supported Catholic emancipation. Its editor was to suffer for his liberal views, but took pride in the fact that 'out of the six or eight prosecutions with which he had been assailed, not a single verdict had been passed against him'. In Cambridge the threat of emancipation was in itself enough to produce in 1825 yet another paper, *The Huntingdon, Bedford and Cambridge Weekly Journal*, to support the Tory opposition. The *Independent Press* survived the challenge. But the most important issue in Cambridge was the corn law. The *Independent Press* continually questioned the notion that rural prosperity could only be achieved on the basis of protection., It urged increased efficiency and production through a rationalisation of farming methods. Its editor, Weston Hatfield, was certainly not afraid to risk hostile public or party reaction: in a predominantly Tory and agricultural area, he was prepared 'to incur the risk of giving offence to a considerable body of our subscribers'. But he was definitely a middle-class reformer, as he demonstrated when, in what might seem a reversal of his earlier principles, he hailed the success of the Tory Peel over Repeal. In an age of revolutions, Peel had, by his statesmanship, saved England:

> By the Reform Bill the predominance of the Middle Classes, in the most active and important branch of our Senate . . . was

solemnly and irrevocably affirmed. And it is by the Middle Classes that our recent important improvement has been commenced, by *them* it has been sustained, and by *them* has it been carried on, to its final triumph over a reluctant Aristocracy . . . The triumph of the Free-trade principle, though a triumph of the people and for the people, has not been a triumph of the populace. We repeat, it proves the actual existence of that, which it was foretold the Reform Bill would eventually find, the Monarchy of the Middle Classes. (5 September 1850.)

Undoubtedly, the provincial Press was developing rapidly, and its political influence growing, although it would seem that no government of the day thought it worth while to subsidise such papers. But the London press was well aware of this new force, and regularly printed extracts from the country newspaper. In 1846 the influential *Reynold's Magazine* printed a whole series of articles on 'The Provincial Press of the United Kingdom' (7 November 1846 to 13 February 1847). Thirty-eight papers were included, with brief accounts of their history, political views, circulation and advertising importance. The comments were often well-informed and succinct:

> *The Manchester Guardian* . . . is the principal organ of the manufacturing and commercial interest . . . In politics it sides with the liberal party, and it is likewise a spirited advocate for public improvements. The friends of public parks, washhouses, etc. are in no small degree indebted to this paper for the able manner in which it has pleaded their cause . . . ; *The Kentish Independent* . . . has rendered considerable service to the artisans of the dockyard and arsenal of Woolwich, by exposing the system of tyranny and peculation carried on by the officials (even of the highest rank); *The Glasgow Herald* . . . is moderately Conservative in tone, but never commits itself against any political party; its aim being to stand well with them all; *The Nation* [an Irish paper] . . . the uncompromising champion of the legislative independence of Ireland . . . The style of the leading articles is peculiar; rapid, epigrammatical, and bearing evidence of a pen of iron, it arrests the attention, pleases the taste, and appeals forcibly to the mind. In perusing these outbursts of stern reasoning, severeness and passionate feeling, the reader is forcibly struck both with the conviction, that they by no means emanate from a common mind.

Most contemporary commentators were convinced that the local newspapers *were* influential. The wealthier manufacturers in the provinces might well subscribe to London newspapers, but for discussion of the problems of the new society they looked to their local newspaper. And here the provincial paper faced a problem: it must include local news – reporting, as *The Leeds Mercury* explained in 1836, 'that this friend has been overtaken by death – that that pretty neighbour is married'. Equally, as the *Brighton Patriot* put it (24 February 1835),

> In regard to Local Affairs we shall give such attention to them as their importance may require, but upon this we are determined: – that the *Patriot* shall never sink down into a mere local vehicle for the conveyance of parochial likings, and dislikings. The *Patriot* is a political Journal, established with the view of communicating great political truths and principles.

The balance was a rather delicate one. But the great question regarding the provincial newspapers (as of all newspapers, up to the present day) is whether they simply reflected a public opinion already formed, or whether they played an effective role in forming that public opinion? The *Sheffield Iris* had its answer: 'Newspapers are first what public opinion makes them; then by a peculiar reaction they make public opinion what they please, so long as they led with discretion, and seem to follow while in reality they lead.' The success of the middle-class papers in following this precept was revealed in the triumph of the various middle-class causes of the period. It was in some ways an indirect influence, for, according at least to a contemporay writer, ministers were largely unaware of this new influence:

> The *North British*, the *British Quarterly*, the *Westminster Reviews*, the *Leeds Mercury*, the *Manchester Guardian*, wide as their circulation and great as their influence is among the miscellaneous and middle classes, they seldom read, and regard little. Sentiments may be fermenting, and doctrines may be spreading for years in the interior of the community, and yet these men may have heard nothing of them till some such startling fact as the Birmingham Political Union, the Anti-Corn Law League, or the Secession of the Free Churches break in upon their apathetic slumbers.

But *Reynold's Magazine* (2 January 1847) was in no doubt as to the remarkable development of the country newspapers:

> The provincial press has made wonderful advances in ability and energy during the last twenty years. How almost invariably has the pen displaced the scissors – the ink supplanted the paste! Some of the best reporters in the country are engaged on the country press; whilst the leading articles of the first country newspapers are quite upon a par with most of the daily London press . . . From the peculiar position and local influence of a country paper, its editor has often the interests of a local party greatly in his power; and I have known invaluable services rendered through this means. How many a member of Parliament has owed his seat to the exertions of the local

journal, which, for concentrating its efforts on one particular spot, and to one great party purpose, has achieved a triumph of which the metropolitan press itself might be proud!

And in 1863 Richard Cobden, looking back over the great changes of the previous fifty years, agreed: the 'half a score of men, the conductors of journals in Leeds, Edinburgh, Liverpool, Manchester, Norwich, Etc.' who had led public opinion had played a part in the Industrial Revolution as important as that of the great inventors. Through the influence of their newspapers they had helped to ensure that the new industrial society dealt intelligently and vigorously with the many problems which the new industry had brought with it.

8 The explosion: from 1855 to the advent of Northcliffe

The 1836 attempt to do something about *The Times* had failed. The reduction of the newspaper stamp from 4*d* to 1*d* had not produced the anticipated results, and *The Times* continued to flourish. It was, as Francis Williams puts it, 'a towering Everest of a newspaper with sales ten times those of any other daily, combining leadership in circulation, in news services especially of the most confidential and exclusive kind – in advertising revenue, commercial profit and political influence to an extent no other newspaper anywhere in the world has ever done before or since'.

In the background, the Sunday newspapers were already laying the foundations of the mass circulation papers of today. Otherwise, there was no competition. Outside London, only Manchester and Liverpool had a bi-weekly paper. Some few country newspapers had become powerful forces, both locally and even nationally; but most were small. *The Times* was, in fact, a colossus, and 'in its gigantic shadow the rest of the press pursued its restless, bustling, querulous and only too frequently short-lived way'.

The reduction of the stamp tax had thus had exactly the opposite effect to that intended by at least some of its promoters. One reason for this (quite apart from the sheer superiority of *The Times*) was the fact that stamped papers were carried free through the post, giving *The Times* with its large country sale a tremendous advantage over all others. Because of its strong commercial position and the great demand for its advertising space, it was able to produce a much bigger newspaper than any of its rivals – twelve or sixteen pages, together with regular advertising supplements, as against their six or eight pages. Yet it paid the same tax, secured the same free carriage, and was sold at the same price of fivepence. At the same time, of course, this postal concession favoured *all* London newspapers at the expense of the provincial ones, which generally circulated through comparatively restricted areas, and benefited little from free distribution through the mail. But they paid the same tax, and had to sell at the same price, and so could hardly hope to compete successfully (although there were always exceptions).

What the opponents of *The Times* now proposed, in alliance with those who had long campaigned against the 'taxes on knowledge', was .

that the compulsory stamp tax be abolished so that those who did not use the mail should not pay for it, while for those papers carried by the Post Office the penny stamp should remain, not as a tax but as a postal charge. This charge would cover the cost of the conveyance of newspapers up to four ounces in weight; those weighing more would have to pay excess postage. Such a change was bound to have two consequences. It would favour all London papers in relation to *The Times*, for that paper was the only one that weighed more than four ounces (and usually far more). So *The Times* would have to pay excess postage and charge more than the other London papers, or reduce to their size and so lose its special character. And the change would assist all provincial papers, for without the tax they would be able to sell locally below the London papers' price. The campaign had a double appeal: it served a great principle, and it hit *The Times*; it combined idealism and sharp practice. It would serve the interests of that ever-growing number of the middle classes in the industrial cities of the north and Midlands. It would serve also those small tradesmen and skilled workers next below them in the social hierarchy. As Cobden said in 1850, 'so long as the penny [stamp duty] lasted there can be no daily press for the middle or working class. Who below the rank of a merchant or a wholesale dealer can afford to take a daily paper at five pence? Clearly it is far beyond the reach of the mechanic and the shopkeeper.'

Whatever their motives, the reformers carried the day. In 1853 the advertisement duty disappeared, and on 20 June 1855 the stamp tax was abolished. *The Times* came out priced fourpence unstamped and fivepence halfpenny stamped. Its rivals charged fourpence and fivepence respectively. It was not a big difference, but it was enough to set the stage for a remarkable development, coming as it did at a time when the press was already expanding and when new techniques in news collection and distribution were beginning to be widely exploited. Reuter's Agency, founded in 1849, was supplying foreign news on the cooperative principle. Printing methods were steadily improving. Railway development was making distribution easier and quicker. And more and more people were being taught to read. The general mood of the economy was confident and expansive. But the reformers had not had things all their own way, and in 1854 a noted economist, J. R. McCulloch, had sounded a warning – one which was to be often repeated down to the present day:

> We much doubt whether the circulation of low-priced journals can ever be of advantage. Such papers are, speaking generally, addressed to the lower and poorer classes of the community; and their writers find it more to their advantage to flatter the prejudices entertained by their readers, and that espouse their peculiar views, how inconsistent soever these may be with the interests of society in general, than to inculcate sounder though less popular principles. Hence the revolutionary character of the greater number of the lower-priced papers, or, at least, of

such of them as are read by the lower orders. This, perhaps, may be a necessary evil in a highly-advanced country like this; but whether it be so or not, there can be no doubt of its existence, and of its formidable magnitude.[1]

Already, men had begun thinking of newspapers in a quite different way. For close on thirty years all other daily papers lived so completely under the shadow of *The Times* that hardly anyone could imagine a paper except in its image. Now, with the removal of the tax, they suddenly found it possible to do so. It was as though a spell had been broken. New papers sprang up all over the country, not at fourpence but at twopence, and very soon at a penny. Mowbray Morris of *The Times* commented that, although there was no reason why a daily newspaper should not be published for a penny, 'it is impossible to produce a first class paper at that price'. Granted *The Times*'s standard of 'first class', this was true enough, although perhaps less so than that paper thought. Even as late as 1861 Lord Robert Cecil was to ask, with aristocratic contempt, 'could it be maintained that a person of any education could learn anything from a penny newspaper?' But penny newspapers *were* being produced in ever-growing numbers – and were appealing more and more to the 'educated classes'.

In the provinces, the removal of the stamp tax brought about an immediate and remarkable transformation. The *Manchester Guardian* and papers like it turned themselves into dailies, reducing their price to twopence, and then to a penny. They began to publish not only their own parliamentary reports but also dispatches from abroad (helped by Reuter's, at first largely ignored by *The Times*, which tended to prefer its own correspondents), and they entered vehemently into the discussion of local and national affairs. In London similar developments were taking place. On Friday, 29 June 1855, appeared the *Daily Telegraph and Courier*, begun by a Colonel Sleigh, price twopence. Its opening editorial declared that

> the gradual improvement in the moral and intellectual conduct of the great masses of the people in this country, within the last half-century, may be ascribed to the more general diffusion of knowledge and the extension of education among the lower classes . . . It is all very well for our older contemporaries of the Morning Press to presage all manner of evil from the moment of the passing of the Newspaper Stamp Bill . . .

The new venture was not an immediate success, and was taken over by J. M. Levy who, undeterred by his predecessor's failure, reduced the price to one penny on 17 September 1855,

> believing that the *Daily Telegraph* has convinced the public that in literature, as connected with the morning press, cheapness is consistent with excellence . . . There is no reason why a daily newspaper, conducted with a high tone, should not be

produced at a price which will place it within the means of all classes of the community. The extension of the circulation of such a journal must prove beneficial to the public at large. If artisan and Peer alike can peruse daily the same wholesome literary matter, produced by first-class writers, the general tone of society must benefit. The working man will feel assured that we consider that he is deserving of having laid before him a newspaper compiled with a care which places it in the Hamlet and secures its perusal in the Palace.

The claim, as Lord Burnham has pointed out, was over-ambitious: the Palace had certainly not been won over – and the hamlet was waiting for Harmsworth. But all that lay between was available: and there was clearly some truth in its announcement in October 1855 that 'people will not now have to buy the day before yesterday's *Times* . . . they can have a first-class newspaper upon their breakfast table as well as the rich. The price of the *Daily Telegraph* places it within the reach of every man.' By 20 September 1855 the paper was proudly announcing that 'the circulation of the DAILY TELEGRAPH EXCEEDS THAT OF ANY LONDON MORNING NEWSPAPER with the Exception of the *Times*. More than that, the Circulation of the DAILY TELEGRAPH is greater than any *four* Morning Newspapers all put together'. Its claims continued to grow: to 27,000 daily in January 1856, 141,700 by 1860, 191,000 by 1871, and 250,000 by 1880.[2]

From its very beginning, the *Telegraph* set out to serve an entirely new public, one which hitherto had not been able to afford a newspaper, and still less a daily newspaper. It was determined to cater for 'the million'. Its model seems to have been the *New York Herald*, which provided reading material more suited to the taste of the new London penny public (as estimated by Levy) than *The Times* or any other London daily. In this way, according to the *History of The Times*, 'began that imitation by London newspapers of sensational New York journalism which, as was feared and prophesised in 1825 and 1855, has since gone far to destroy the English type of popular newspaper and periodical'. The criticism is hardly fair. The *Telegraph* was not the first paper to adopt a lighter style of journalism: the pioneers in that field had been the *Morning Post* and the *World*. 'What we want is a human note', Levy told his staff, and politics must not be assumed to be the sole interest of the readers. The approach was lighter, the news dramatised, the style colloquial. Matthew Arnold called it 'the new journalism'. In terms of content, there was little new about it, but there was a change of emphasis. Politics lost the primary place it had hitherto held – and, when included, was treated with a new liveliness. And Lord Burnham writes that 'reviewing the files, the honest biographer cannot dispute that the *Daily Telegraph* thrived on crime'.

But the *Telegraph* also enlivened its pages with spirited crusades. The Tractarian Movement received particularly rough handling, with its followers being described as 'the little finicking man-milliners who duck and bob before crucifixes': 'Every verminous libertine who can creep into the establishment will mentally manipulate his parishioners with the prying sensuality of the Confessional, gorged with the promiscuous unbosomings of vice, will over flow like an inundation of disease upon society.'

Politicians were not spared. The House of Lords was 'the chartered lords of misrule ogling in the ancient face of bigotry'. Disraeli was a 'windbag of surfeited acrimony and undigested sophisms', and Gladstone a 'voluble casuist' and a man of 'Jesuitical cunning'. Nor were the arts neglected. Tennyson was accused of affectation, his *Idylls of the King* 'jingling without music, obsolete . . . sham mediaeval panoply': 'Let it be hot, Mr Tennyson, or not at all.'

According to George Augustus Sala, who adorned the *Telegraph* from 1857 to 1893,

> the idea of the proprietors was that it should be not only a thoroughly comprehensive newspaper, but also a miscellany of human and descriptive social essays, and in these respects a kind of daily *Household Words* . . . and what they yearned for was a staff of writers who possessed, first of all a lively style, and who next, had seen something of the world.

In fact, it was the eighteenth-century formula of 'intelligence, instruction and entertainment' brought up to date. The news was presented in a more entertaining and arresting manner; and there were magazine and feature articles for weekend reading – on lines not always what one would expect in a popular newspaper, dealing with such topics as 'The Velocity of Light' and 'Spontaneous Generation'. Readers of *The Times* found it all vulgar and crude. The *Daily Telegraph* has the credit as the leader of the 'new journalism'. But very soon there were rivals in the field – particularly the *Standard*, which in the late 1860s and 1870s was the most serious rival of *The Times*. It had been an evening paper since 1821, but became a morning daily in 1857, consisting of eight full-sized pages, price twopence. On 4 February 1858 it reduced its price to one penny.

The Times was not unduly impressed. With the vast majority of its readers, it shared the view that cheap newspapers were or would be nasty papers. Certainly, the penny papers differed too much from it to secure its readers. But the other dailies were feeling the pinch: the *Morning Chronicle* was to die in 1862, and the *Herald* in 1869. But the anticipated deterioration of the *Standard* did not take place, and soon that paper was competing with *The Times* almost at its own level, and at a quarter the price. Well edited, well produced, the *Standard* gradually brought down the sale of its great opponent; by 1861 its circulation was 65,000 – well ahead of *The Times*. But John Walter III was determined to retain the leading position of *The Times* by the exercise of the highest standards. Says *The History of the Times*, (II, 348), 'for Walters' sake the *Times* was read by proof-correctors as if it were the text of the Holy Bible'. He declined competition with the penny press, and disregarded the new journalism and the new prices. And *The Times* still did well. Occasionally, its sales reached remarkable heights: its issue of 16 December 1861 reporting the death of the Prince Consort sold 90,000; that of 9 March 1863 on the reception of the Princess Alexandra, 98,000; and that of 11 March on the marriage of the Prince of Wales, 108,000. Delane could still dictate his own terms to politicians: he could secure their information, while refusing to pay for it with uncritical support. While Palmerston lived, the authority of *The Times* was as great as ever, and this despite the fact that it had often alluded to his private gallantries, calling him 'a juvenile old Whig, nicknamed Cupid'. But his death in 1865 destroyed this unique degree of intimacy with public affairs and public men.

Another London newspaper which refused to enter into competition with the new cheap press – and which prospered – was the *Morning Post*, still pursuing its curious career of ups and downs. In 1849 its quarterly balance was only £250. But under Peter Borthwick, with his emphasis on news as against views – there was, he said, 'nothing which gives a journal so much power and influence as early and exclusive intelligence' – the paper's position began to improve. By 1852, when the sale of *The Times* was over 40,000, the *Post* had less than 3,000. But influence was not to be measured in mere figures. In prestige, if not in circulation, the paper was beginning to stand high again. Its new reputation rested upon its political reporting. On 2 November 1872 it stated its policy: 'Independence is the first condition of influence, and a Journal to be listened to must speak in its own name alone, and with the weight which years of experience in public affairs free from ties and trammels of mere party can alone give to its utterance.' Algernon Borthwick, who became editor in 1852, had translated these words into deeds. Supporting Palmerston, he declined to follow him in all things – such as his divorce and in particular his policy on the Indian Mutiny. And when in 1884 the Central Conservative Association invited the 'editors of Conservative newspapers' to attend a conference, he replied that he was 'not altogether willing to attend at the beck and call of the Conservative Central Office'. The project, he thought, was

> a futile one . . . and will certainly be treated as an instance of 'nobbling' the Press . . . We of the Press can be of infinite service, but only on condition of absolute freedom from all trammels. We report, narrate, and comment, but have nothing to do with central associations and banquets . . . A weak journal subsidised is only a mockery of public opinion.[3]

The Times had said very much the same thing. It was the somewhat arrogant claim to power without responsibility.

The great political idol of the *Post* was Disraeli – a curious choice for a paper with a reputation of being ultra-English. But he won its support by the way he summed up and directed the spirit of England in the mid-

Victorian age, fostering imperialism, and restoring English prestige on the continent. In the period of his eminence, the *Morning Post* maintained more positively than hitherto the High Tory policy of 'kind and careful government of the working classes'. It approved measures for the promotion of public education and health even when they were the work of Liberal Governments; it was prepared to support the cooperative movement in spite of its connection with socialism. 'Children are removed from school at too early an age', it declared on 23 July 1857, 'We may not be able to compel parents to keep their children at school till they are 14 years old, but we may in many ways encourage them to do so.' And it warmly congratulated the government on the 1870 Education Act, having 'no doubt that it will be the groundwork of a system of national education from which great results may be expected'. But it was Disraeli's imperial policies that really won the *Post*'s admiration. Earlier in the century the paper had regarded colonies as a nuisance, and had objected strongly to what it called 'those "little wars" which tell so heavily upon the purse as well as upon the prestige of England' (18 July 1863). It had tended to support the Maoris in the Maori Wars of the 1860s, and it had welcomed the movement towards imperial autonomy begun by the creation of the Dominion of Canada, stating that 'in conceding to our fellow-citizens in the more advanced colonies the right to manage their domestic concerns in their own way, the Government and people of this country have got rid of a responsibility which, in former times, led to many embarrassments' (21 February 1867). But thereafter, the *Post*'s 'Little England' sentiments gave way to the new imperialism. It approved Disraeli's melodramatic conferment of the title of Empress of India on the Queen, and the purchase of the Suez Canal shares in 1875. 'Little wars' in Africa were no longer a nuisance. For once, it had chosen the 'right' side – and it prospered. By 1870 it was claiming the 'second place in London journalism' – from being the last when Peter Borthwick took over. Less popular were two other High Tory paths which it followed: the repression of Irish nationalism (on which subject it was the most reactionary of all English newspapers) and, in the 1880s, its return to the attack on free trade.

The *Morning Post* scorned the 'new journalism'; but in 1881 it reduced its price to one penny – to the horror of *Punch*:

> Sir Halgernon, Sir Halgernon! I can't believe it true,
> They say the *Post*'s a penny now, and all along of you;
> The paper that was once the pride of all the swells in town
> Now like a common print is sold for just a vulgar brown.

'We ought', Borthwick had written some years earlier,

> to have become the first penny paper, and we should then have taken a higher ground and have claimed a better place than the *Telegraph*. The creation of the penny press has naturally dwarfed us. *The Times* is always *The Times*, but the *Standard*

and the *Telegraph* are great powers, while the *Pall Mall* and
Echo are no insignificant journals. When there is a crisis I can
always have, as you see, the best news; but crises only come
rarely and in the meantime a new generation has come to look
on the *Post* as a mere fashionable paper and are consequently as
amazed at real news appearing its columns as if it had been
published in the Court Journal. I have to work as of old against
the prejudices which I conquered fifteen years ago, but which I
have now anew to combat.[4]

In fact, despite the excellence of its news and its literary distinction, the
paper was dogged always by its earlier 'Society' reputation.

The Sunday papers continued to flourish. And, as always, there
was a whole host of periodicals appealing to every taste. Some were
humorous, such as *Falstaff* (1855), *Quiz. A Journal of Laughter* (1859), and
Mr Merryman (1864). Most were far more serious. Not neglected,
however, was one of the traditional tastes: the first issue of *The Penny
Satirist. A Paper for the People* (probably 1860, but undated) had a
frontispiece depicting a woman stripped to the waist being flogged by
Austrian soldiers – presumably during the Hungarian rising of 1849. But
the second issue illustrated 'Females flogged by order of his Grace the
Duke of Wellington from *Times* newspaper, September 16, 1850' – about
a dozen this time, all stripped to the waist and tied to triangles. The
editor obviously thought that he was on a good thing! *Paul Pry*, which
appeared on 11 October 1856, also price one penny, had a different
approach. Two pages were devoted to the 'Secret Memoirs of Mrs.
Howard, The Friend and Mistress of Louis Napoleon III . . . revelling in
all the carnal delights of Mrs. Billing's Brothel in Norton-street . . . Her
appetite for sexual recreation is described as being insatiable.' There
followed a page of libellous gossip, with the names given only the most
transparent of disguises; and an article on 'The Mysteries of Prostitution:
or Revelations of Cyprian Life'. The advertisements included

> Secrets of Young Men, married Men and Single Men by which
> certain Diseases may be cured without Medical Aid. Price 2d.
> A Private Hint . . . how to prevent an Increase in your Family.
> 2d.
> The Book without a Name, or a Nameless subject of delicate
> importance to the Ladies, and addressed privately to the
> Gentlemen.

This type of journalism was clearly still popular, and was to remain
so. It had a strong advocate in Henry Dupré Labouchère, another of
those eccentric characters who adorn the history of the Press. Educated at
Eton, a Member of Parliament and strong supporter of Mr Gladstone, he
achieved journalistic fame with his reports in the *Daily News* from
besieged Paris during the Franco-Prussian War. He also founded a paper
called *Truth* in 1876 with the idea of satisfying the permanent curiosity of

the lower classes about the way of life their betters were leading. It was the formula used so successfully by the *Morning Post* in its very early years. High Society was, apparently, populated by adulterers and nympho-maniacs, cuckolds and homosexuals, drunkards and swindlers. As a recent writer remarks, 'in the course of his journalistic career, Labouchère was horse-whipped and caned, beaten up and boxed on the ears by the victims of his aggression, and no other newspaper of the period ever appeared so many times in Court charged with libel'[5]. And in the background were even more salacious journals, such as *The Pearl* (1879–82), which catered for birch enthusiasts as they had never been catered for before, providing also stories with such titles as 'Lady Pokingham or They All do It'; *The Cremorne* and *The Boudoir*.

Very different in tone, if not in subject matter, was the approach of W. T. Stead, who was responsible for one of the greatest journalistic scoops of all time. In 1880 he joined the *Pall Mall Gazette*, an evening paper, price one penny, but with an influence out of all proportion to its modest circulation. He became much concerned over juvenile prosti-tution, at a time when the age of consent was thirteen. According to the legend, he interviewed a police officer on the subject:

> 'Do you mean to tell me,' he asked, 'that actual violation, in the legal sense of the word, is constantly being perpetrated in London on unwilling virgins, purveyed and procured to rich men at so much a head by brothel-keepers?' – 'Certainly', replied the officer, 'there is no doubt about it. If a girl over thirteen can be inveigled into a house of ill-repute she can be said to have consented freely, although she may be absolutely ignorant of what is in store for her in such a house.' – 'Why, the very thought is enough to raise hell', cried Stead. – 'True, but although it ought to raise hell it does not even arouse the neighbours'. – 'Then *I* will raise hell', declared Stead. He certainly did.

He purchased a girl for £5. And on 6 July 1885, as the second item in the *Pall Mall Gazette*, appeared the first article on 'The Maiden Tribute of Modern Babylon. The Report of our Secret Commission' – five and a half pages of it (the *Gazette* was a sixteen-page paper). The main heading was 'The Violation of Virgins'; but there were such subheadings as 'The Confessions of a Brothel-Keeper', 'How Girls are Ruined', 'Why the Cries of the Victims are not heard', 'Strapping Girls down', and 'A Child of Thirteen bought for £5'. The following day, another five pages dealt with such topics as 'Unwilling Recruits', 'The Story of an Escape', 'Procuration in the West End', 'How Annie was Poisoned', 'You want a Maid, do you?', 'I order five Virgins', 'The Virgins Certified', and 'Delivered from Seduction'. Not until 8 July did the series achieve the distinction of becoming the leading article, when, with the comment that 'The Report of our Secret Commission, it is now very evident, has procured an effect unparalleled in the history of journalism', the paper devoted another four pages to 'The Ruin of the very young', 'The Child Prostitute', 'Juvenile Prostitutes', 'Entrapping Irish Girls', and 'Ruining Country Girls'.

It was no idle boast when the paper claimed that the series had 'procured an effect unparalleled in the history of journalism'. The issue of 9 July reported that a prosecution had been threatened, and followed with a section entitled 'Public Feeling on the Subject', consisting of extracts from letters received from peers, Members of Parliament, bishops, clergy and others. Most supported the campaign, but there were some very hostile criticisms, and a mention of the fact that 'W. H. Smith and Son and one or two other agents' were refusing to sell the *Gazette*. The series ended officially on 10 July with a 'Conclusion' very critical of the police – and an announcement that the four previous issues were out of print. But the controversy was very far from being finished. As Larsen puts it,

> Thousands of readers of the *Pall Mall Gazette* could not believe their eyes when they found words used and things described which had never before been used and described in a British newspaper . . . A hostile crowd threatened to storm the paper's offices, and police had to throw a cordon around the house. An indignant M.P. asked in Parliament whether Stead could not be prosecuted for obscene libel.

And Lord Henry Snell wrote:

> England was stripped naked and shamed before the world, and she did not like it. Such things might happen on the wicked Continent, but that anyone should say that these infamies occurred in Pimlico, under the very shadow of the home of 'our dear Queen', was an indefensible and wanton outrage. Patriots and brothel-keepers gave an united shout of angry protest, and the accusation that girl children could be bought from their parents in London and sold to rich men for seduction was stoutly denied by an offended and injured public – until Stead proved it by facts which were conclusive. And then there was a savage cry of resentment against the man who had exposed the loathsome traffic.

Undoubtedly, many *Gazette* readers and advertisers cancelled their orders. At the same time, of course, the series brought the paper many new readers, if only temporary ones. Inevitably, Stead's motives were questioned: was he a genuine crusader, or a muck-raker, or was he simply out for profit by playing upon the age-old love of sex and sensationalism? The *Gazette* very naturally played up the controversy. On 11 July it began a new section, 'The Press on the Question of the Hour', with extracts from both London and provincial papers. This particular issue included reports from *The Times*; the *Methodist Times* (very favourable: 'the great event of the week has been the revelation in the columns of the *Pall Mall*

Gazette of the indescribable atrocities of the traffic in young girls'); the *Tablet*; the *Weekly Times* (very hostile: the series was 'a public outrage'); the *Liverpool Echo; Northern Echo; Weekly Dispatch; Reynold's News* (very favourable: '*The Pall Mall Gazette* has done one of the most courageous and noblest works of our time'); and *Justice* ('the sensation of the week, we may say of the year or many years'). Stead was quick to refute the insinuations that his articles were deliberately sensational and written for profit. He announced on 17 July that the profits of the reprints 'now selling . . . by the hundred thousand' were to go into a fund to continue the good work. He went on,

> as to the profits on the exceptional sale of last week's paper, we should be very happy to hand them over to the same fund, if they existed. It is no doubt natural that the general public which bought up thousands of copies at prices ranging from 3d. to 20s. each should imagine that we have reaped a golden harvest by last week's business. The fact is exactly the reverse. The profit on the sale of a penny newspaper is very trifling. Of all the fancy prices charged for the *Pall Mall Gazette* last week, we never fingered a farthing . . . In so far as the commercial department of the *Pall Mall Gazette* is concerned, it is out of pocket by the enterprise.

In fact, the hawkers had made a rich killing. Nevertheless, the paper did well, stating on 20 July that 400,000 copies of the reprints had been struck off. Increasingly it reported public meetings – and the subscriptions pouring in. The interest now switched to the debate on the Criminal Law Amendment Bill – given three pages in every issue, and including (7 August 1885) the speech of a Mr Staverly Hill:

> Under the auspices of a certain wretched journal, this is the Augustan era of obscene literature (hear, hear) . . . a newspaper which had great difficulty in maintaining its circulation sought by a sensational course to galvanise itself into a greater circulation . . . It is no secret that not only in the streets but in the most private rooms of almost every household throughout the country, this filthy literature has penetrated . . . smut . . . for which the proprietor shovels tens of thousands into his pocket.

The campaign culminated in a mass demonstration in Hyde Park. Stead himself was prosecuted and spent two months in gaol. His reward was the passing of the Bill, which raised the age of consent from thirteen to sixteen years.

Stead's methods were undoubtedly an anticipation of later journalism: but the *Pall Mall Gazette* was a 'class' newspaper, and a modern journalist has expressed distress at its whole approach:

> Even the greatest stroke of his career, 'The Maiden Tribute of

Modern Babylon', was not heralded with bold captions. The first of a series that produced an unparalleled sensation in the country was begun only a few lines from the foot of a column. Imagine an editor of today, even of the most conservative papers, tucking away his biggest feature in the bottom corner of a paper![6]

Another authority on the press agrees:

It remains one of the oddest things in newspaper history that Stead's 'Maiden Tribute' campaign, a magnificent piece of muck-raking with all the right ingredients, only put up the newspaper's sale from 8360 to 12,250 . . . A campaign like that would be worth not 4000 but more like 40,000, if not 400,000 for a 'popular' paper today.[7]

But perhaps Stead's motives were rather different.

In the relative – if only temporary – brightness of the *Gazette* there was a presage of revolution. Another such appeared in 1888 with T. P. O'Connor's *Star* – according to the experts, the first modern evening paper. Its first issue, dated 17 January, announced its 'Confession of Faith':

The STAR will be a Radical journal. It will judge all policy – domestic, foreign, social – from the Radical standpoint. This, in other words, means that a policy will be esteemed by us good or bad as it influences for good or evil the lot of the masses of the people. The rich, the privileged, the prosperous, need no guardian or advocate . . . In our view, then, the effect of every policy must first be regarded from the standpoint of the workers of the nation, and of the poorest and most helpless among them. The charwoman that lives in St. Giles, the seamstress that is sweated in Whitechapel, the labourer that stands begging for work outside the dockyard gate . . .

The policy which annexes even an empire, wins an immortal battle, raises this man or that to the Premiership, sweeps the board at a General Election, shall appear to us infamous, not glorious, evil not good – a thing to weep over, not to acclaim, if it do nothing towards making the lives of the people brighter and happier. On the other hand, the policy will appear to us worthy of everlasting thanks and of ineffaceable glory, that does no more than enable the charwoman to put two pieces of sugar in her cup of tea instead of one; and that adds a farthing a day to the wages of the seamstress or the labourer.

This was stirring stuff indeed – and would have won the full support of Cobbett and Hetherington. O'Connor went on to explain his general approach:

We shall have daily but one article of any length, and it will usually be confined within half a column. The other items of the day will be dealt with in notes terse, pointed and plain-spoken. We believe that the reader of the daily journals longs for other reading than mere politics, and we shall present him with plenty of entirely unpolitical literature – sometimes humorous, sometimes pathetic; anecdotal, statistical, the craze for fashions and the arts of house-keeping – now and then, a short dramatic and picturesque tale . . .[8]

The *Star* was perhaps the first newspaper to acknowledge the *fact* of a new reading public. It was an immediate success and, according to Francis Williams, was 'unlike anything seen on the streets before. Everything about it was bright, brisk and human. Its longest article was only half a column – and there was only one of that length. It was . . . crisp, cheerful, humorous and commensensical'. There were already halfpenny London evening papers, but none to rival it in its bold headlines and its impudent street bills. 'The Pope: No News' it shouted one dull day, and sold thousands to those who believed that this strictly truthful statement must mean something very different. By 3 February 1888 it was claiming a daily circulation of 125,000. The *Daily Telegraph* was around 300,000 and the *Standard* about 255,000.

The other newspapers remained strangely insensitive to such developments. The 'new journalism' had become heavy and sedate. As Francis Williams says,

> Such papers were for men established in their station in society, or on the way to being so; men with morning coats and top hats – at least on Sundays . . . They were heavily political, long-winded, and restricted in interest; much more so in the 'nineties than they had been in the first exuberence of the new journalism of forty years previously, a great deal more so than the journalism of the eighteenth century.

But below, ignored by the newspaper proprietors, the new literates of the Board Schools were emerging, the reading public of the shop assistant, the artisan, the man and girl on a bicycle on a Saturday afternoon. There had been a major reorganisation of education to suit the needs of a radically changing society. Said Robert Lowe, with reference to the extension of the franchise in 1867, 'I believe it will be absolutely necessary that you should prevail on our future masters to learn their letters'. More down to earth was the argument of Forster himself: 'Upon the speedy provision of elementary education depends our industrial prosperity'. After 1870 reforms followed rapidly. In 1876 and 1880 elementary schooling was made compulsory; in 1893 the leaving age was raised to eleven, in 1893 to twelve, and in 1900 to a permissive fourteen. More and more people were able to read and write. Earlier journalists had been aware of a growth of the reading public: Cobbett had written for it, as had Hetherington and Charles Knight. But they were writing for a rather different kind of reader. The real potentialities of this new public of the late nineteenth century were left to be discovered – and exploited – not by a journalist, but by a representative of a London fancy-goods firm living in Manchester: George Newnes. His taste was for snippets of information and odd facts about people and things – the same taste which, in fact, inspired the early *Athenian Mercury* and inspires the *Reader's Digest* today. According to the established legend, as noted by Francis Williams, he said to his wife one evening, reading a paragraph from an evening paper, 'Now that is what I call an interesting tit-bit. Why doesn't someone bring out a whole paper made up of tit-bits like that?' – 'Why don't you?' she replied, being a practical woman. And so, on 30 October 1881, price one penny, appeared *Tit-Bits from all the Interesting Books, Periodicals, and Newspapers of the World*. Its impact was immediate, and lasting. Before any of the established publishers woke up to what was going on around them, it had a sale of 900,000. Newnes gave the new reading public exactly what it wanted: potted, easily assimilated information. Everything was short and written simply and clearly: a predigested literary breakfast food for the family. And there were exciting 'stunts', such as the burying of bags of golden sovereigns for the discovery of those readers clever enough to spot the clues in a serial story.

The lesson was ignored by the newspaper proprietors. Not until 1888 was the possibility that the readers discovered by *Tit-Bits* might like a *news*paper of their own explored by O'Connor in his *Star*. Otherwise, the ranks of the serious – and for the most part dull – morning papers remained unbroken. The makers of the 'New Journalism' had grown set in their ways, and for all the *Daily Telegraph*'s talk of a newspaper for 'the million', they were not much interested in it. Interestingly enough, Newnes himself failed to realise the full possibilities of his discovery. He began an evening paper, the *Westminster Gazette*, in 1896, completely inside the orthodox tradition, and losing heavily. His *Daily Courier* lasted only a few months. It was fifteen years before his discovery found expression in a morning newspaper – set up not by one of the established proprietors but by Alfred Charles William Harmsworth.

Harmsworth began his career in the periodical press. In 1883, he is reported as having told Max Pemberton that

> The Board Schools are turning out hundreds of thousands of boys and girls annually who are anxious to read. They do not care for the ordinary newspaper. They have no interest in society, but they will read anything which is simple and is sufficiently interesting. The man who produced this *Tit-Bits* has got hold of a bigger thing than he imagines. He is only at the beginning of a development which is going to change the whole face of journalism. I shall try to get in with him.[9]

Get in he did – with *Answers* in 1888. This sold 12,000 copies of its first issue, and by the end of the year was selling 48,000. Then came the offer of £1 a week for life for winning a guessing competition (Newnes had begun with an offer of free insurance). Harmsworth's competition was later declared illegal but sales climbed to 352,000 in the second year. His profits from *Answers* enabled him to expand – always with the same type of audience in mind. There followed *Comic Cuts* for the children, *Chips* for the errand boy, *Forget-me-Not*, for the factory girl, *Home Chat* for the housewife, and many more. Another competitor, Pearson, entered the field in 1890 with *Pearson's Weekly*. All were highly successful.

According to a modern biography of Northcliffe (as Harmsworth was later to become),

> A symbolic reader-figure only vaguely emerges from the early *Answers* volumes. It is a predominantly male figure . . . This typical reader appears to be given to wearing the white collar of the clerk with the rolled-up sleeves of the artisan, a class composite reflecting social change . . . He has an appetite for processed mental meals in the form of one-sentence paragraphs of information 'about everything under the sun'. To his arbitrary fear of sudden death is joined a recurring dream of sudden wealth . . . With a relish for details of the hangman's private life there goes an aspiration to the higher knowledge, hinted at in articles on the careers of artists and scientists and the successes of self-educated persons in realms other than commerce. His gambling instincts are provided for by competitions ranging from those involving spectacular guesses to others requiring him to count accurately the total number of words or the number of times the letter 'b' occurs in a given issue . . . The total impression received . . . is of an ingenious exploitation of the popular mind, which has been taught to read but not to think. The periodicals which owe their prosperity to that fact were a powerful and constant force in the growth of modern democracy. Not that any of them could boldly proclaim a political faith, even that which mirrored the hopes of the widest class of reader. 'We do not care to express an opinion on Socialism', it was stated in *Answers* for June 29 1889, a year in which the streets of London were thronged with processions of dockers on the march to better times. A reader of 'Radical sympathies' who wrote deploring the many references to 'the Conservative gang' received the reply that 'politics play no part whatsoever in the management of this paper'.[10]

More controversial was the cultural influence of these periodicals – a controversy which still continues. Somewhat dauntingly, the same biographers of Northcliffe remark that

> the best that can be said for the newcomer [*Chips*] was that it helped to restrict the scope of the still less desirable types of publication. These Harmsworth papers were published for immature minds but in those days, as always afterwards, Alfred

and Harold Harmsworth were unyielding in their policy of not pandering to the lowest tastes of all. Alfred wrote in *Answers*, 'It is always a gratifying thought to us that it is universally admitted that no harm can come from the reading of any of our publications, and that by encouraging the taste for pure literature we are rendering a service to the times in which we live'.

In fact, if there was little in the periodicals that was positively high-minded, there was nothing that was obscene. A sourer note was struck by A. A. Milne, who declared that 'Harmsworth killed the penny dreadful by the simple process of producing a halfpenny dreadfuller'. His opinion was obviously shared by *Punch*, which reacted with all too little humour when Alfred spoke of *Comic Cuts* as 'the poor man's *Punch*'. They sent him a solicitor's letter. A more sympathetic view was expressed by Lord Randolph Churchill:

> Your new literature is simple, but it is none the less instructive and valuable for that . . .Let us take the case of one fresh from school, who reads in your pages not only interesting things about everyday life, but gathers also interesting facts about literature itself. What is he likely to do? Certainly not to relinquish the reading habits he has acquired. There is no reason at all why he should not go from your pages to the pages of the monthly magazines, from those to the quarterlies, and again from those all through the English classics.

This had been the aim of Charles Knight. There is indeed a marked emphasis on popular education in the Harmsworth periodicals which places them right in the tradition which goes back to such pioneers. At the same time, it can hardly be denied that there was a marked lowering of standards. But what contemporary critics (and their modern counterparts) tend to overlook is the fact that, then as now, there were immature minds for which the printed word in itself had little attraction, readers who had learned how to read but not what to read. The awful disparity between what the general public *was* reading and what, according to its 'betters', it *ought* to be reading had been a matter of controversy since the very early days of the press. It remains so today.

The discoveries in popular psychology made by Newnes, Harmsworth and Pearson had opened up an immense field for the newspaper press, but one only nibbled at until Harmsworth, using the huge profits of all his various enterprises, launched the *Daily Mail* on 4 May 1896 and applied his techniques to a morning newspaper. And this event has always been regarded as one of the great turning-points in the history of the press. By present standards of popular journalism, the new paper was conservatively presented. Even in comparison with the Sunday newspapers, its appearance was relatively traditional, with advertisements on the front page. Where it differed from its rivals was in its lively and brief treatment of news, its descent from high politics to the interestingly trivial, its emphasis upon persons, and its 'stunts'. On 4 May 1896 leading articles in *The Times* filled 81 inches of space, in the *Daily Telegraph* 32 inches, in the *Morning Post* 53 inches, in the *Daily Chronicle* 55 inches, and in the *Daily News* 41½ inches. The leading articles in the *Daily Mail* of that day took up only 17 inches. There was the same change in parliamentary reporting. Most newspapers gave up pages to this. But the new class of reader who had been enfranchised by the Third Reform Bill had little interest in the long speeches which filled the newspaper columns: they bored him. The *Daily Mail* had a different approach: and it cost only a halfpenny, when most other London dailies cost a penny or more. Its success was immediate: by 1898 its average sale was over 400,000 and by 1900 it had reached 989,000 – and a new period had definitely begun.

The dominance of the *Daily Mail* was as complete as that of *The Times* before it. Indeed, striking parallels may be drawn between the two – which neither would probably have been prepared to accept. Like *The Times*, the *Mail* was based on a clear concept of the economics of journalism, with a large volume of advertising interacting with circulation (although again, interestingly enough, Harmsworth had originally wanted to run *Answers* without advertisements). Like *The Times*, it was technically in the lead in both production and distribution methods. And it pursued a popular policy, its Imperial sentiment corresponding with the Reform sentiment in *The Times*. Just as *The Times* reached its first peak with the Reform Bill agitation, so the *Mail* reached its first peak with the Boer War. But they appealed to a different public. What Harmsworth had done was to produce a cheap and interesting newspaper which won over part of that lower middle class of small businessmen, clerks and artisans which had hitherto been unable to afford a daily newspaper. And, spectacular as his success was, it can easily be exaggerated. For all the talk of 'the millions', there was certainly no 'mass' public as yet for newspapers; nor was there to be until well into the next century.

There was a price to be paid for this expansion of the press – one which, according to many critics, was far too high. What one may call 'the Opposition' in this controversy maintains that the press before Northcliffe had been responsible and serious, serving an educated minority. After him, it became trivial and degraded. The historian R. C. K. Ensor speaks of what he calls 'a dignified phase of English journalism', which

> reigned unchallenged till 1896 and indeed beyond. Yet the seed
> of its destruction was already generating. In 1880, ten years
> after Forster's Education Act . . . Newnes became aware that
> the new schooling was creating a new class of potential readers
> – people who had been taught to decipher print without
> learning much else, and for whom the existing newspapers, with
> their long articles, long paragraphs, and all-round demands on

the intelligence and imagination, were quite unsuited. To give them what he felt they wanted, he started *Tit-Bits*.[11]

Even more 'aristocratic' in approach is Q. D. Leavis, who writes:

> The popular Press about 1850 has the dignity of the best papers of the age. The standards of journalism were set from above . . . The daily papers catered for the government and professional classes, intelligently interested in politics, the money market, the law and current affairs, adopting towards their readers the only tone which those readers would have permitted, and if other classes found them dull, they must go without, there was no choice.

In a sense, of course, Leavis is right: there was no choice, so far as the daily newspapers were concerned. But from 1840 onwards the most widely selling newspaper was not *The Times* but one or other of the Sunday papers – and whether they could be classed as 'dignified' remains a matter of some doubt. In many ways there was little new about Harmsworth's approach: he was simply reviving an old journalistic tradition stressing interest and entertainment as against instruction, but applying it now to a daily newspaper. But other factors were involved: the age of the 'Press lord' had arrived, with increasing emphasis on high finance. With masterly understatement, Wadsworth comments that 'the effects of the Harmsworth revolution have not yet been studied as fully as they should'.

They certainly merit a separate study in their own right.

Conclusion

Essentially the story of the press is based on three main themes: intelligence, instruction and entertainment. All have meant different things to different people at different times. 'Intelligence' for many years meant bald accounts of events on the Continent, without comment of any kind. Domestic news was treated with extreme caution, and politics was out. With the excitement of the seventeenth century 'intelligence' came increasingly to mean politics, with the savage private war of *Mercurius Aulicus* and *Mercurius Britannicus* in the Civil War period, and the even more scurrilous newsbooks of the Popish Plot crisis. Authority hastened to re-impose its system of control. It had seen the dangers as early as 1530, when the first licensing machinery was set up, but the Popish Plot revealed beyond any shadow of doubt the subversive potentialities of the Press and its influence over the dreaded London mob. In 1695 the Printing Act was allowed to lapse, although Authority had every intention of formulating more stringent and effective measures. But again the excitement of the time was too great, and the freedom of the Press rapidly came to be regarded as one of the classic freedoms – and a subject to be treated with care. No government dared to try to re-establish a licensing system, although governments did what they could in the way of stamp taxes and advertisement duties, together with harsh prosecutions for libel. The early eighteenth century was to become a golden age of the political pamphlet, aimed at a reasonably wealthy and politically conscious elite, and the pamphlet was to remain a powerful force for many years to come. But the political newspaper also flourished, with the polished essays of Bolingbroke's *Craftsman*, the far more reckless diatribes of Nathaniel Mist, the invective of John Wilkes and of the mysterious Junius, and the almost incredible scurrility of such lesser-known papers as *The Parliamentary Spy*, *The Whisperer*, and *The Scotchman*. All made politics *exciting* and did much to stir up popular interest. In the same period, the Press also won, although not without heavy casualties, the practical right to report parliamentary debates. The stage was being set for the development of a Radical newspaper press in the disturbed years after 1815, and particularly in the 1830s.

'Instruction' was similarly to go through various phases. It first really blossomed in the early eighteenth century, with the elegant essays of *The Tatler* and *The Spectator* – essays designed to give merchants and gentry a certain social polish. But with the increased size of the more 'popular' weekly newspapers which was an unintended result of the Stamp Act of 1712, more and more printers turned to 'instruction' to fill their pages. The instruction was often somewhat heavy, with such mammoth enterprises as 'A Brief Historical and Chronological Account of all the Empires, Kingdoms, and States of the World . . . from the Creation to the present Time' and what was called 'An Abridgement of Geography'. The main emphasis otherwise was on the moral essay. Significantly for the future, readers often complained: they did not want to be instructed but to be entertained. The great days of instruction were to come in the nineteenth century.

'Entertainment' has always been one of the main features of the Press, although whether the term is altogether apt is a matter of opinion. The sixteenth-century reader apparently never wearied of descriptions of miracles, prodigies and wonders. But already the emphasis on 'blood and sex' had appeared, with unusually ghastly crimes assured of a splendid coverage. After the Civil Wars some papers made such topics their speciality, although, to do them credit, they did try to emphasise the humorous angle. One Crouch took the lead: his paper, *Mercurius Fumigosus*, which made its appearance in 1654, was perhaps one of the smuttiest papers in the history of the Press. It was an eight-page newsbook: but its 'news' rarely took up more than half a page, the rest being devoted to a masterly collection of what can only be called 'dirty jokes'. It is amazing that, in this particular period, the paper was not instantly suppressed. But the tradition was firmly established. Most newspapers could always find room for the particularly spicy tit-bit, and some continued to emphasise it. One might mention John Dunton's *The Night Walker: Or, Evening Rambles in search after Lewd Women* in 1696–97, *The Rambler's Magazine* of 1783, and *The Bon Ton Magazine* of 1791, with its early emphasis upon what was later to be known as 'the Victorian vice'. This pornographic tradition was to be upheld in the next century by such publications as *Paul Pry, The Town* and *The Age*, to mention only a few. Most eighteenth-century papers avoided such extremes and confined their entertainment to fiction and to extracts from the fashionable Society periodicals, although, with the appearance of the *Morning Post* in 1772, these extracts were a form of blackmail, and the *Post* made a great profit of fees for suppressing some embarrassing item altogether, or for contradicting a story which had already appeared in print. The *Post* was essentially an organ of the leisured classes: but the lower classes have always been very ready to read about the private affairs of their betters, particularly when served up in a titillating way. This flippancy was, however, to lose ground in the next century.

Hitherto, the Press can only have appealed to a minority, although as early as 1649 *The Perfect Weekly Account* could state that 'in these our dayes the meanest sort of people are not only able to write Etc. but to argue and discourse on matters of highest concernment.'. Sir Roger

L'Estrange, Surveyor of the Press in 1663, declared that 'a Publick Mercury . . . makes the Multitude too familiar with the actions and counsels of their superiors, too pragmatical and censorious, and gives them not only an itch but a kind of colourable right and license to be meddling with the government'. Whether the 'meanest sort of people' could read or were interested in high politics, save in times of quite unusual excitement, must remain a matter of debate. But the whole situation was to change decisively with the problems presented by the French Revolution and, closer to home, the Industrial Revolution. Issues were beginning to emerge which people could feel deeply about – political, social and economic. And a Radical Press sprang into life, a Press increasingly violent in tone. This time there was no doubting the fact that the working classes were reading newspapers (or having them read out to them), and were learning dangerous ideas from them. The clamour reached its height with the so-called 'Battle of Peterloo' in 1819, when Radical papers openly advised their readers to arm themselves. The government tried counterpropaganda and physical repression, without success. It soon found a more effective solution. Hitherto, only newspapers proper had been subject to the stamp tax, and the Radical papers claimed to present *views* (a device first used by Cobbett in his famous 'Two-penny Trash'). One of the notorious Six Acts of 1819 closed that loophole: henceforward all papers were to pay the fourpenny tax. Temporarily, the cheap Radical Press collapsed. But it was to revive again in 1830 with the 'War of the Unstamped Newspapers', when dozens of papers appeared openly defying the law, preaching what often amounted to revolution. The 'common reader' had suddenly become a very real threat to the nation's security, for it is clear that more working-class people could read than can ever be statistically proved. The high circulation figures claimed by the leading Radical papers (and not disputed) indicate this. Again, repression became the order of the day; but the problem of the Radical papers was not really solved until the reduction of the stamp tax in 1836. That measure was aimed primarily at *The Times*, but it reduced the difference in price between the stamped and the unstamped papers, making it less profitable to produce the latter, particularly at the risk of prosecution. As the *Northern Star* of Leeds put it in 1838, 'it has made the rich man's paper cheaper, and the poor man's dearer'. Chartism was to witness the final flare-up of Radical journalism, led by the *Northern Star*.

But another basic problem remained. More and more members of the working class were able to read, inadequate as the educational opportunities might appear to be. And it was *what* they were reading which alarmed the ruling classes. Already a new threat to what was called the 'respectable Press' had appeared: the Sunday newspaper, usually opening with the noblest of moral aims, but very quickly adapting itself to the old blood and sex tradition – an adaptation assisted by the 'Queen's Affair' of 1820, when the Press as a whole wallowed in hitherto unplumbed depths of obscenity and scurrility. What working-class readers obviously needed was cheap and wholesome literature. Very early in the field was Hannah More with her tracts: but to tell the workers to be content with their lot and hope for rewards in the hereafter was hardly a message suited to a period of unemployment and social and economic ferment. Then came the Utilitarians, emphasising 'the diffusion of useful knowledge' (in the shape of good solid facts about mechanics, metallurgy and hydraulics) and hopelessly out of touch with their intended audience. Out of these earlier experiments sprang one of the most spectacular movements in the history of the Press, with the appearance in 1832 of *Chambers's Edinburgh Journal*, price 1½d, and Charles Knight's *Penny Magazine*. Both stressed useful instruction, leavened occasionally by carefully selected 'entertainment', but excluding politics and fiction. Their immediate success was extraordinary: but very soon the question was raised as to whether they were in fact reaching the lower classes they had been intended for. They were not: they appealed mainly to a middle-class audience. The new reading public did not want to be instructed: it wanted to be amused and entertained. The 'family magazine' – perhaps the typical product of the Victorian press – persisted; it was personified by Eliza Cook and Charles Dickens, still stressing moral instruction, but with a lighter touch. But even Dickens proved too heavy for most working-class readers: they wanted adventure and excitement – not so much to keep up with the world as to escape from it. They turned to chapbooks and ballads – heartily vulgar, and immensely popular (in 1826 the 'Last Dying Speech and Confession' of William Corder who had killed Maria Marten reputedly sold over a million copies). They turned to such periodicals as the *Terrific Register* and the *Death Warrant*, and to the Sunday newspapers of Reynolds and Lloyd. And it has always to be remembered that the most widely read newspapers were the Sunday newspapers, not *The Times*.

Most histories of the Press have been written round *The Times* and have tended to ignore the growth of the reading public in the background, and what its interests were. Undoubtedly, the power of *The Times* in the mid-nineteenth century was extraordinary: it could literally make and unmake governments. It was a new and dangerous factor in politics. Lord Lyndhurst said in 1834: 'Why, Barnes [the editor] is the most powerful man in the country.' The *Saturday Review* agreed: 'No apology is necessary for assuming that this country is ruled by *The Times*. We all know it.' This sheer power raises the whole question as to whether newspapers guide or merely reflect public opinion – still a matter of controversy today. One of Queen Adelaide's ladies-in-waiting maintained that *The Times* would change its policy if its sale dropped by ten copies. Perhaps Le Marchant put the case more fairly when he said that Barnes was remarkable 'for the quickness with which he caught the earliest sign of public opinion' – though that public opinion was not that of the masses but of the new aristocracy of wealth. The classic statement was the report of the French ambassador in 1851:

It is an axiom among the founders of this paper that to retain a
great number of readers one must anticipate public opinion,
keep it alive, animate it, but never break a lance against it, and
give way every time it declares itself in any direction and even
when it changes its attitude to change with it.

The *Sheffield Iris* had its own somewhat ambiguous answer to the
fundamental question: 'Newspapers are first and foremost what public
opinion makes them; then by a peculiar reaction they make public
opinion what they please, so long as they lead with discretion, and seem
to follow while in reality they lead.'

In 1855, the stamp tax was abolished, again mainly in an attempt to
hit *The Times*. The tax was only one penny, but its abolition produced
something of a revolution. Daily papers sprang up for the first time in the
provinces, reducing their price to twopence, and then to one penny. In
London appeared the *Daily Telegraph*, soon priced at a penny. It was
aimed at 'the million' and heralded in what was to become known as 'the
New Journalism', with its lighter style, its spirited crusades, and the
absence of the former heavy emphasis on politics. By 1880 its daily sale
was 250,000. Then came Harmsworth with his *Daily Mail* in 1896. Its
success was immediate, with the daily sales reaching over 400,000 by
1898. The cheap newspaper thus flourished: but it did not reach down
very far in the social scale. There had been a major reorganisation of the
educational system to meet the changing demands of a radically-
changing society, and a new reading public was emerging, composed of
the new literates of the Board Schools. It was a public with severe
limitations for which the printed word in itself had little attraction, which
was bored by politics and wanted only to be entertained. This public
remained untouched by the expansion of the newspaper press. Instead it
turned to such weekly periodicals as *Tit-Bits* and Harmsworth's own
Answers, whose sales achieved astonishing heights – to the horror of those
critics whose sensitive souls were outraged by what they regarded as sheer
trash. It was the old problem of the difference between what the lower
classes were reading, and what, according to their social superiors, they
ought to be reading. The fact remains that these periodicals did more to
encourage the reading habit than all the newspapers combined.

The story of the Press has had its moments of excitement, its
martyrs and heroes – and its villains. Northcliffe and the *Daily Mail* must
take their place among a long line of 'stirrers': a line which includes such
individuals as Marchamont Needham, Crouch, Defoe, Addison, Wilkes,
Junius, Charles Knight and Reynolds; and such publications as *Mercurius
Aulicus*, the *Craftsman*, the *North Briton*, *Cobbett's Weekly Register*, the *Poor
Man's Guardian*, *The Times*, and the *News of the World*. The list is endless.
All played their part in the story, either in the winning of that great
principle, 'The freedom of the Press', or in encouraging the reading habit
among the lower classes. All were affected by the changes in the society of
their time, and all, in their different ways, contributed to those changes.

Sources and references

Principal sources of facts and quotations are given for each chapter, with supplementary notes. Publication details are given at first reference and in the Bibliography which follows.

Chapter 1. From the beginnings to 1695

Principal sources

For references to sixteenth-century printing the author is deeply indebted to the following: F. W. Bateson, ed. *The Cambridge Bibliography of English Literature*, Cambridge University Press, 1941, vol. ii, 736 ff; and D. C. Collins, *A Handlist of News Pamphlets, 1590–1610*, London, South-West Essex Technical College, 1943.

For the early corantos see F. Dahl, *A Bibliography of English Corantos and Periodical Newsbooks, 1620–1642*, London, The Bibliographical Society, 1952.

See also J. Frank, *The Beginnings of the English Newspaper, 1620–1660*, Harvard University Press, 1961; F. S. Siebert, *Freedom of the Press in England, 1476–1776*, University of Illinois Press, 1952.

1. *Cal. State Papers, Domestic* Ja.s I, 1619–1623.
2. *Mercurius Britannicus*, 4 August 1645.
3. Quoted in H. Herd, *The March of Journalism*, Allen and Unwin, 1952, p. 21.
4. For Muddiman see P. Fraser, *The Intelligence of the Secretaries of State & Their Monopoly of Licensed News, 1660–1688*, Cambridge University Press, 1956; and J. G. Muddiman, *The King's Journalist, 1659–1689*, The Bodley Head, 1923.
5. *The Intelligencer*, 31 August 1663.
6. See R. B. Walker, 'The newspaper press in the reign of William III', *The Historical Journal*, **17**, no. 4 (1974), 691.
7. *True Domestick Intelligence*, 30 March 1680.
8. See Fraser, p. 131.
9. Walker, p. 697.

Chapter 2. Intelligence, instruction and entertainment, 1695–1760

Principal sources

Milton Percival, ed., *Political Ballads Illustrating the Administration of Sir Robert Walpole*, Oxford Historical and Literary Studies, vol. viii, 1916.
F. S. Siebert, *Freedom of the Press in England, 1476–1776*, University of Illinois Press, 1952.
Francis Williams, *Dangerous Estate*, Longmans, 1957; paperback, Arrow Books, 1959.

1. J. R. Sutherland, 'Circulation of newspapers and literary periodicals, 1700–1730', *The Library*, 4th ser. **15** (1934–35), 110.
2. L. Hanson, *The Government and the Press, 1695–1763*, Oxford University Press, 1936, p. 94.
3. Siebert, p. 271
4. See F. L. Mott, *American Journalism*, New York, 1949, p. 6.
5. C. H. Timperley, *Encyclopaedia of Literary and Typographical Anecdote*, 1842, pp. 630–3.
6. See T. N. Brushfield, 'Andrew Brice and the early Exeter newspaper press', *Trans. Devonshire Association*, **20** (1888) 18.
7. *Cal. State Papers, Domestic* 35, vol. 29 (67).
8. G. A. Cranfield, *The Development of the Provincial Newspaper, 1700–1760*, Clarendon Press, 1962, pp. 144–5.
9. Samuel Negus, *Complete List*, in Timperley, pp. 630–3.
10. For a study of the paper see G. A. Cranfield, 'The London Evening Post, 1727–1744', *Historical Journal*, **6**, no. 1 (1963), 20–37.
11. R. L. Haig, *The Gazetteer, 1735–1797*, Southern Illinois University Press, 1960, p. 6.
12. See generally, G. A. Cranfield, 'The London Evening Post and the Jew Bill of 1753', *Historical Journal*, **8**, no. 1 (1965), 32–62.
13. *House of Commons Journals*, vol. xxvii, 769

Chapter 3. Liberty, licentiousness and venality

Principal sources

R. R. Rea, *The English Press in Politics, 1760–1774*, University of Nebraska Press, 1963, is the main authority for this period and except where otherwise noted is the source for the following paragraphs, to p. 72.
See also: A. Aspinall, *Politics and the Press, 1780–1850*, Home and Van Thal, 1949; W. Hindle, *The Morning Post, 1772–1937*, Routledge, 1937; F. S. Siebert, *Freedom of the Press in England* (see ch. 1 above); L. Werkmeister, *The London Daily Press, 1772–1792*, University of Nebraska Press, 1963.

1.   See G. Rudé, *Wilkes and Liberty*, Clarendon Press, 1962, p. 46.
2.   F. Williams, *Dangerous Estate*, p. 60.
3.   Lepaux was a minor figure in the French Revolution, but much esteemed by English Radicals; quoted Hindle, p. 70.
4.   A. P. Wadsworth, 'Newspaper circulations, 1800-1954', *Trans. Manchester Statistical Society*, 9 March 1955, p. 7.
5.   *History of The Times*, London, The Office of the Times, 1935, vol. i, 38-44.
6.   *Ibid*, vol. i, 108.
7.   S. Morison, *John Bell, 1745-1831*, Cambridge University Press, 1930, p. 5n.
8.   See B. J. Hurwood, *The Golden Age of Eroticism*, London, Tandem, 1968, for a lively, if superficial, account of these magazines; also, for the quotation, J. Graham, *Gentlemen's Relish or The Buyer's Guide to Young Ladies*, Tandem, 1968.

Chapter 4. The early Radical Press and the Sunday newspapers

Principal sources

A. Aspinall, *Politics and the Press*, 1949.
R. D. Altick, *The English Common Reader*, University of Chicago Press, 1957.
R. K. Webb, *The British Working-class Reader, 1798-1848*, Allen and Unwin, 1955.
W. H. Wickwar, *The Struggle for the Freedom of the Press, 1819-1832*, Allen and Unwin, 1928.

1.   A specimen of this placard is in the British Museum.
2.   Morison, *John Bell*, p. 5n.
3.   F. Williams, *Dangerous Estate*, p. 94.
4.   Asa Briggs, *Press and Public in Nineteenth-century Birmingham*, Oxford, Dugdale Society, 1949, (quoted in Webb, p. 33).
5.   A. Aspinall, 'The circulation of newspapers in the early nineteenth century' quoted in Altick, p. 330.

Chapter 5. The growth of a new reading public - and the struggle to control it

Principal sources

Altick, *The English Common Reader*.
Aspinall, *Politics and the Press*.

J. W. Dodds, *The Age of Paradox: a biography of England, 1841–1851*, Gollancz, 1953.
Webb, *The British Working-class Reader, 1790–1848*.

1. R. Williams, *The Long Revolution*, Chatto and Windus, 1961, p. 135.
2. Wickwar, *The Struggle for the Freedom of the Press*, p. 296.
3. Quoted in Cyril Pearl, *Victorian Patchwork*, Heinemann, 1972, p. 71.
4. *Ibid*, pp. 60 ff.

Chapter 6. The age of 'The Times'

Principal sources

Aspinall, *Politics and the Press*.
Dodds, *The Age of Paradox*.
Hindle, *'The Morning Post'*.
History of The Times.
F. Williams, *Dangerous Estate*.

1. *Annual Register*, 1822.
2. *Public Ledger*, quoted by the *Standard*, 29 July, 1833.
3. Quoted F. Williams, p. 81.
4. R. Williams, *The Long Revolution*, p. 54.
5. Pearl, *Victorian Patchwork*, pp. 89–90.
6. *Ibid*, pp. 90–1.
7. *Penny Magazine*, 1846, quoted Dodds, p. 111n.
8. See *Illustrated London News Anniversary Issue*, 13 May 1967.
9. Pearl, *Victorian Patchwork*, p. 88.
10. G. R. Porter, *Progress of the Nation*, 1847, quoted Dodds, p. 176.

Chapter 7. The provincial Press, 1701–1854

Principal sources

Cranfield, *Development of the Provincial Newspaper*.
D. Read, *Press and People, 1790–1850*, Edward Arnold, 1961 (a major source for this chapter).
Wickwar, *The Struggle for the Freedom of the Press*.

1. *Newcastle Journal*, 8 September 1739.
2. The anecdote originated in Timperley, *Encyclopaedia*, p. 680.
3. Samuel Negus, *Report of the Printing Houses*, 1724.
4. *Cal. Treasury Books and Papers, 1729–30* (17 April 1730); and *1735–38* (6 July 1737).
5. Cranfield, p. 209; and K. G. Burton, 'The early newspaper Press in Berkshire', M.A. thesis, University of Reading, 1949, pp. 259–60.

6.   W. J. Murphy, 'Newspapers and opinion in Cambridge, 1780–1850', *Trans. Cambridge Bibliographical Society*, **6** (1972), 39.
7.   H. Butterfield, *George III, Lord North and the People*, Geo. Bell, 1949, p. 216.
8.   Wadsworth, 'Newspaper circulation . . .', p. 5.
9.   *Illustrated London News Anniversary Issue*, 13 May 1967.
10.   In 1836 each newspaper *was* given a stamp of distinctive hue and thereafter the stamp returns may be taken as a guide to actual sales.

Chapter 8. The explosion: from 1855 to the advent of Northcliffe

Principal sources

Lord Burnham, *Peterborough Court* (The Daily Telegraph), Cassell, 1955.
Hindle, *The Morning Post.*
R. Pound and G. Harmsworth, *Northcliffe*, Cassell, 1959.
F. Williams, *Dangerous Estate.*
R. Williams, *The Long Revolution.*

1.   Wadsworth, 'Newspaper circulations', p. 4.
2.   *Ibid*, p. 20.
3.   Quoted Hindle, p. 217–18.
4.   Quoted *ibid*, p. 219.
5.   E. Larsen, *First with the Truth*, John Baker, 1968, p. 80; and, for the following extracts, pp. 10–14.
6.   H. Herd, *The Making of Modern Journalism*, quoted in Q. D. Leavis, *Fiction and the Reading Public*, Chatto and Windus, 1939, p. 310.
7.   Wadsworth, 'Newspaper circulations', p. 23.
8.   Quoted R. Williams, p. 198.
9.   R. Williams, p. 174.
10.   Pound and Harmsworth, p. 99.
11.   R. C. K. Ensor, *England, 1870–1914*, Clarendon Press, 1952, p. 145.
12.   Leavis, pp. 177–8.

Bibliography

Altick, R. D., *The English Common Reader*, University of Chicage Press, 1957.

Aspinall, A., *Politics and the Press, 1780–1850*, Home and Van Thal, 1949.

Bateson, F. W., ed. *The Cambridge Bibliography of English Literature*, Cambridge University Press, 1941.

Brewer, J., *Party Ideology and Popular Politics at the Accession of George III*, Cambridge University Press, 1976.

Brushfield, T. N., 'Andrew Brice and the early Exeter Newspaper Press', *Trans. Devonshire Association*, 20 (1888).

Burnham, Lord, *Peterborough Court*, Cassell, 1955.

Burton, K. G., *The early newspaper Press in Berkshire*, M.A. thesis, University of Reading, 1949.

Butterfield, H., *George III, Lord North and the People*, Geo. Bell, 1949.

Cole, G. D. H., *The Life of William Cobbett* reprint by Greenwood Press, 1971. (first edition, London 1947).

Collins, D. C., *A Handlist of Pamphlets, 1590–1610*, London, South-West Essex Technical College, 1943.

Cranfield, G. A., *The Development of the Provincial Newspaper, 1700–1760*, Clarendon Press, 1962.

Cranfield, G. A., '*The London Evening Post*, 1727-1744', *Historical Journal*, **6,** no. 1 (1963).

Cranfield, G. A., '*The London Evening Post* and the Jew Bill of 1753', *Historical Journal*, **8,** no. 1 (1965).

Dahl, F., *A Bibliography of English Corantos and Periodical Newsbooks, 1620–1642*, London, The Bibliographical Society, 1952.

Dodds, J. W., *The Age of Paradox: a biography of England, 1841–1851*, Gollancz, 1953.

Ensor, R. C., *England 1870–1914*, Clarendon Press, 1952.

Ewald, W. B., *The Newsmen of Queen Anne*, Oxford, Basil Blackwell, 1956.

Fox Bourne, H. R., *English Newspapers*, London, 1887.

Frank, J., *The Beginnings of the English Newspaper, 1620–1660*, Harvard University Press, 1961.

Fraser, P., *The Intelligence of the Secretaries of State and Their Monopoly of Licensed News, 1660–1688,* Cambridge University Press, 1956.

Graham, J., *Gentleman's Relish or The Buyer's Guide to Young Ladies,* London, Tandem, 1968.

Haig, R. L., *The Gazetteer, 1735–1797,* Southern Illinois University Press, 1960.

Hanson, L., *The Government and the Press, 1695–1763,* Oxford University Press, 1936.

Herd, H., *The March of Journalism,* Allen and Unwin, 1952.

Hindle, W., *The Morning Post, 1772–1937,* Routledge, 1937.

Hoggart, R., ed. *Your Sunday Paper,* University of London Press, 1967.

Hone, J. A., 'William Hone, 1780–1842, publisher and bookseller: an approach to early 19th century London radicalism' *Historical Studies,* **16**, 62–65, 1974–75.

Hurwood, B. J., *The Golden Age of Eroticism,* London, Tandem, 1968.

The Illustrated London News Anniversary Issue, 13 May 1967.

Larsen, R., *First with the Truth,* London, John Baker, 1968.

Leavis, Q. D., *Fiction and the Reading Public,* Chatto and Windus, 1939.

Morison, S., *John Bell, 1745–1831,* Cambridge University Press, 1930.

Mott, F. L., *American Journalism,* New York, 1949.

Muddiman, J. G., *The King's Journalist, 1659–1689,* The Bodley Head, 1923.

Murphy, M. J., 'Newspapers and opinion in Cambridge, 1780–1850', *Trans. Cambridge Bibliographical Society,* **6**, pt 1 (1972).

Neuberg, V. E., *Popular Literature: A History and Guide,* Penguin, 1977.

Pearl, Cyril, *Victorian Patchwork,* Heinemann, 1972.

Percival, Milton, ed. *Political Ballads Illustrating the Administration of Sir Robert Walpole* (Oxford Historical and Literary Studies, vol. viii) Oxford, 1916.

Pound, R., and **Harmsworth, G.,** *Northcliffe,* Cassell, 1959.

Price, J. M., 'A note on the circulation of the London Press, 1704–1714', *Bulletin of the Institute of Historical Research,* **31**, no. 84 (November 1958).

Rea, R. R., *The English Press in Politics, 1760–1774,* University of Nebraska Press, 1963.

Read, D., *Press and People, 1790–1850,* Edward Arnold, 1961.

Rudé, G., *Wilkes and Liberty,* Clarendon Press, 1962.

Siebert, F. S., *Freedom of the Press in England, 1476–1776,* University of Illinois Press, 1952.

Sutherland, J. R., 'Circulation of newspapers and literary periodicals, 1700–1730', *The Library,* 4th series, **15** (1934–35).

History of The Times, London, The Office of The Times, 1935.

The Times Tercentenary Handlist of English and Welsh Newspapers, Magazines and Reviews, London, 1920.

Timperley, C. H., *Encyclopaedia of Literary and Typographical Anecdote,* Bohn, 1842.

Wadsworth, A. P., 'Newspaper circulations, 1800–1954', *Trans. Manchester Statistical Society*, 9 March 1955.

Walker, R. B., 'The newspaper Press in the reign of William III', *Historical Journal*, **17**, no. 4 (1974).

Wardroper, J., *Kings, Lords and Wicked Libellers: Satire and Protest, 1760–1837*, Murray, 1973.

Webb, R. K., *The British Working Class Reader, 1790–1848*, George Allen and Unwin, 1955.

Werkmeister, L., *The London Daily Press, 1772–1792*, University of Nebraska Press, 1963.

Wickwar, W. H., *The Struggle for the Freedom of the Press, 1819–1832*, Allen and Unwin, 1928.

Williams, Francis, *Dangerous Estate*, Longmans 1957; Arrow Books, 1959.

Williams, R., *The Long Revolution*, Chatto and Windus, 1961.

Index

Considerations of space have limited the entries to those newspapers actually quoted, or which have some special significance. The short titles are given, together with dates and page references to circulation (circ.) and finance (fin.). A plus sign indicates that a paper continued after 1896. Similar restrictions have been placed upon the individuals included.